RUBENS' ANTWER
A GUIDE

Irene Smets

LANNOO

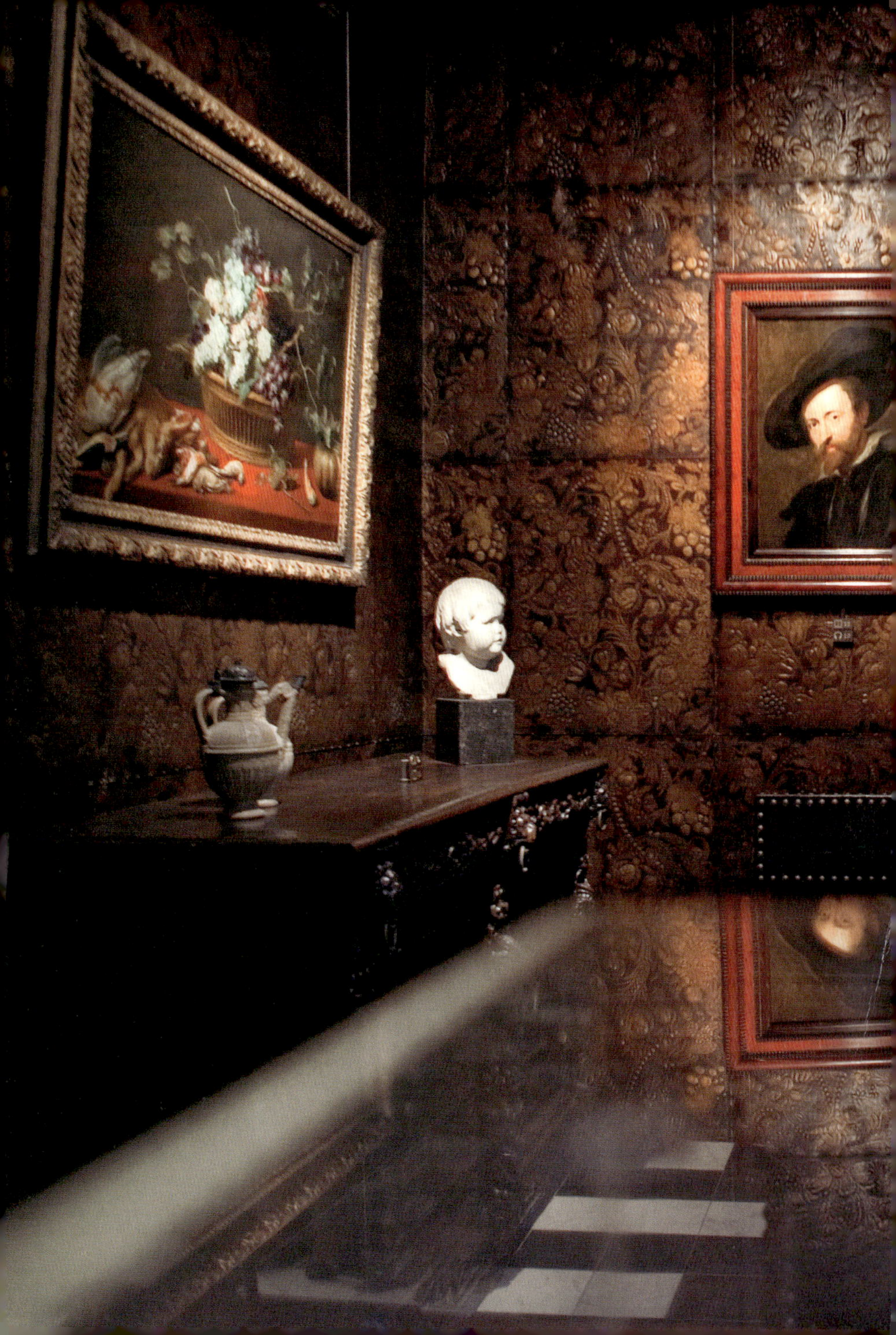

RUBENS' ANTWERP

Irene Smets

A GUIDE

How to use this guide

A guide to Rubens' Antwerp is an ideal companion to discover the artist in the city he loved so much. As well as being a practical guide, which will unerringly lead you to the many great masterpieces made by Rubens in Antwerp, it is also a book that will teach you about the man behind the artist and the fascinating Baroque period in which he lived.

Chronological summary of the most important dates in Rubens' life

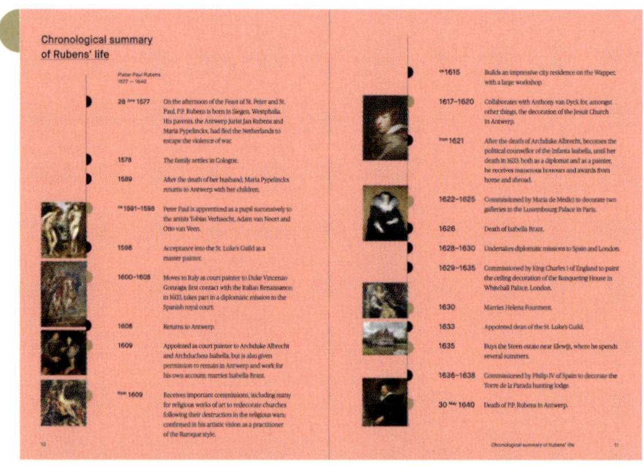

Chronological summary of Rubens' life

Pieter Paul Rubens

28 June 1577	On the afternoon of the Feast of St. Peter and St. Paul, P.P. Rubens is born in Siegen, Westphalia. His parents, the Antwerp jurist Jan Rubens and Maria Pypelinckx, had fled the Netherlands to escape the violence of war.
1578	The family settles in Cologne.
1589	After the death of her husband, Maria Pypelinckx returns to Antwerp with her children.
ca 1591–1598	Peter Paul is apprenticed as a pupil successively to the artists Tobias Verhaecht, Adam van Noort and Otto van Veen.
1598	Acceptance into the St. Luke's Guild as a master painter.
1600–1608	Moves to Italy as court painter to Duke Vincenzo Gonzaga; first contact with the Italian Renaissance; in 1603, takes part in a diplomatic mission to the Spanish royal court.
1608	Returns to Antwerp.
1609	Appointed as court painter to Archduke Albrecht and Archduchess Isabella, but is also given permission to remain in Antwerp and work for his own account; marries Isabella Brant.
from 1609	Receives important commissions, including many for religious works of art to redecorate churches following their destruction in the religious wars; confirmed in his artistic vision as a practitioner of the Baroque style.
ca 1615	Builds an impressive city residence on the Wapper, with a large workshop.
1617–1620	Collaborates with Anthony van Dyck for, amongst other things, the decoration of the Jesuit Church in Antwerp.
from 1621	After the death of Archduke Albrecht, becomes the political counsellor of the Infanta Isabella, until her death in 1633; both as a diplomat and as a painter, he receives numerous honours and awards from home and abroad.
1622–1625	Commissioned by Maria de Medici to decorate two galleries in the Luxembourg Palace in Paris.
1626	Death of Isabella Brant.
1628–1630	Undertakes diplomatic missions to Spain and London.
1629–1635	Commissioned by King Charles I of England to paint the ceiling decoration of the Banqueting House in Whitehall Palace, London.
1630	Marries Helena Fourment.
1633	Appointed dean of the St. Luke's Guild.
1635	Buys the Steen estate near Elewijt, where he spends several summers.
1636–1638	Commissioned by Philip IV of Spain to decorate the Torre de la Parada hunting lodge.
30 May 1640	Death of P.P. Rubens in Antwerp.

10 · Chronological summary of Rubens' life · 11

Learn about the life and multi-faceted work of Rubens, the most brilliant exponent of the Baroque

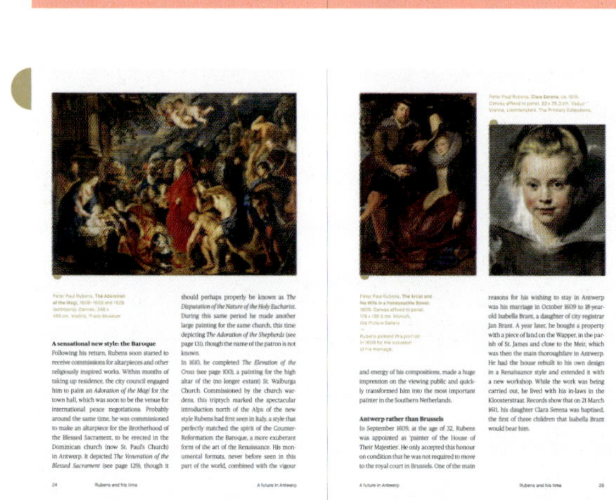

A sensational new style: the Baroque

Following his return, Rubens soon started to receive commissions for altarpieces and other religiously inspired works. Within months of taking up residence, the city council engaged him to paint an *Adoration of the Magi* for the town hall, which was soon to be the venue for international peace negotiations. Probably around the same time, he was commissioned to make an altarpiece for the Brotherhood of the Blessed Sacrament, to be erected in the Dominican church (now St. Paul's Church) in Antwerp. It depicted *The Veneration of the Blessed Sacrament* (see page 129), though it should perhaps properly be known as *The Disputation of the Nature of the Holy Eucharist*. During this same period he made another large painting for the same church, this time depicting *The Adoration of the Shepherds* (see page 131), though the name of the patron is not known.

In 1610, he completed *The Elevation of the Cross* (see page 100), a painting for the high altar of the (no longer extant) St. Walburga Church. Commissioned by the church wardens, this triptych marked the spectacular introduction north of the Alps of the new style Rubens had first seen in Italy, a style that perfectly matched the spirit of the Counter-Reformation: the Baroque, a more exuberant form of the art of the Renaissance. His monumental formats, never before seen in this part of the world, combined with the vigour and energy of his compositions, made a huge impression on the viewing public and quickly transformed him into the most important painter in the Southern Netherlands.

Antwerp rather than Brussels

In September 1609, at the age of 32, Rubens was appointed as 'painter of the House of Their Majesties'. He only accepted this honour on condition that he was not required to move to the royal court in Brussels. One of the main reasons for his wishing to stay in Antwerp was his marriage in October 1609 to 18-year-old Isabella Brant, a daughter of city registrar Jan Brant. A year later, he bought a property with a piece of land on the Wapper, in the parish of St. James and close to the Meir, which was then the main thoroughfare in Antwerp. He had the house rebuilt to his own design in a Renaissance style and extended it with a new workshop. While the work was being carried out, he lived with his in-laws in the Kloosterstraat. Records show that on 21 March 1611, his daughter Clara Serena was baptised, the first of three children that Isabella Brant would bear him.

24 · Rubens and his time · A future in Antwerp · A future in Antwerp · Rubens and his time · 25

The walk takes you to different places in Antwerp where the work of Rubens can still be seen

—

Information about Rubens sites of interest

WALK

From St. James's Church, you can reach the Rubens House on the Wapper. This means that after passing through the Eikenstraat, you have to cross over the busiest shopping street in Belgium: the Meir.

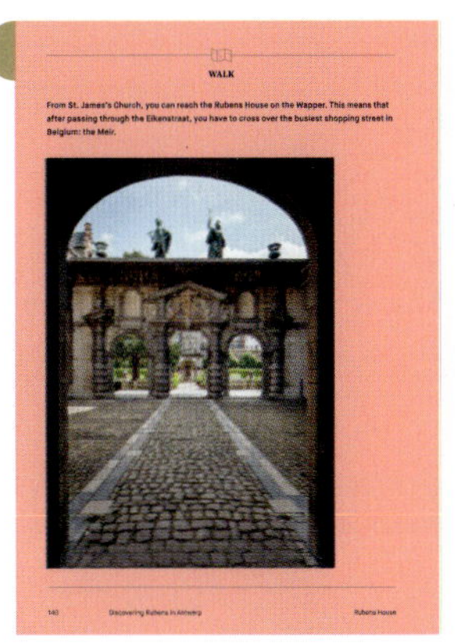

140 Discovering Rubens in Antwerp Rubens House

Rubens House

Wapper 9-11
+32 (0)3 201 15 55
www.rubenshuis.be
Tue-Sun 10:00-17:00, closed 1 Jan, 1 May, Ascension Day, 1 Nov, 25 Dec

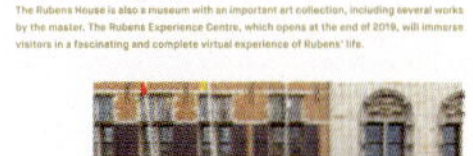

It is impossible to ignore the fact that you are now in the commercial heart of Antwerp. The Wapper connects the Meir, where you can find branches of all the major chain stores, with the parallel streets of Hopland and Schuttershofstraat, home to the more exclusive shops and boutiques. The Rubens House is an oasis of calm amidst the hustle and bustle of the city. Behind its elegant facade, you will discover the artist's mansion and workshop, a courtyard, a portico and a garden with a pavilion. Rubens lived here from 1615 until his death in 1640. It was also the place where he painted most of his masterpieces.

The monumental building in Renaissance and Baroque style was carefully restored and in part rebuilt during the 20th century, using original sources, such as contemporary descriptions and prints, as a guideline. Since art historians know a great deal about Rubens, based on his own copious correspondence and the many testimonies of his peers, it was possible to decorate and furnish the house in a manner that closely matches the tastes and the spirit of his times. Within this authentically reconstituted whole, the original architectural elements, such as the Baroque portico and the garden pavilion, are enhanced to maximum effect.

The Rubens House is also a museum with an important art collection, including several works by the master. The Rubens Experience Centre, which opens at the end of 2019, will immerse visitors in a fascinating and complete virtual experience of Rubens' life.

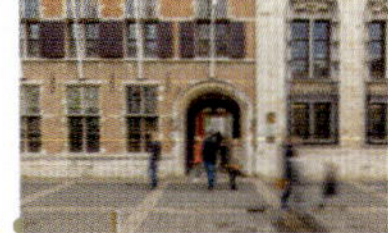

Rubens House Discovering Rubens in Antwerp 141

Discussion of the Rubens works you can still admire in Antwerp

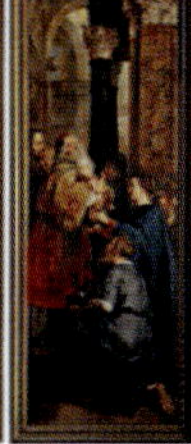

The Descent from the Cross 1611-1614

In 1611, the Antwerp Guild of Harquebusiers commissioned a 'descent from the Cross' for their altar in the city's cathedral from their celebrated fellow citizen, Peter Paul Rubens. The captain of the guild at that time was burgomaster Nicolaas Rockox, who is shown in profile on the far left of the right-hand panel.

The central panel depicts Christ's descent from the cross against the background of a louring sky. With great care, a number of men - Joseph of Arimathea, Nicodemus, St. John the Evangelist and two helpers - are lowering the body of Jesus onto a shroud. Several women, including the Virgin Mary, are helping them. Jesus' left foot rests on the shoulder of Mary Magdalene, who once dried his feet with her hair. The left-hand panel illustrates the Blessed Virgin's visit to her cousin, Elisabeth. Mary is pregnant with Jesus, and Elisabeth with John the Baptist. The women and their husbands, Joseph and Zacharias, greet each other under a portico. Behind them, on the stairs, a serving girl carries a basket with their travel belongings. The right-hand panel shows Jesus' presentation in the temple in Jerusalem. The ageing Simeon holds the Christ Child in his arms, while in the background, between the priest and the Virgin, the prophetess Anne looks on with joy. Joseph, who has brought two sacrificial doves with him, is kneeling at Simeon's feet.

At first sight, this triptych contains three highly divergent subjects, but there is, in fact, a connection between them. Rubens painted the legend of St. Christopher, the patron saint of the Harquebusiers, on the rear panels. According to medieval tradition, this saint once carried the Infant Jesus on his shoulders across a river, finding his way by a light shone by a hermit. When the triptych was closed, the depiction of this legend was all that was visible. However, the symbolism becomes clear when you know that the saint's name in Greek, Christophorus, means 'bearer of Christ'. This explains the key to the entire composition: the friends and holy women in the central panels and Mary and Simeon in the side panels are all 'bearers of Christ'.

The Descent from the Cross was Rubens' first masterpiece - and also the first Baroque painting - to be installed in the cathedral.

106 Discovering Rubens in Antwerp Cathedral of Our Lady

Cathedral of Our Lady Discovering Rubens in Antwerp 107

An easy-to-follow walking route on a detachable map that shows all the Rubens sites of interest

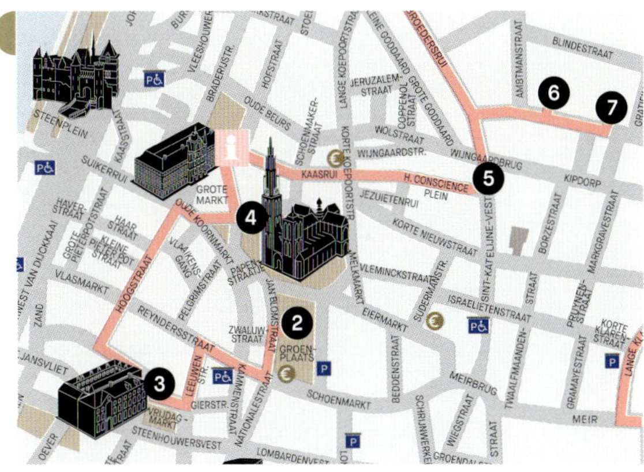

Contents

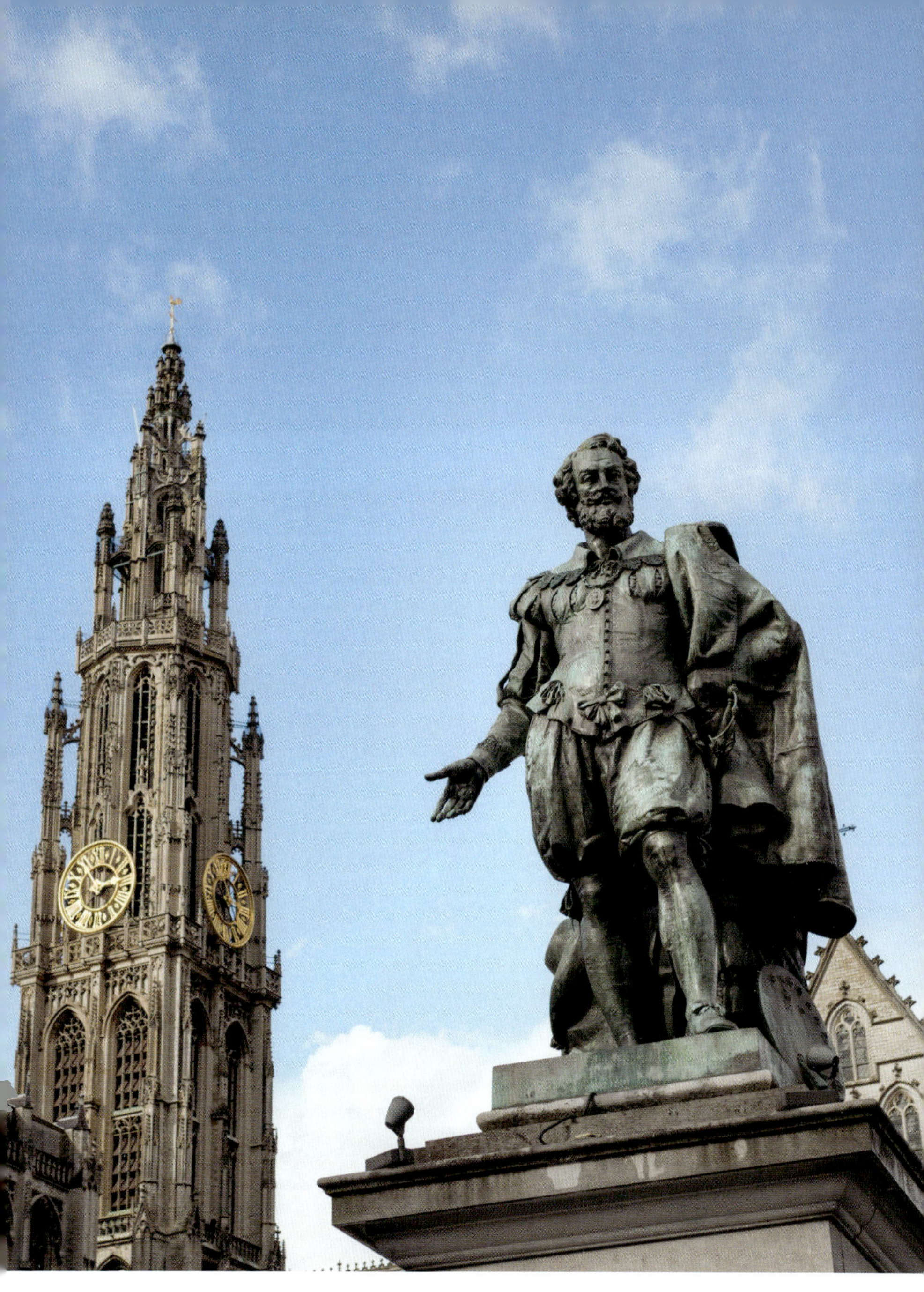

With Rubens through Antwerp

Peter Paul Rubens was one of the most important representatives of the art of his time, the Baroque. More than that, he was also one of the most productive artistic geniuses who ever lived. His talents were remarkably varied: in addition to the magnificent religious and mythological canvases for which he is most famous, he also painted landscapes and portraits, as well as making designs for book illustrations, tapestries, buildings and sculptures. He was an outstanding colourist, who raised the skilled use of a rich palette of shades and tints to a new and important form of expression. He also understood the techniques necessary to create dramatic scenes that were capable of seizing and holding the imagination of the viewer. For this reason, the Romantic French painter Eugène Delacroix once called him the 'Homer of art'. He found the perfect balance between unbridled imaginative power and well-ordered, harmonic composition.

You can find his works in almost all the world's leading museums, but there is only one city that can truly be described as his 'biotope': Antwerp. It is in Antwerp that you can visit his house and workshop, where nearly all of his great masterpieces were crafted. It is in Antwerp that you can find the homes of his friends, Balthasar I Moretus and Nicolaas Rockox. It is in Antwerp that you can admire his canvases in the historical churches and other locations for which they were originally intended.

This book is devoted to exploring Rubens' presence in 'the city on the Scheldt'. It examines Rubens' life and the development of his art, and it discusses in depth the artist's most important paintings that can still be viewed in Antwerp today. In short, the book is a guide to the environment in which one of the world's great masters of art lived and worked.

Irene Smets

Chronological summary of Rubens' life

Pieter Paul Rubens
1577 — 1640

28 June 1577	On the afternoon of the Feast of St. Peter and St. Paul, P.P. Rubens is born in Siegen, Westphalia. His parents, the Antwerp jurist Jan Rubens and Maria Pypelinckx, had fled the Netherlands to escape the violence of war.
1578	The family settles in Cologne.
1589	After the death of her husband, Maria Pypelinckx returns to Antwerp with her children.
ca 1591–1598	Peter Paul is apprenticed as a pupil successively to the artists Tobias Verhaecht, Adam van Noort and Otto van Veen.
1598	Acceptance into the St. Luke's Guild as a master painter.
1600–1608	Moves to Italy as court painter to Duke Vincenzo Gonzaga; first contact with the Italian Renaissance; in 1603, takes part in a diplomatic mission to the Spanish royal court.
1608	Returns to Antwerp.
1609	Appointed as court painter to Archduke Albrecht and Archduchess Isabella, but is also given permission to remain in Antwerp and work for his own account; marries Isabella Brant.
from 1609	Receives important commissions, including many for religious works of art to redecorate churches following their destruction in the religious wars; confirmed in his artistic vision as a practitioner of the Baroque style.

ca 1615	Builds an impressive city residence on the Wapper, with a large workshop.
1617–1620	Collaborates with Anthony van Dyck for, amongst other things, the decoration of the Jesuit Church in Antwerp.
from 1621	After the death of Archduke Albrecht, becomes the political counsellor of the Infanta Isabella, until her death in 1633; both as a diplomat and as a painter, he receives numerous honours and awards from home and abroad.
1622–1625	Commissioned by Maria de Medici to decorate two galleries in the Luxembourg Palace in Paris.
1626	Death of Isabella Brant.
1628–1630	Undertakes diplomatic missions to Spain and London.
1629–1635	Commissioned by King Charles I of England to paint the ceiling decoration of the Banqueting House in Whitehall Palace, London.
1630	Marries Helena Fourment.
1633	Appointed dean of the St. Luke's Guild.
1635	Buys the Steen estate near Elewijt, where he spends several summers.
1636–1638	Commissioned by Philip IV of Spain to decorate the Torre de la Parada hunting lodge.
30 May 1640	Death of P.P. Rubens in Antwerp.

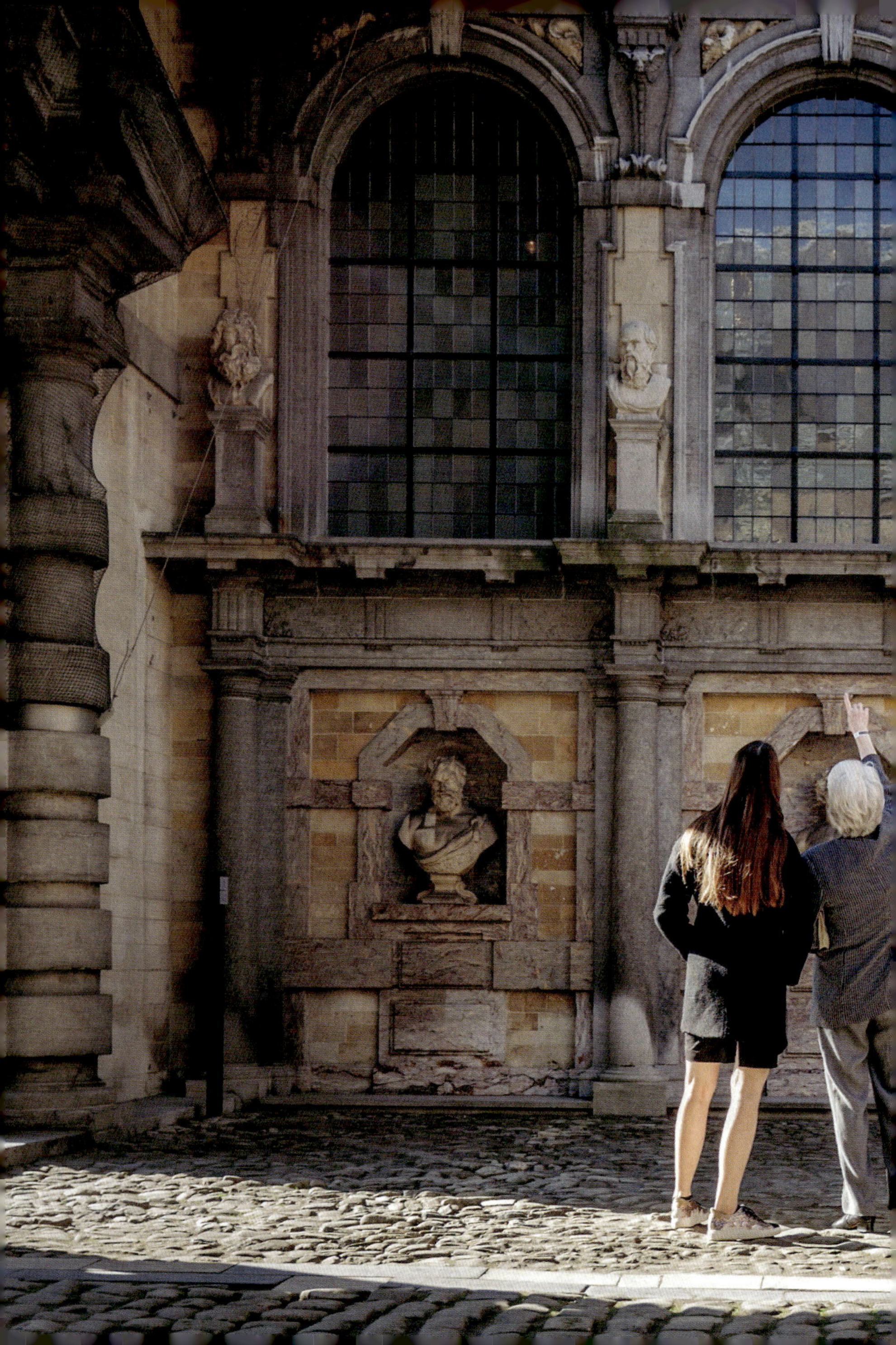

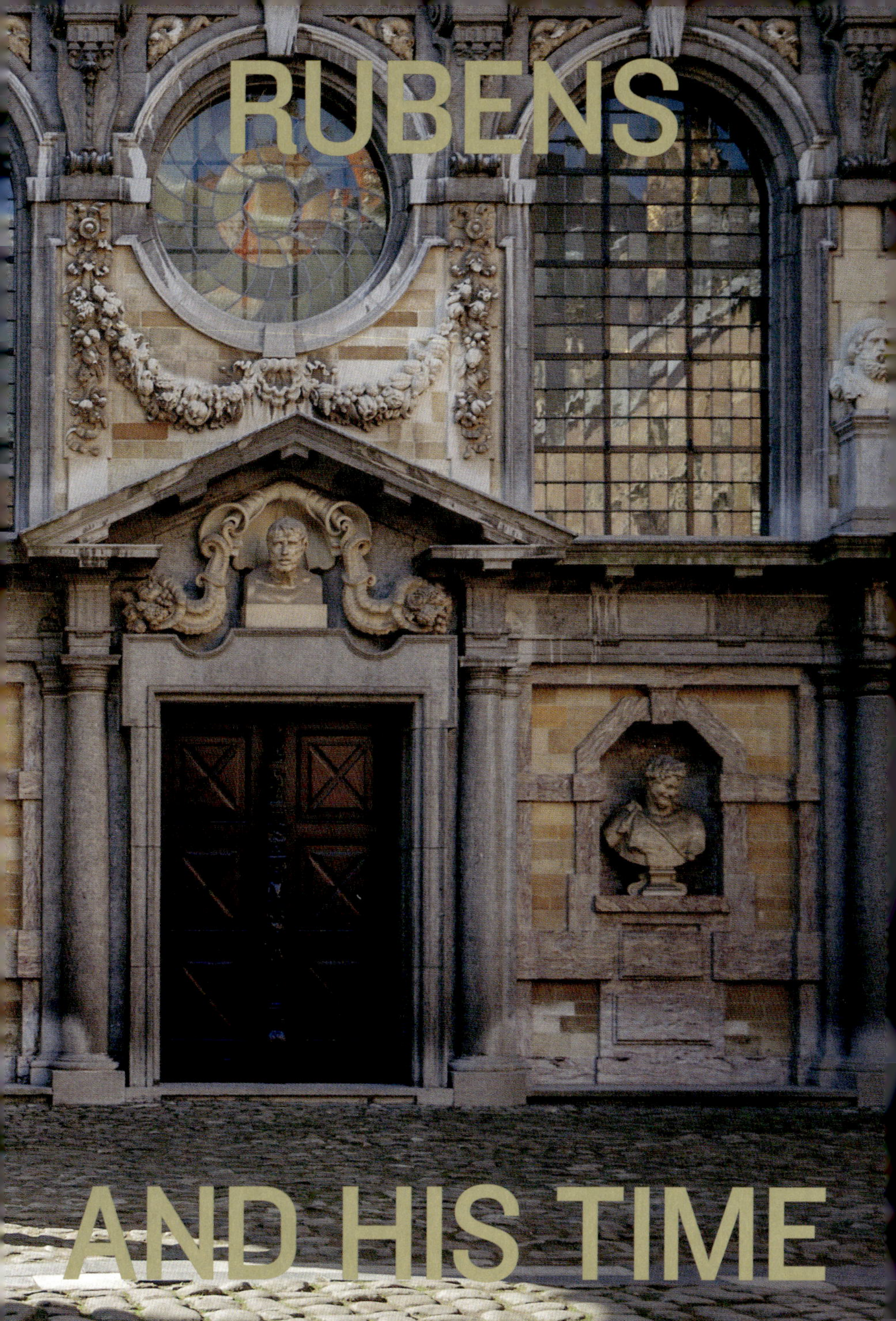
RUBENS
AND HIS TIME

Childhood

I knew your brother when he was a child at school and I loved that boy with his sweet and noble nature.

Balthasar I Moretus to Philip Rubens, November 1600

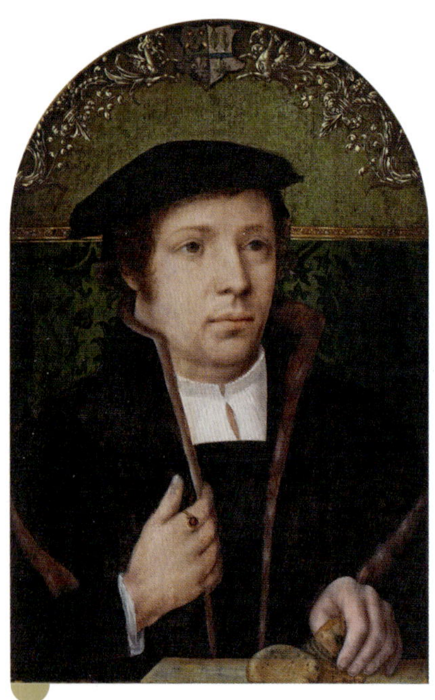

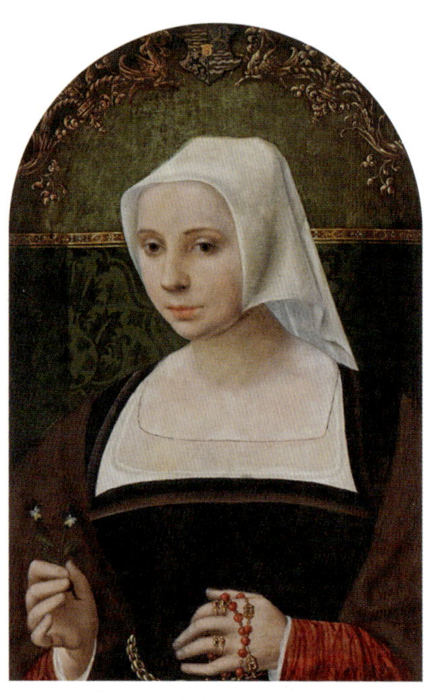

Jacob Claesz. van Utrecht, **Bartholomeus Rubens** and **Barbara Arents, also named Spierinck**, 1529–1530. Panel, both 56 x 36.5 cm. Antwerp, Rubens House

—

These pendant portraits depict Rubens' grandparents on his father's side ca. 1529, the year of their marriage. Bartholomeus was a spice merchant and apothecary in Antwerp. Barbara came from a family belonging to the minor nobility. Their son Jan, the father of Peter Paul, was born in 1530.

Son of political refugees

Peter Paul Rubens was born on the afternoon of 28 June 1577 - the Feast of St. Peter and St. Paul - in Siegen, a small town in Westphalia. His parents - the Antwerp jurist Jan Rubens and his wife Maria Pypelinckx - had fled the Scheldt city in 1568. Jan Rubens, who was one of the city aldermen, was suspected of having Protestant sympathies, which could be highly dangerous in those perilous times, when a bloody religious war was being fought out in the Netherlands between the Catholic Spanish overlord and the various supporters of the Protestant cause. The family moved to Cologne, where Jan Rubens became the legal adviser to Anna of Saxony, wife of Prince William of Orange, also known as William the Silent, who was one of the leaders of the anti-Spanish resistance. After experiencing a number of trials and tribulations, including a period of imprisonment for Jan, the Rubens household settled in Siegen, but was eventually able to return to Cologne just a short time after Peter Paul's birth. It was in this city that the future artist spent the early years of his childhood, until he was almost 12 years of age. He grew

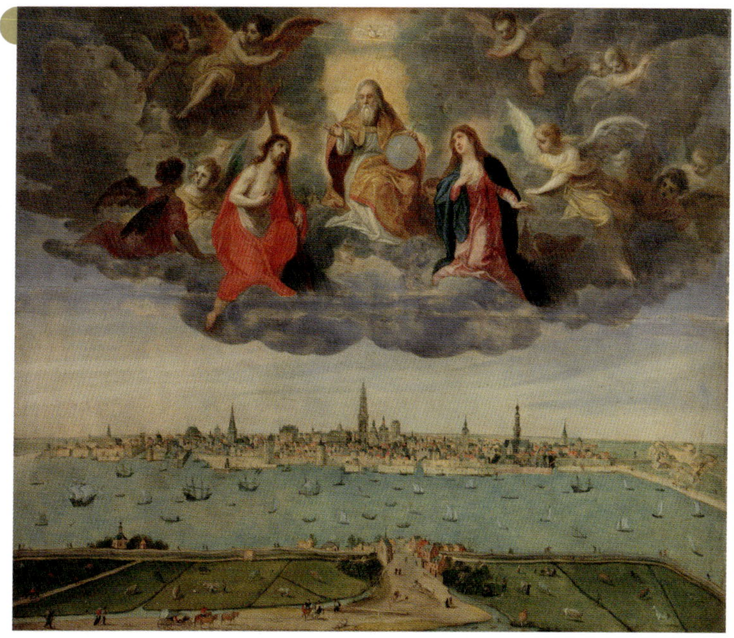

Abel Grimmer and Hendrik van Balen, **Antwerp, with part of the Flemish Head fort**, 1600. Panel, 37 x 44 cm. Antwerp, Royal Museum of Fine Arts

up in a large family with many siblings, but he was particularly close to his brother Philip, who was three years older.

Return to Antwerp

Jan Rubens died in 1587. A short while later, Maria Pypelinckx returned with her children to Antwerp. During the intervening years, the political situation had changed. In 1585, the military commander Alexander Farnese had captured the city for the Spanish king and the Catholic faith. This led to the final and irreversible separation of the Northern and Southern Netherlands. The North was organized as the Republic of the United Provinces, headed by a Council of State and a 'stadtholder'. The South remained under Spanish rule and was administered by a governor. Rubens' mother was allowed to take up residence in Antwerp, provided that she converted to Catholicism.

Unfortunately, the partition between North and South failed to bring peace: both sides continued to harry each other wherever possible. This meant that the young Rubens grew up against a constant backdrop of political and religious division, often resulting in new outbreaks of fighting. To make matters worse, France also intervened in the conflict, in the hope of one day incorporating the Southern Netherlands into the French kingdom. The various phases of this struggle for supremacy in the Low Countries is now known to history as the Eighty Years' War (1568-1648), a war in which all of Europe would eventually become involved.

Back in Antwerp, Peter Paul attended the Latin school in the Papenstraatje, not far from the Cathedral of Our Lady. There he learnt both Latin and Greek, and later expanded his knowledge of the culture of classical antiquity through his own self-study. When he was 13 or 14 years old, he left school to become a page to Marguerite de Ligne, widow of Count Philip de Lalaing, who lived near the town of Oudenaarde. However, after just a few months he returned to Antwerp to start his apprenticeship as a painter.

City plan of Antwerp in the commemorative book **Pompa Introitus Ferdinandi**, published by Theodoor van Thulden at the printing house of Jan van Meurs in Antwerp, 1642. Antwerp, Plantin-Moretus Museum

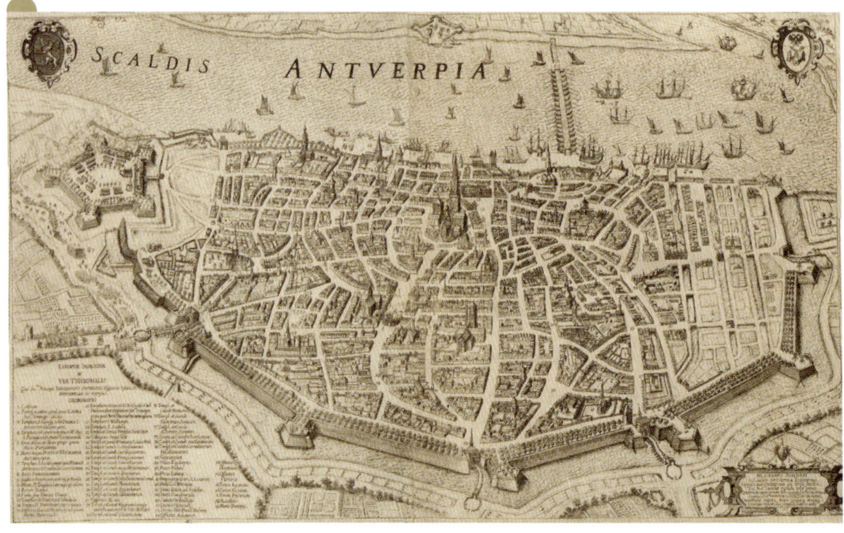

Artistic training and his stay in Italy

Finally, after he [Otto van Veen] had taught him a great deal in a very short space of time, and when the fame of the renowned pupil had become so great that people no longer knew which of the two was the more skilful, him or his master, Rubens decided to go to Italy.

Roger de Piles, *Conversations sur la Connaissance de la Peinture...*, Paris, 1677

Early training in Antwerp

Rubens studied first under the landscape artist Tobias Verhaecht and then under Adam van Noort, a painter of dull and uninspired religious scenes, but neither of these two masters had a far-reaching influence on their pupil's later development. More significant for his future were the three years he spent in the workshop of Otto van Veen, who was best known for his robust altar pieces and his allegories with mythological figures in a cool and somewhat detached classicist style. Interesting examples of his work in Antwerp can be seen in the Cathedral of Our Lady (*The Last Supper*, 1592) and in St. Andrew's Church (*The Martyrdom of St. Andrew*, 1599).

One of the few surviving works from Rubens' early years as a painter - *The Fall from Grace*, sometimes known as *Adam and Eve in Paradise* (see page 143) - displays strong stylistic similarities with the work of Van Veen, but is more powerful and more plastic in its approach.

To Italy, a mecca for artists

In 1598-1599, shortly after completing his training with Van Veen, Rubens was admitted

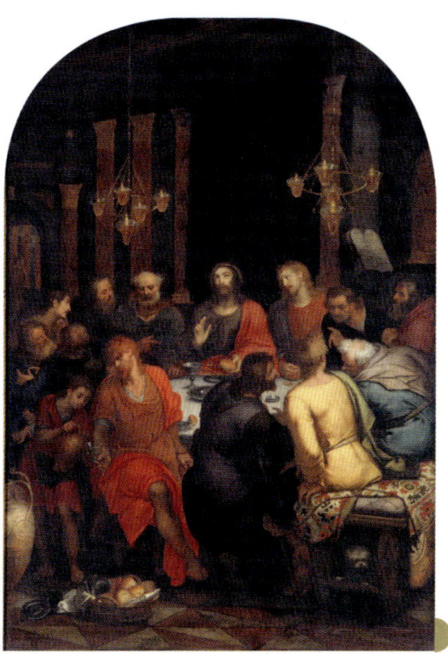

Otto van Veen, **The Last Supper**, 1592. Canvas, 350 x 247 cm. Altarpiece for the Brotherhood of the Most Blessed Sacrament. Antwerp, Cathedral of Our Lady

—

This painting was regarded by contemporaries as the high point of Van Veen's oeuvre.

An important teacher

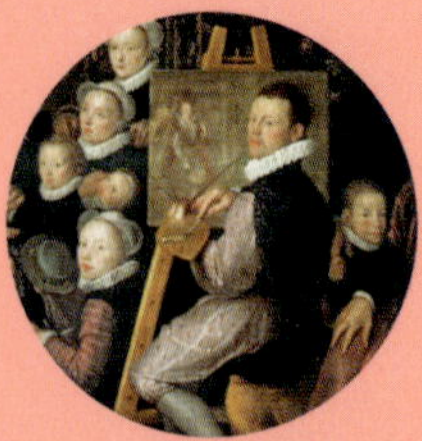

Otto van Veen, **The artist at work, surrounded by his family**, 1584. Canvas, 176 x 250 cm. Detail. Paris, Louvre Museum

Otto van Veen, often Latinized as Otto Vaenius, was born in 1556 in Leiden, where he also received his first artistic training. Out of loyalty to the Spanish king and the Catholic faith, Van Veen's father, who was burgomaster of Leiden, fled with his family to Antwerp in 1572. However, because the city at that time was largely under the dominance of the reformers, the family moved on to Liege, where the young Otto was apprenticed to the humanist artist Dominicus Lampsonius. Van Veen later completed his artistic education with five years in Rome, following which he returned to the Southern Netherlands, working first for the Prince-Bishop of Liege and later for the Spanish governor, Alexander Farnese. By 1590, he was back in Antwerp and in 1594 he was admitted to the St. Luke's Guild. It was in that same year (or possibly the next) that the young Rubens joined his workshop as an apprentice. 'Their shared interest in literature soon led them to become friends and the master willingly passed on all his knowledge and the secrets of his art to his pupil, teaching him above all how to position his figures and to distribute the fall of light to best advantage,' wrote Rubens' biographer Roger de Piles in 1677. Van Veen later moved to Brussels, where he died in 1629.

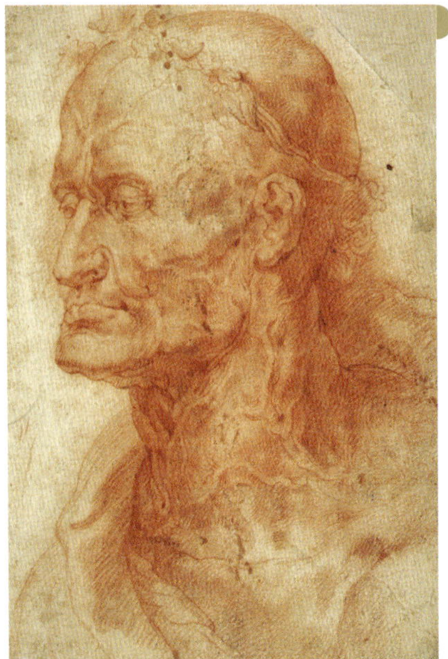

Peter Paul Rubens, **Study of the head of an old man**, 1600–1608. Red chalk on paper, 23.3 x 15.5 cm. Antwerp, Rubens House

as a master to the St. Luke's Guild in Antwerp. The following year, 1600, he left for Italy to complete his artistic education. He soon found a position at the court of Vincenzo I Gonzaga, Duke of Mantua. In the duke's magnificent Renaissance style palace, the young Rubens was able to admire the masterpieces of the greatest 'modern' artists of his day. Not that he stayed there for long. He was given a degree of freedom by the duke - who was notoriously slow to pay his salary - to travel and to learn as much as he could. Taking advantage of this liberty, he made lengthy sojourns to Florence, Genoa and, above all, Rome.

He was eager to expand his artistic horizons

and threw himself into the study of topics as varied as the classical sculpture of Ancient Greece and Rome, the art of the Italian High Renaissance, local architecture and even gemstones. While he was in Rome, he made numerous copies and study drawings of famous classical statues, such as the *Belvedere Torso* and the *Laocoon*, but also of the paintings of the great masters of the Renaissance, like Mantegna, Leonardo da Vinci, Raphael, Michelangelo, Titian, Tintoretto, Correggio and others. At the same time, he was open to new ideas and in particular was fascinated by the Baroque movement, which was bursting onto the scene in Rome at that time thanks to the works of Carracci and Caravaggio. When in Genoa, he collected a large number of architectural plans and facade drawings of the city's many palaces, which he later engraved and published in Antwerp in 1622 as a book of prints, titled *Palazzi di Genova*.

In March 1603, the duke asked Rubens to accompany a convoy of gifts that he wished to send to the court of the Spanish king, Philip III. These

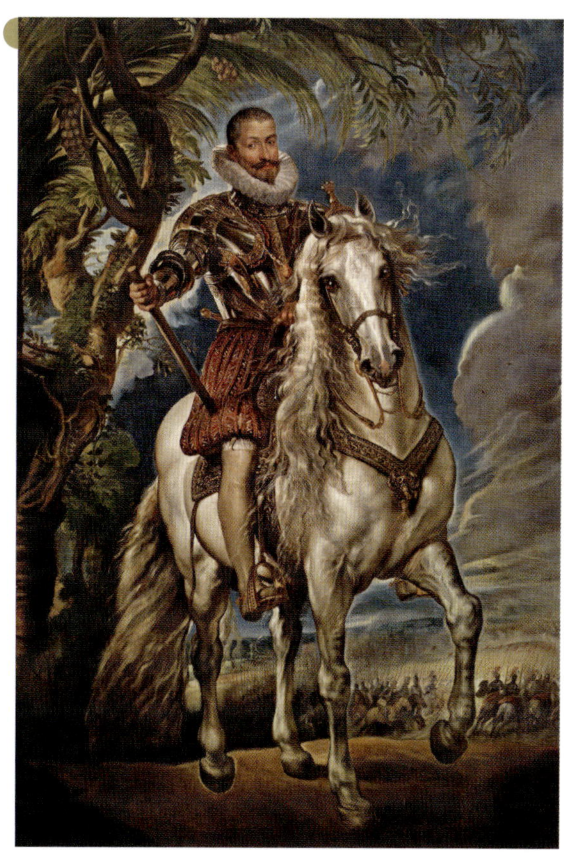

Peter Paul Rubens, **Equestrian Portrait of the Duke of Lerma**, 1603. Canvas, 290.5 x 207.5 cm. Madrid, Prado Museum

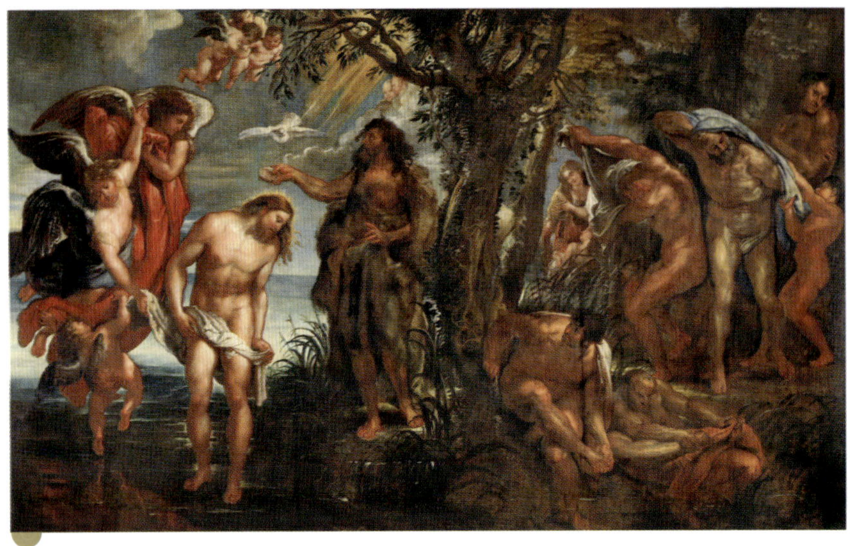

Peter Paul Rubens, **The Baptism of Christ**, 1604–1605. Canvas, 411 x 675 cm. Antwerp, Royal Museum of Fine Arts

gifts were intended not just for the king, but also for a number of other influential figures in the royal circle, such as the powerful Duke of Lerma. The visit allowed Rubens to discover further works by the Renaissance greats in the king's collection, especially Titian, but it also gave him an excellent opportunity to impress with his own painting. Whilst in Valladolid, he made his famous *Equestrian Portrait of the Duke of Lerma*, the lively and lifelike execution of which marks a turning point in the development of his art.
After his return from Spain to Italy, he was finally given the major commission he had long been waiting for from Vincenzo Gonzaga, who until then had been content to impose on him tasks of minor importance and copies. This commission involved the creation of three large-scale canvases for the Jesuit Church in Mantua: *Vincenzo Gonzaga and His Family in Adoration of the Holy Trinity* (Ducal Palace, Mantua), *The Baptism of Christ* and *The Transfiguration* (Museum of Fine Arts, Nancy). During various visits to Genoa at that time, he also painted portraits for members of the aristocracy.
From 1605 onwards, Peter Paul lived mostly in Rome with his brother Philip, who was in the service of one of the Vatican's cardinals as a secretary and librarian. During his stay in the Eternal City, he made several new works, one of the most impressive of which was for the main altar of the Oratorian Church. When the painting was installed above the altar, it became apparent that it could not be viewed properly because of an irritating reflection. The young artist immediately began to make a new version of the three panels, but this time on slate, a less reflective material.

A lifelong source of inspiration

In October 1608, Rubens hurriedly left Rome

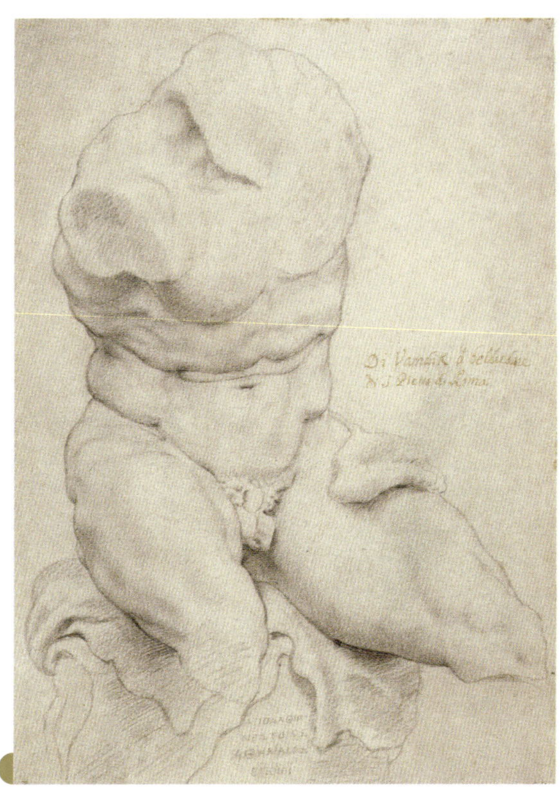

Peter Paul Rubens, **Belvedere Torso**, before 1608. Pencil and black chalk on paper, 37.5 x 26.9 cm. Antwerp, Rubens House

when he received news that his mother was dying. By the time he arrived back in Antwerp, she was already dead. He had spent eight years in Italy and was destined never to return. Even so, what he had seen there continued to influence him for the rest of his life.

The works he made in Italy initially showed traces of what he had learnt under Otto Van Veen, but these were soon merged with and eventually replaced by new creative impulses: the art of classical antiquity, the warm silvery palette of the Venetian School, the influence of artistic giants like Michelangelo, Raphael, Tintoretto, Titian and others. His style became freer, his colours more vibrant and more richly nuanced, and his compositions more heroically monumental in the manner of Graeco-Roman sculpture.

The sketchbooks and design folders he brought back from Italy, packed as they were with drawings and studies of ancient statues and Renaissance masterpieces, later provided him with inspiration for the religious and mythological scenes for which he was to become so famous. Working in combination with sketches made from live models, he used this Italian material as a kind of reference book on which he could draw for the rest of his career. But he was always able to integrate these 'borrowed' elements into his canvases in a vivid and original way.

A future in Antwerp

... They endeavour with all kinds of complements to keep me here. The Archduke and the Most Noble Infanta have even sent letters in the hope of convincing me to remain in their service.

P.P. Rubens to Johannes Faber, April 1609

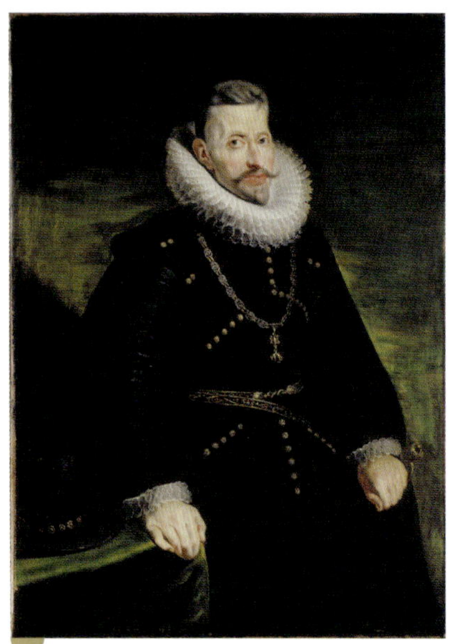

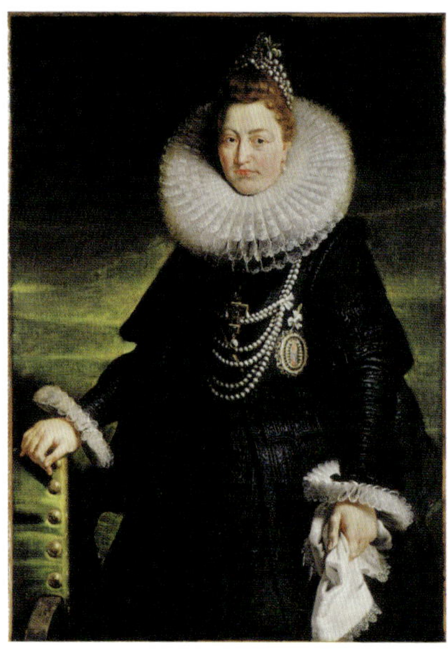

Workshop of P.P. Rubens, **Portrait of Archduke Albrecht** and **Portrait of Archduchess Isabella**, 1616–1617 or later. Canvas, both 119 x 86 cm. Antwerp, Rubens House

The Twelve Year Truce

Even though he missed the company of his friends in Italy ('those fine conversations that will often make me long to be back in Rome'), Rubens decided to stay in Antwerp. The political and military situation in the Low Countries was becoming clearer and more stable. Shortly before his death in 1598, the ageing Spanish king, Philip II, had entrusted the administration of the Netherlands (which in practice meant the Southern Netherlands, since the Northern Netherlands had already seceded) to his Austrian nephew, Albrecht, who in 1599 married the Infanta Isabella, Philip's oldest daughter. As the new governors, Albrecht and Isabella's first wish was to secure a lasting peace as quickly as possible with the Republic of the United Netherlands.

When Rubens arrived back in Antwerp in 1608, he found that people had high expectations for the peace treaty that seemed imminent. On 10 April 1609, he wrote to a friend: 'The peace, or rather a truce for a number of years, will no doubt be concluded in the near future and people think that this will herald in a period of renewed prosperity for the land. It is rumoured that it will be announced throughout all the provinces next week.' And he was right. Before the end of April, the Twelve Year Truce was proclaimed and all hostilities in the Low Countries were brought to an end. This policy of pursuing peace made the archduke and the archduchess much loved by the common people.

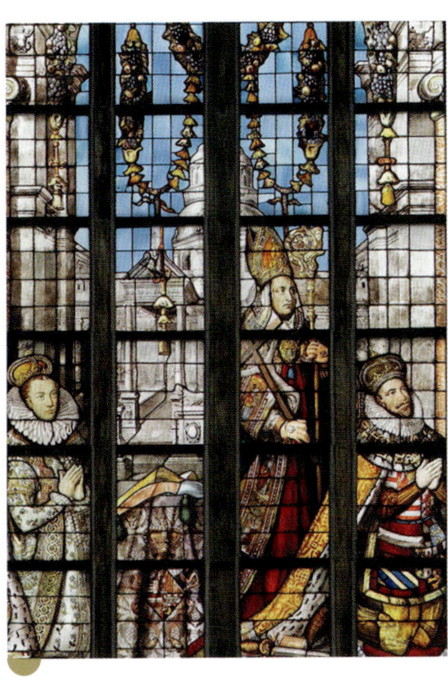

Archduke Albrecht and Archduchess Isabella in Adoration of the Cross, 1616. Stained glass. Antwerp, Cathedral of Our Lady

—

This stained glass panel was a gift from Albrecht and Isabella to the cathedral.

Rubens was also right about the renewal of prosperity. Once peace had been restored, the economy soon began to pick up again. This period of 'reconstruction' was defined by a re-emergent and triumphant Catholicism, a movement that came to be known as the Counter-Reformation. Churches and monasteries that had been damaged during the religious troubles or whose works of art had been stolen were now rebuilt and redecorated with a new grandeur. Religious art in the broadest sense of the term - buildings, painting, sculpture, tapestry-making, engraving and many other skills and crafts - flourished in the Southern Netherlands with a vigour and a lustre never previously seen.

This was particularly true in the trading metropolis of Antwerp, where many artists and wealthy art-lovers resided, creating a climate that was highly favourable towards this new artistic élan. Guilds and brotherhoods of many different kinds were anxious to have their own beautifully embellished altar in the cathedral or in their local parish church, while rich merchants and the aristocracy were keen to display their wealth by making donations to religious establishments in the form of art.

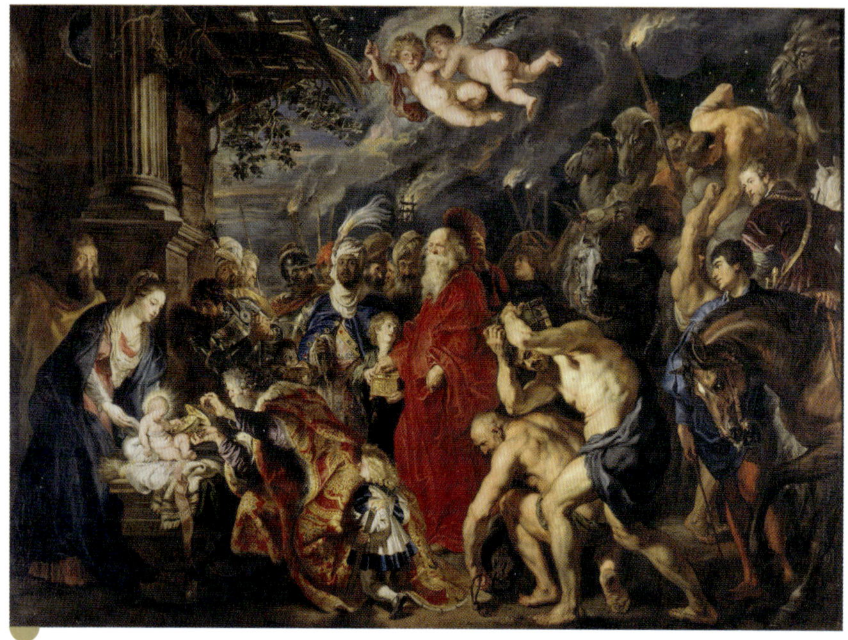

Peter Paul Rubens, **The Adoration of the Magi**, 1608–1609 and 1628 (additions). Canvas, 346 x 488 cm. Madrid, Prado Museum

A sensational new style: the Baroque

Following his return, Rubens soon started to receive commissions for altarpieces and other religiously inspired works. Within months of taking up residence, the city council engaged him to paint an *Adoration of the Magi* for the town hall, which was soon to be the venue for international peace negotiations. Probably around the same time, he was commissioned to make an altarpiece for the Brotherhood of the Blessed Sacrament, to be erected in the Dominican church (now St. Paul's Church) in Antwerp. It depicted *The Veneration of the Blessed Sacrament* (see page 129), though it should perhaps properly be known as *The Disputation of the Nature of the Holy Eucharist*. During this same period he made another large painting for the same church, this time depicting *The Adoration of the Shepherds* (see page 131), though the name of the patron is not known.

In 1610, he completed *The Elevation of the Cross* (see page 100), a painting for the high altar of the (no longer extant) St. Walburga Church. Commissioned by the church wardens, this triptych marked the spectacular introduction north of the Alps of the new style Rubens had first seen in Italy, a style that perfectly matched the spirit of the Counter-Reformation: the Baroque, a more exuberant form of the art of the Renaissance. His monumental formats, never before seen in this part of the world, combined with the vigour

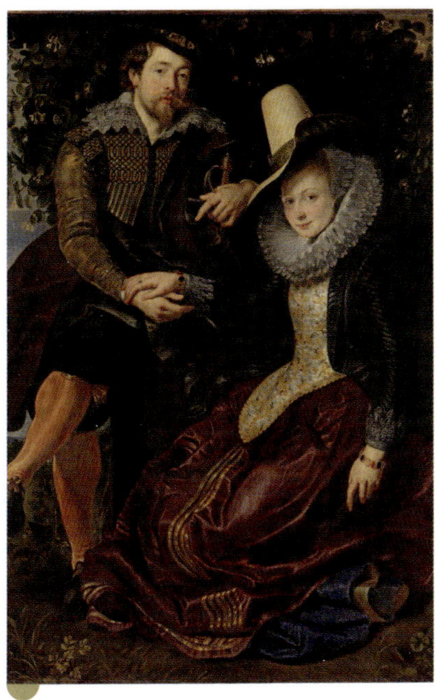

Peter Paul Rubens, **The Artist and his Wife in a Honeysuckle Bower**, 1609. Canvas affixed to panel, 178 x 136.5 cm. Munich, Old Picture Gallery

—

Rubens painted this portrait in 1609 for the occasion of his marriage.

Peter Paul Rubens, **Clara Serena**, ca. 1616. Canvas affixed to panel, 33 x 26.3 cm. Vaduz-Vienna, Liechtenstein, The Princely Collections.

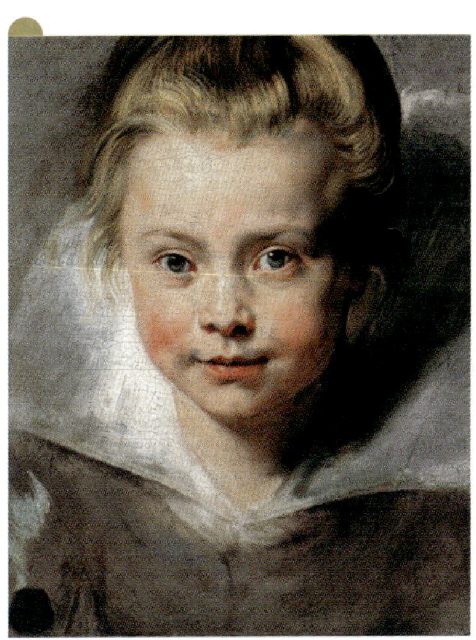

and energy of his compositions, made a huge impression on the viewing public and quickly transformed him into the most important painter in the Southern Netherlands.

Antwerp rather than Brussels

In September 1609, at the age of 32, Rubens was appointed as 'painter of the House of Their Majesties'. He only accepted this honour on condition that he was not required to move to the royal court in Brussels. One of the main reasons for his wishing to stay in Antwerp was his marriage in October 1609 to 18-year-old Isabella Brant, a daughter of city registrar Jan Brant. A year later, he bought a property with a piece of land on the Wapper, in the parish of St. James and close to the Meir, which was then the main thoroughfare in Antwerp. He had the house rebuilt to his own design in a Renaissance style and extended it with a new workshop. While the work was being carried out, he lived with his in-laws in the Kloosterstraat. Records show that on 21 March 1611, his daughter Clara Serena was baptised, the first of three children that Isabella Brant would bear him.

The unfolding of a great talent

> I do not know what I should most praise in my friend Peter Paul Rubens: his skilfulness in the art of painting, where experts say he has achieved perfection - if anyone today is capable of such a thing - or his wide knowledge of literature, or his fine insight that he combines with a remarkably pleasing verbal skill and congenial conversation.
>
> The Bavarian theologian Gaspar Scioppius writing about P.P. Rubens, 1607

Bravura and pathos

Initially, Rubens continued to be strongly influenced by examples from Italy. His *Elevation of the Cross* was a synthesis of everything he had learned during his stay in that country: a monumental composition expressed in the muscular, sculptural style of Michelangelo (as can be clearly seen, for example, in the depiction of the executioners' assistants in the central panel) and rendered in the dazzling tones of the vibrant Venetian palette. The diagonality of the composition is full of dynamism and displays a subtle interplay of colours.

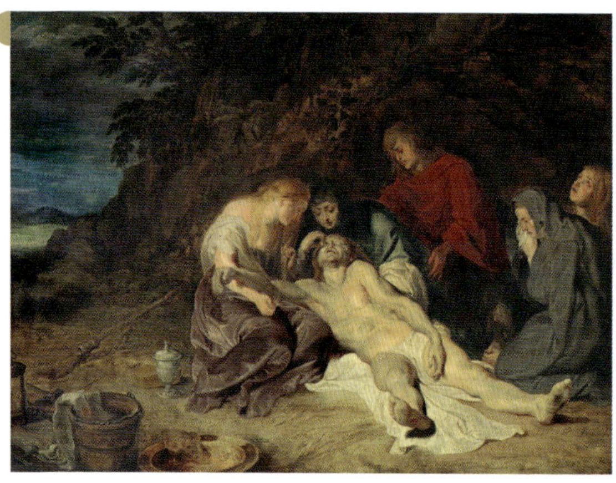

Peter Paul Rubens,
The Lamentation, 1614.
Panel, 55 x 73 cm. Antwerp, Royal Museum of Fine Arts

—

St. John the Evangelist and the holy women mourn the dead Jesus, whose body is laid out in front of the grave in the rock. The small dimensions of the work suggest it was intended for private devotion. The background landscape was painted by another Antwerp artist.

The figures are depicted in twisted, backward-leaning or bent postures, in which they make pathetic gestures of sorrow and anger, with the bright reflections of light on the bodies contrasting sharply with the darker shades of the robes, while the curls of the women and the mane of the horse add a clear sense of movement. This bravura style can generally be said to characterize Rubens' work during the period between 1609 and 1612. As a result, this first 'turbulent' period is often referred to as the '*Sturm und Drang*' phase of his artistic career.

The classical period

After just a few years, his style began to show more control and composure, as is clear from his *Descent from the Cross* (see page 106), which he painted between 1611 and 1614 for the altar of the Guild of Harquebusiers in Antwerp cathedral. The composition shows greater simplicity and clarity, while the postures and gestures are more restrained than in his earlier works. This marked the start of a new phase in his stylistic development:

Peter Paul Rubens, **The Four Continents**, ca. 1615–1616. Canvas, 208 x 283 cm. Vienna, Art History Museum

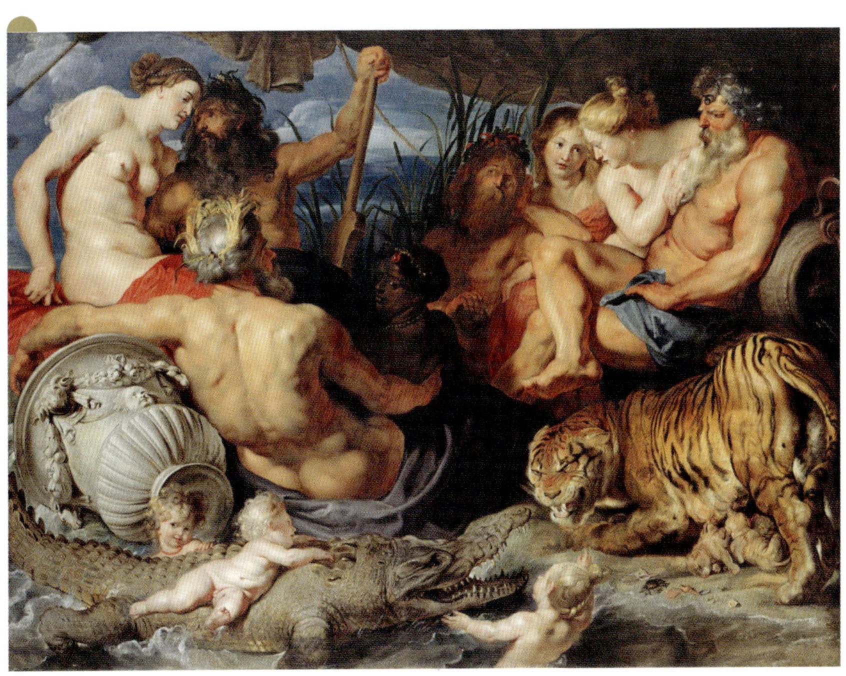

the classical period. The colouring is clearer and with fewer contrasts, while the contours are softer and less starkly defined. The light is cooler and more evenly distributed, adding relief to the forms that are often depicted against a neutral background. It is almost as if a silvery sheen has been added over the colours. These characteristics can be found in the mythological and religious scenes painted by Rubens in the years between 1612 and 1615. Examples include his *Resurrection of Christ*, also known as the Moretus Triptych (see page 102), the allegorical *Venus Frigida* (see page 78) and *The Four Continents*, *The Epitaph for Nicolaas Rockox and His Wife Adriana Perez*, also known as *The Doubting of St. Thomas* (see page 76), which Rubens painted for his friend and patron, Nicolaas Rockox, and *The Blessed Virgin in Adoration Before the Sleeping Infant Jesus* (see page 120), a small panel for personal devotion.

A philosophical conversation piece

It was also during this period that Rubens painted the group portrait of *Justus Lipsius and His Pupils*, also known as *The Four Philosophers*. Behind a table strewn with books sits the

Bust of 'Seneca', marble sculpture, Roman, first century A.D. Antwerp, Rubens House

—

When Rubens returned to Antwerp in 1608, he brought with him this ancient bust, in the belief that it depicted Lucius Annaeus Seneca. As such, he painted it in a number of his works. However, in 1813 archaeologists were able to show that it did not, in fact, portray Seneca, but an unknown Greek from the classical period. It is possible that the bust, which was gifted to the Rubens House in 1952, is Rubens' original 'Seneca', though it may only be a faithful copy.

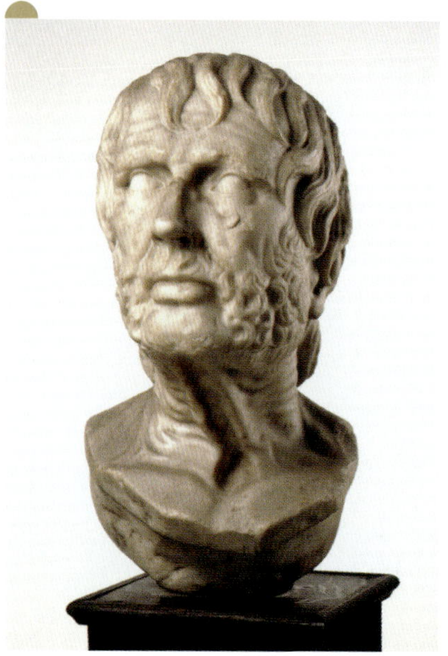

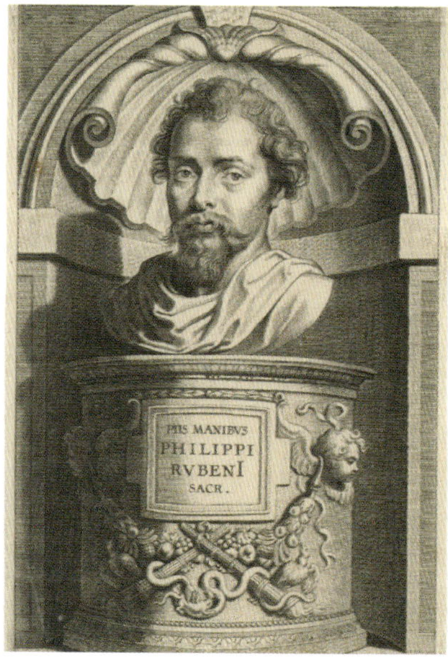

South Netherlands humanist Justus Lipsius, who is in the act of instructing two of his pupils, Johannes Woverius (right) and Rubens' brother, Philip (left). A little further in the background on the left, partly in shadow, the artist has added a portrait of himself. He was not a pupil of Lipsius, but was certainly an admirer and shared his philosophical beliefs. In the niche on the right stands a classical bust, which is thought to be of Seneca (it is known that Rubens had such a bust in his own art collection). The four tulips symbolize the four people in the portrait, two of whom were already dead by the time the work was completed. This explains why two of the tulips are still in bud, while two are fully open. Peter Paul most probably painted *The Four Philosophers* (the fourth is Seneca, not Rubens himself) to commemorate his brother, who died in 1611.

This painting is an illustration of the Neo-Stoic ideas that the artist had in common with his cultivated circle of friends all over Europe. In Antwerp, he kept the company of a group of humanist-inclined patricians, rich businessmen, religious dignitaries and senior civic officials, such as burgomaster Nicolaas Rockox, town registrar Jan Gaspar Gevartius, the merchant

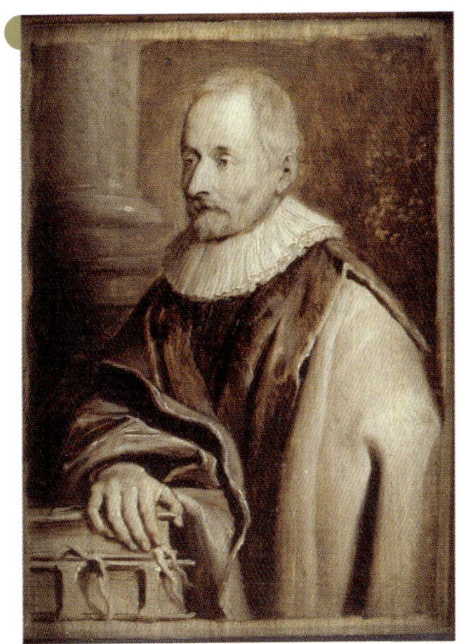

Erasmus II Quellinus, **Portrait of Balthasar I Moretus.** Grisaille on panel, for the engraver Cornelis Galle. Antwerp, Plantin-Moretus Museum

Portrait of Philip Rubens, engraving by Cornelis Galle after P.P. Rubens, in Ph. Rubens, **S. Asterii Amaseae Homeliae,** Antwerp, 1615. Antwerp, Plantin-Moretus Museum

A philosophy of life based on a classical model

Lipsius, who died in 1606, was a highly respected philosopher, philologist and historian. He taught in Leiden and Leuven, and was responsible for printed editions of the works of Roman writers, like Tacitus and Seneca. In his *De constantia libri*, published in 1584, he expounded his philosophy of Christian stoicism, a way of living that regarded 'fortitude' as the highest virtue, based on an all-embracing spirit of reasonableness, resulting in an unshakeable peace of mind. His thinking was influenced by the texts of the Roman philosopher Seneca (1st century A.D.), whose vision was compatible in many respects with the ideas of Christendom.

Lipsius also wrote Latin poems and political treatises. In 1637, his collected works were published under the title *Justus Lipsius, Opera Omnia* by Balthasar I Moretus, who was then head of the Gulden Passer (Golden Compass), the Plantin printing workshop in Antwerp. Rubens designed the title page for this publication. For his contemporaries, Lipsius was the leading modern interpreter of the much-admired culture of classical Roman antiquity in its most exalted moral form. Philip Rubens and Balthasar I Moretus had both studied under him at Leuven.

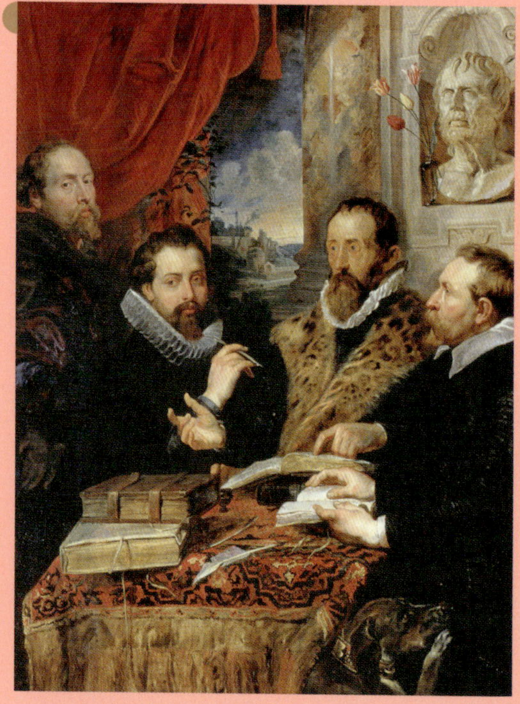

Peter Paul Rubens, **Justus Lipsius and His Pupils (The Four Philosophers)**, 1611–1612. Panel, 67 x 143 cm. Florence, Pitti Gallery

Cornelis van der Geest, the printer Balthasar I Moretus and the prior of the Antwerp Dominicans, Michael Ophovius. Together, they shared a passion for the culture and art of classical antiquity and the Italian Renaissance, which had its origins in that culture.

Valued as an artist and as a person

Rubens' family ties and intellectual upbringing meant that he was well connected within the higher circles of Antwerp society. It was here that he also found his earliest patrons. Nicolaas Rockox was captain of the Harquebusiers when its guild commissioned *The Descent from the Cross*; a painting of *Samson and Delilah* hung above the fireplace in the drawing room of

Peter Paul Rubens, **Samson and Delilah**, ca. 1609. Panel, 185 x 205 cm. London, National Gallery

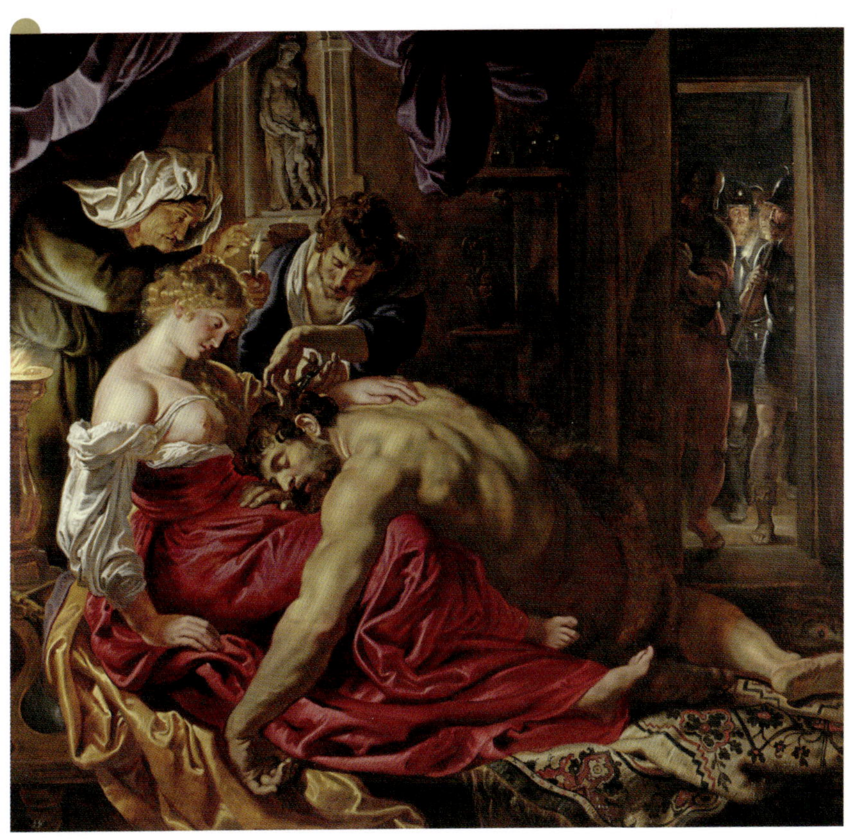

his home; and he also had Rubens paint a triptych for his future burial chapel. The Moretus family also gave him various commissions, including a triptych for the burial chapel of Jan I Moretus, the father of Balthasar. Michael Ophovius was prior of the Antwerp Dominicans, who acquired several of Rubens' paintings for their church. As an influential parishioner of the St. Walburga Church, it was Cornelis van der Geest who was able to ensure that Rubens received the commission for *The Elevation of the Cross*. These are just a few examples of the patronage he received from Antwerp's elite. In addition, throughout the years he made numerous portraits of his fellow citizens, relatives and friends, such as Gevartius, Ophovius and many others.

As well as being a highly respected artist, Rubens must have been charming as a person. His few surviving self-portraits show a man of refined and attractive appearance. In 1677, Roger de Piles described him as follows: 'He was tall of stature with a dignified bearing, regular facial features, rosy cheeks, chestnut brown hair, eyes that sparkled, but with a tempered glow, and a cheerful, gentle and honest appearance.' About his personality, the same biographer wrote: 'He had a friendly demeanour, an accommodating character, was relaxed in conversation, clear and perceptive

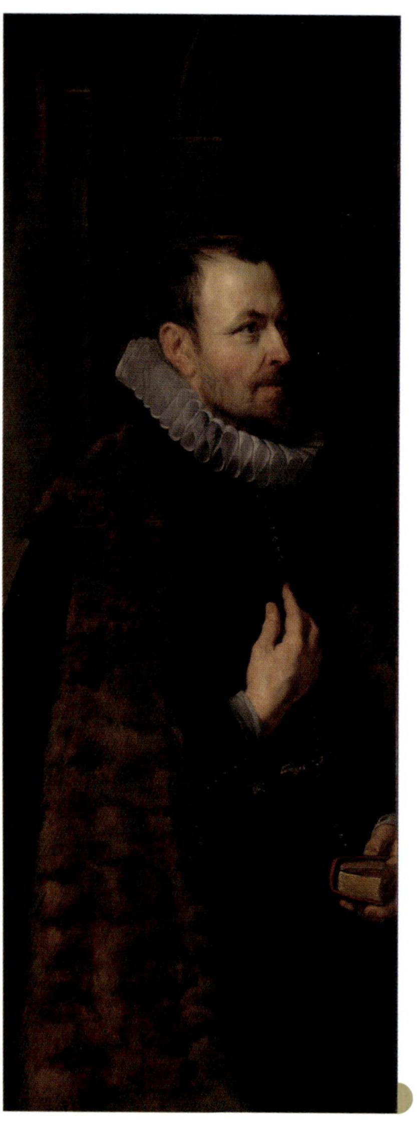

Portrait of Nicolaas Rockox on the left panel of the epitaph triptych (with **The doubting of St. Thomas**), which Rubens painted for the future burial chapel of the Rockox couple in the Church of the Friars Minor in Antwerp.

in thought, and prudent in speech, with a pleasing voice; this all combined to make him naturally eloquent and persuasive.' De Piles based his comments on the testimony of one of the artist's sons and a nephew.

Numerous surviving documents of the day also testify to the high esteem in which Rubens was held. He maintained a busy correspondence with his learned friends abroad and was an interesting and entertaining letter-writer. This is clear, for example, from his correspondence with Nicolas-Claude Fabri de Peiresc, a French humanist and expert in classical antiquity. Thanks to his intrinsic nobility, his pleasing manner and his wide-ranging knowledge, Rubens not only enjoyed the respect of his coterie of friends in Antwerp, but also of his correspondents abroad, many of whom moved in the highest royal circles.

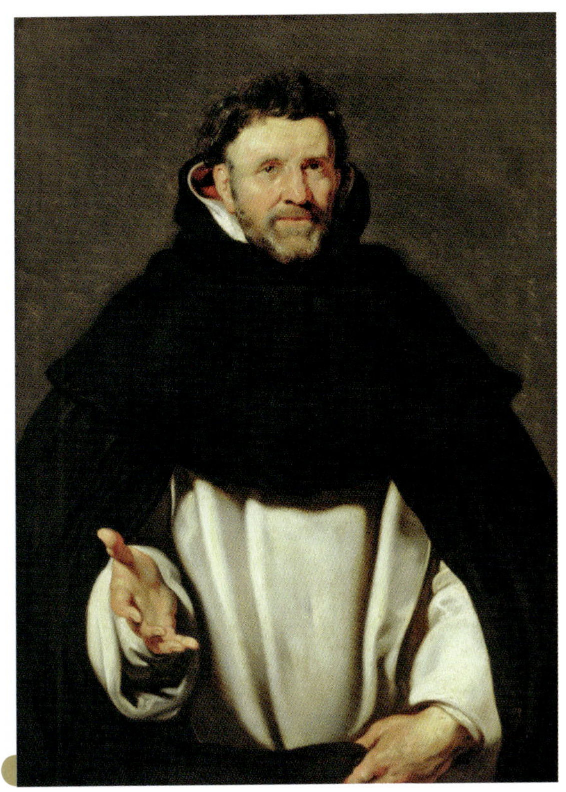

Peter Paul Rubens or workshop, **Portrait of Michael Ophovius**, 1617. Canvas, 114.5 x 85 cm. Antwerp, Rubens House

—

The priest Michael Ophovius (or van Ophoven) was the prior of the Antwerp Dominicans when he was painted by Rubens in 1617. He is wearing the habit of the Mendicant Order of Preachers, who were also known as the Dominicans after their founder, St. Dominic. Ophovius's ceremonial tomb is in St. Paul's Church and was probably designed by Rubens in 1631, at the prior's request. The artist was well known to the priest, who may have been his confessor.

—

This painting is a copy made in Rubens' workshop under his personal supervision. The original is on display in the Maurits House in The Hague.

Protagonist of the Baroque

His mansion is newly built to his own design in the Italian style, in the Doric order and using the finest grey stone. Amongst other things, the interior contains many outstanding paintings and other artefacts, and there is also a small round room, lit only by daylight from the lunette in the vault; it is full of antique marble statues: busts and whole figures of gods and goddesses, emperors, generals, Greek and Roman senators, and beautiful children in all shapes and sizes [...] It is said that Rubens earns 50,000 pounds a year, because he works non-stop and sells his paintings for high prices.

Pierre Bergeron, the secretary of a French nobleman, describing the Rubens House, 1619

Peter Paul Rubens, **The Crowning of the Virtuous Hero**, 1613–1614. Panel, 221.5 x 201 cm. Munich, Old Picture Gallery

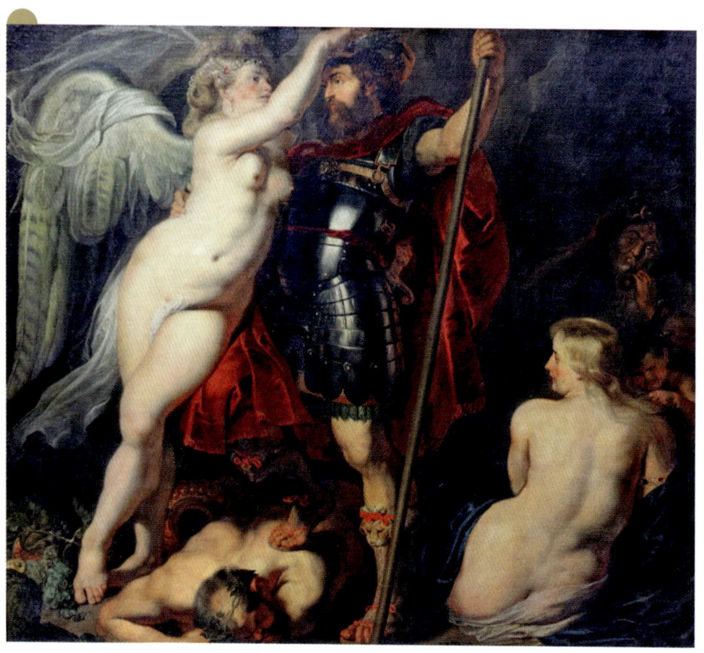

A variety of themes, from the religious to the erotic

Once the Twelve Year Truce came into effect, the number of travellers in the Southern Netherlands began to increase, with many of them keen to visit the magnificent churches in Antwerp. Here they were confronted with Rubens' magnificent paintings, and the artist soon began to receive new commissions for similar 'counter-reformational' altarpieces from churches in Brussels, Ghent, Lille, Mechelen, Lier and elsewhere. This was followed a few years later by a new surge of more important commissions from abroad.

Of course, Rubens' work was not confined to religious subjects, although this genre is strongly represented in his oeuvre. The members of the upper class and nobility wanted to decorate their drawing rooms and reception rooms with paintings. In addition to religious themes, this wealthy public also had interest for landscapes, still lifes, genre pieces, hunting scenes and portraits, usually of small to medium size. Mythological and allegorical subjects were particularly popular. He often celebrated nudity, especially female nudity, in these works, which he depicted with an unparalleled sensuality and elegance that was both tangible and elevated, and increased in sensitivity as time passed.

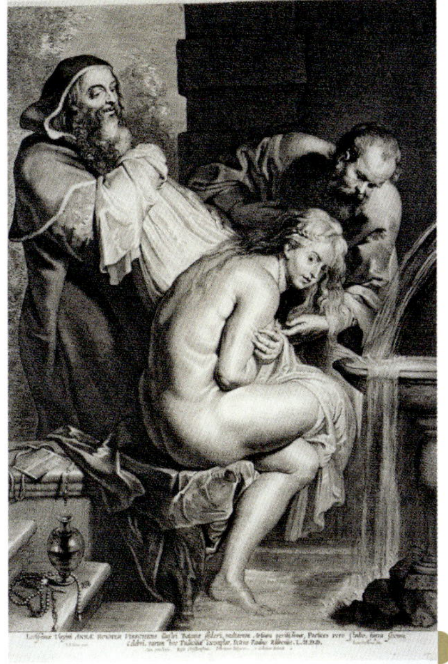

Susanna and the Elders, woodcut by Christoffel Jegher after P.P. Rubens, 1630s (?). Antwerp, Plantin-Moretus Museum

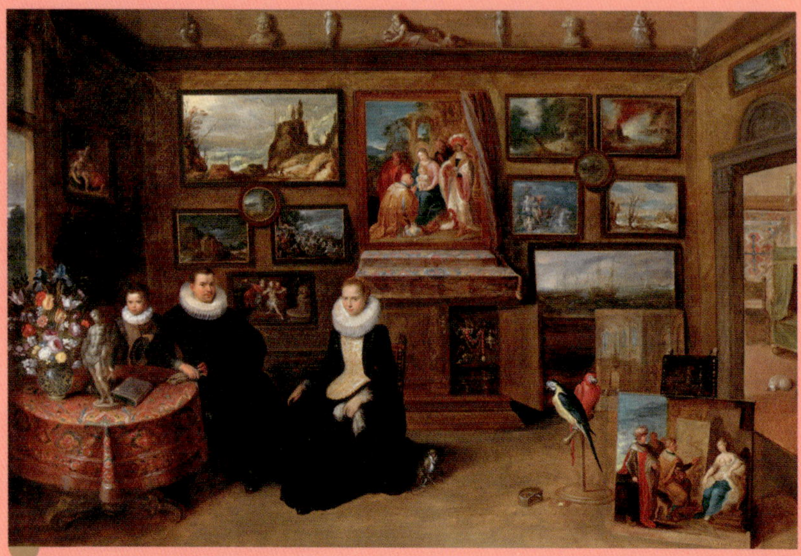

Frans Francken the Younger, **The Art Cabinet of Sebastiaan Leerse**, ca. 1630. Panel, 77 x 114 cm. Antwerp, Royal Museum of Fine Arts

Antwerp, centre of the Flemish Baroque

In the first half of the 17th century, art in general – and not just religious art in the wake of the Counter-Reformation – enjoyed a powerful revival in various cities in the Southern Netherlands. In particular (and as had also been the case in the 16th century), there was a strong concentration of artists and capital in the commercial metropolis of Antwerp. Because the economy stagnated as a result of the religious wars, the lack of any other alternative persuaded wealthy merchants and capitalists to invest their money heavily in works of art. This allowed some of Antwerp's richer citizens to build up fabulous collections, which were displayed in the 'art cabinets' of their homes. These cabinets contained not only paintings, drawings and engravings by contemporary artists and old masters, but also ancient sculptures, Roman coins, medallions and other curiosities.

To satisfy this huge demand, the city's workshops produced a large and varied range of paintings and sculptures. Rubens was certainly a trendsetting figure in these developments, but we should not forget that there were many other first-rate artists in the Southern Netherlands at this time. They made the new Baroque forms of expression their own, but used their personal skill and virtuosity to give the style a uniquely individual character. Their works not only found their way into the mansions of rich art-lovers, but also into the courts of governors and nobles, and even into the palaces of foreign princes and kings, since the style and compositional repertoire enjoyed the same popularity everywhere.

Antwerp display cabinet, first half of the 17th century. Lime wood and ebony, decorated with small paintings. Antwerp, Rubens House
—
This 'art cabinet' is decorated with mythological scenes, most of which are inspired by Rubens' work.

Jan Brueghel the Elder, **Flowers in a Vase**, early 17th century. Panel, 101 x 76 cm. Antwerp, Royal Museum of Fine Arts

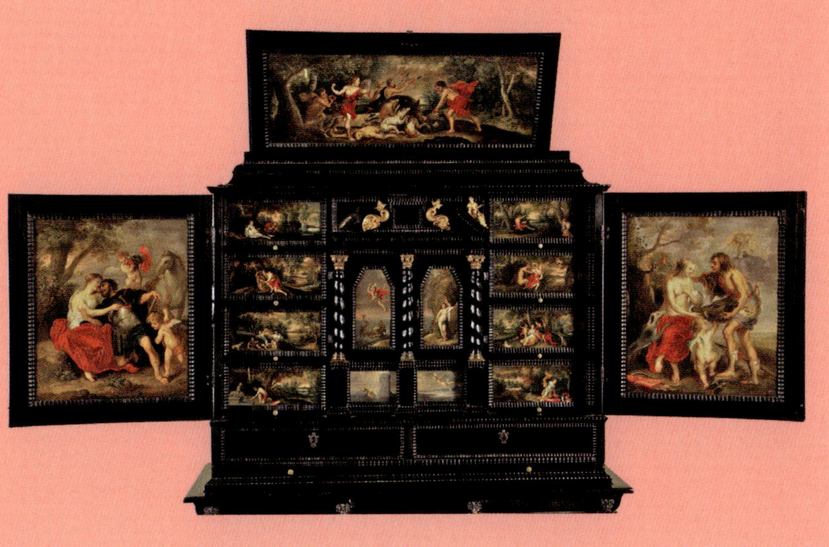

The Rubens House on the Wapper

Thanks to these favourable conditions and his tireless creative energy, Rubens was able to pay for the major renovation work to his property on the Wapper. It was around 1615 that he finally took up residence in this spacious mansion, which he refurbished completely in the Renaissance style. One wing contained his private living quarters, the other housed his workshop. With a frontage of 36 metres and grounds measuring more than 1,200 square metres, it was one of the grandest homes in Antwerp, as befitted one of the city's richest residents. The entire complex reflected both his artistic ideas and his personality.

A triple-arched Baroque portico divided the inner courtyard from a delightful garden. This portico was decorated with two statues of divinities from classical antiquity - a helmeted Athena (Minerva) and Hermes (Mercury) with his herald's baton - while the cartouches above the two side arches bore texts from the Roman poet Juvenal: *'Permittes ipsis expendere numinibus, quid / conveniat nobis, rebusq[ue] sit utile nostris / carior est illis homo quam sibi'* (Leave it to the gods to provide what is good and useful for us, for man is dearer to them than he is to himself) and *'Orandum est ut sit mens sana in corpore sano / fortem posce animum et mortis terrore carentem / nesciat irasci, cupiat nihil'* (Our prayer must be for a healthy mind in a sound body. Ask for a brave soul that has no fear of death and knows neither anger nor desire). Beyond the portico stood a balustrade, and beyond that the garden, laid out in a geometric pattern reminiscent of both classical

The façade of Rubens' workshop

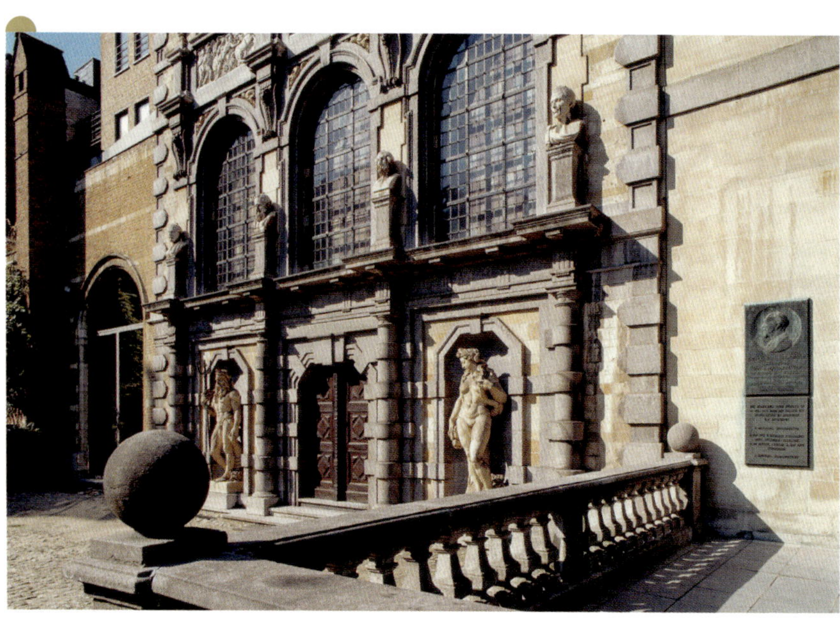

antiquity and the Renaissance. The central path led to a small temple, adorned with statues designed by Rubens in the classical style. To complete this classical picture, there was a fountain and a pergola supported by caryatids, sileni and nymphs.

The Baroque building, its interior and the garden were all altered after the artist's death and it later fell into disrepair for many years. It was only in 1937 that a major programme of renovation was initiated, with the aim of restoring the property as far as possible to its original state. Some parts needed to be rebuilt, but other parts are authentic, such as the portico and the garden pavilion.

Today, the Rubens House is home to a fascinating museum. The interior has been outfitted with authentic period furniture and other household items, so that visitors can get a sense of both the way Rubens lived and of his multifaceted personality. There are various works of art by the master himself, his mentors, his pupils and his contemporaries, and attention is also devoted to his own art collection, since like many of the wealthy citizens of 17th century Antwerp he was a fervent collector, not only of the art of his day, but also of ancient statues, coins and gemstones. Pride of place goes to the workshop where he created most of his huge output, an output that allowed him to write a new chapter in the history of art. Temporary exhibitions (and from the end of 2019 the brand new Rubens Experience Centre) ensure that a visit to the Rubens House always has something new and surprising to offer.

The portico in the Rubens House

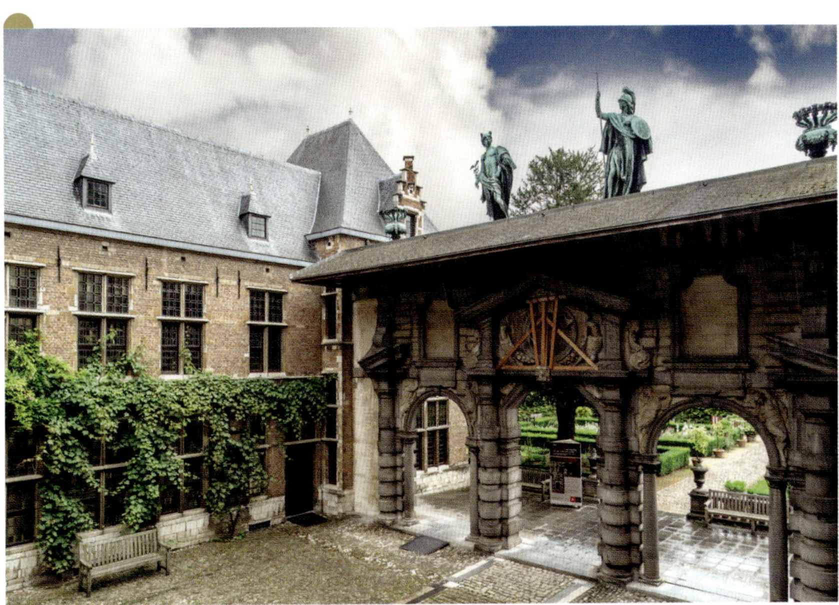

Spectacular productivity - with the help of his workshop

It seems that during the period 1615-1620, Rubens was able to alternate his use of the skills he had acquired in the previous phases of his artistic development to suit the requirements of the subject he was painting. Since his return from Italy, he had significantly enhanced the range of pictorial options available to him. This allowed him, as it were, to play different registers at the same time, providing him with the desired tonalities for the matter in hand, whatever it might be.

Frans Baudouin in *P.P. Rubens*, 1977

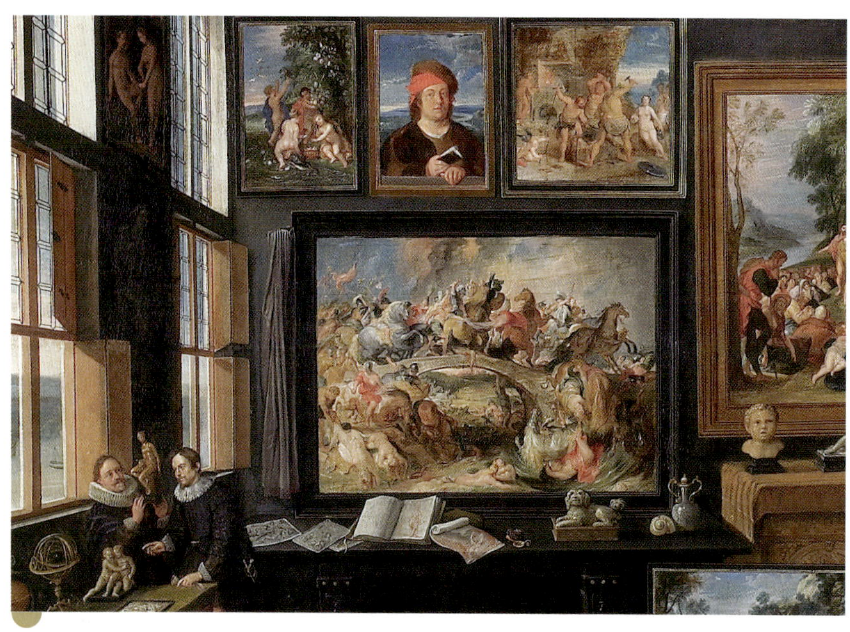

Willem van Haecht, **The Picture Gallery of Cornelis van der Geest**, 1628. Panel, 100 x 130 cm. Detail with **The Battle of the Amazons** by P.P. Rubens. Antwerp, Rubens House

With a first-class team, everything is possible

When Rubens finally moved into his new workshop on the Wapper in 1615 or 1616, it became possible for him to improve the overall organization of his work. By this time he was so famous and so overwhelmed with commissions that he was increasingly turning to assistants for help. The problem was that he had nowhere to put them. In his own words, from 1611 onwards he had been obliged to refuse the requests 'of more than a hundred pupils'. The new workshop changed all this. He could now employ a large and well-trained group of apprentices and assistants, allowing him to significantly boost his output while

Peter Paul Rubens,
The Hippopotamus and Crocodile Hunt, 1615–1616.
Canvas, 248 x 321 cm.
Munich, Old Picture Gallery

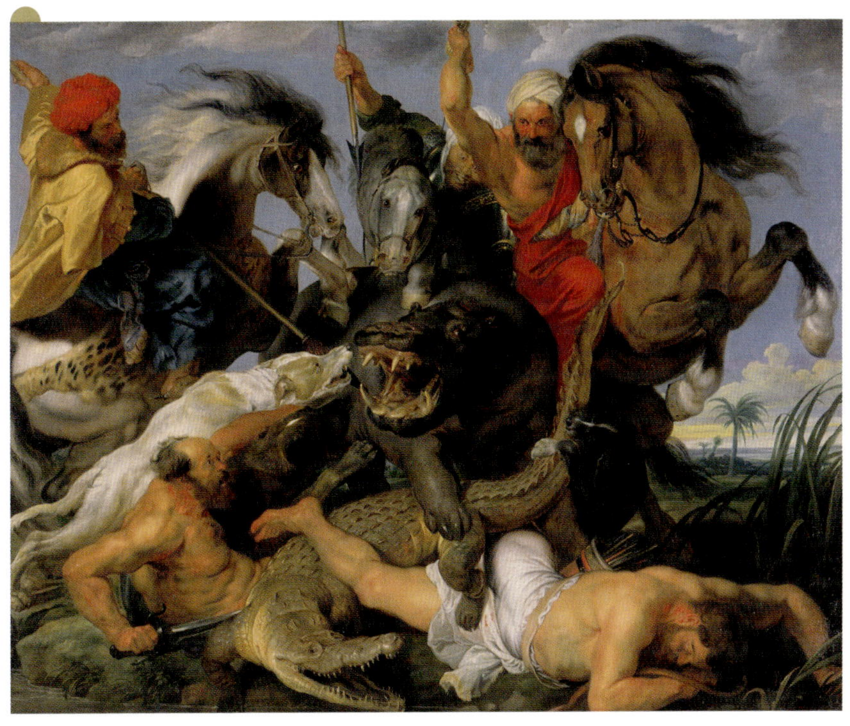

still maintaining the same high quality. It also made it easier for him to fulfil one of his formal obligations as court painter to the archduke and archduchess: the painting of official state portraits, which needed to be copied many times for senior court officials and public administrations.

The input of the workshop assistants varied from work to work. Some paintings - even some of the monumental ones - were completed in their entirety by Rubens himself. Others were prepared by the assistants, before being radically revised by the master. Sometimes, Rubens painted just the key elements, leaving the rest for his team to finish off. The assistants also made copies of popular subjects that were in great demand.

Harmony, nuance and dynamism

After 1615, Rubens' paintings again became more dramatic and mobile. He developed a theatrical High Baroque style in a series of works for aristocratic patrons at home and abroad that ranged from imposing (and sometimes ecstatic) religious themes to turbulent hunting and battle scenes, such as *The Battle of the Amazons* (Munich, Old Picture Gallery), a painting that was given pride of place in

Peter Paul Rubens, **Christ on the Straw**, ca. 1618. Panel, 138 x 98 cm (central panel), 136 x 40 cm (side panels). Antwerp, Royal Museum of Fine Arts

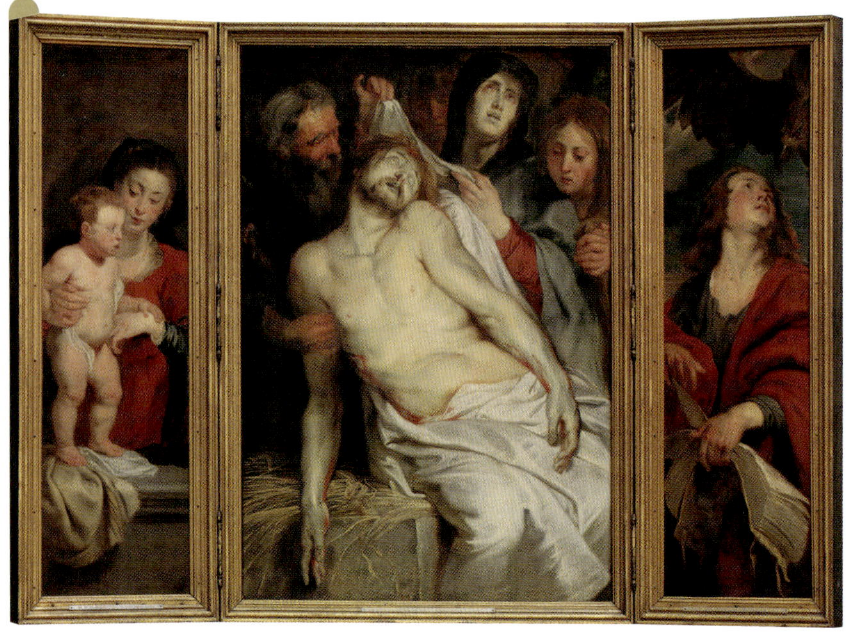

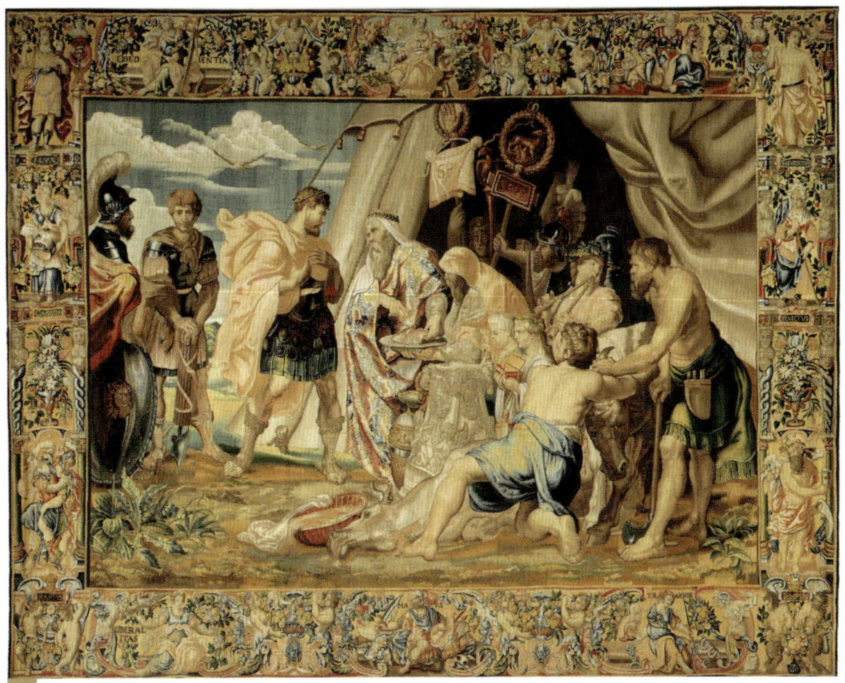

Decius Mus Consults the Oracle, tapestry by Jan Raes (Brussels) after a design by P.P. Rubens for the series **The Life of Decius Mus**, 1616–1617 (the designs). Antwerp, Rubens House

—

The tapestries tell the life story of the Roman consul Publius Decius Mus, as recounted by the Roman writer Livy. According to the contract, Rubens not only had to make the designs for the tapestries, but also supervise the quality of their execution in one of Brussels' foremost weaving studios.

Cornelis van der Geest's private art collection. Within the space of a few years, Rubens developed his talents to such an extent that he was master of a wide range of styles and tonalities, which he could adjust to suit his subject. The movements of the figures became more fluid, the colouring more nuanced, and the outlines and the zones of colour less clearly defined. His use of contrast, so severe in the first years following his return from Italy, was now less pronounced. It was replaced by softer harmonic transitions and subtle gradations of shading, sometimes in bright tones, sometimes in darker tones, but always within a dynamic composition that was built up with a clear sense of balance.

Examples of his work from this period that can still be seen in Antwerp include: *The*

Flagellation of Christ (see page 132), donated by a member of the Guild of Harquebusiers to the Dominican Church; *The Prodigal Son* (see page 81), a fine depiction of rural life; *The Last Communion of St. Francis of Assisi* (see page 82), purchased by a rich merchant for the St. Francis Chapel in the Church of the Friars Minor; and *The Lance* (see page 83), a work commissioned by Nicolaas Rockox for the high altar of the same church.

Tapestries and ceilings

A fine illustration of Rubens' sense of dramatic expression is the cycle of tapestries depicting *The Life of Decius Mus*. At the end of 1616, he received a commission from an Antwerp tapestry maker on behalf of a Genoese nobleman to paint the designs for this seven-part series. He personally painted the first sketches in oils on panel, before working with his assistants to transfer the designs onto larger canvases, the so-called cartoons, which would serve as patterns for the tapestry weavers to follow.

One of the assistants who worked on the cartoons was Anthony van Dyck. In 1620, just months before his departure from Antwerp, he was also involved in another major project: the decoration of the ceiling in the new Jesuit Church. By this time, the Baroque style was also making its appearance in architecture and the first church in Antwerp with a Baroque facade was the Jesuit Church (now the St. Charles Borromeo Church). The church's ground plan was the work of the Jesuit François Aguilon, but the remainder of the building was designed by Peter Huyssens, a Jesuit lay brother, in collaboration with Rubens. The artist not only made

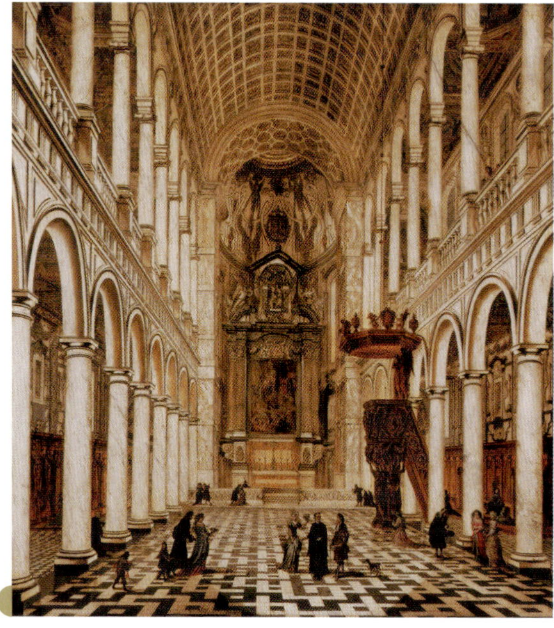

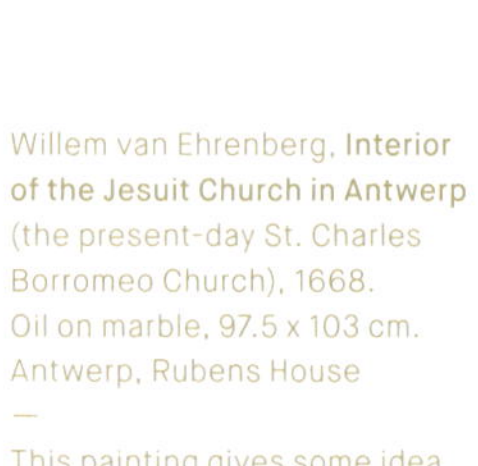

Willem van Ehrenberg, **Interior of the Jesuit Church in Antwerp** (the present-day St. Charles Borromeo Church), 1668. Oil on marble, 97.5 x 103 cm. Antwerp, Rubens House

—

This painting gives some idea of the interior before the fire of 1718, which destroyed the ceiling paintings of Rubens and his assistants.

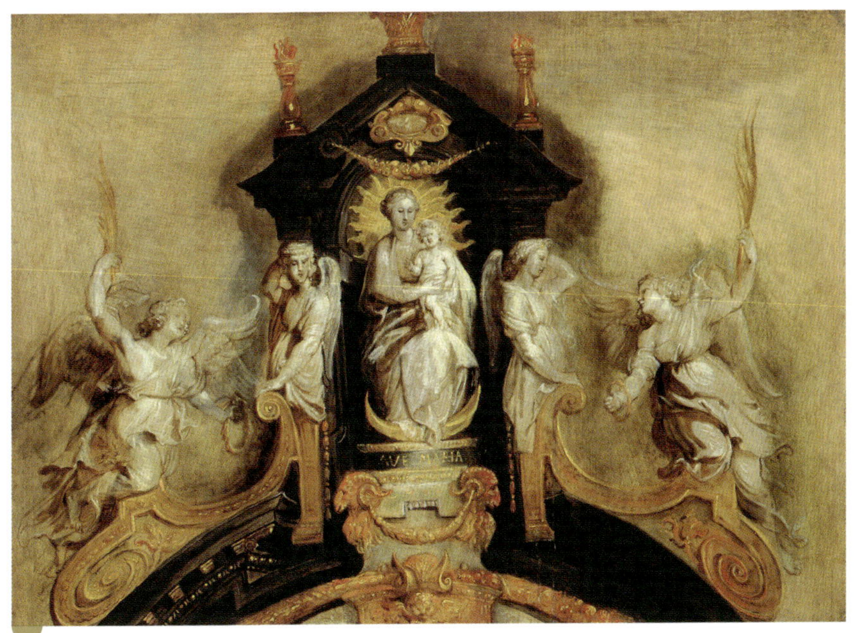

Peter Paul Rubens, **Design sketch for the crown work of the high altar in the Jesuit Church in Antwerp (?)**, ca. 1617. Oil sketch on panel, 44.5 x 64.8 cm. Antwerp, Rubens House

—

Until recently, it was thought that this detailed oil sketch in greyish tints (grisaille) was a design for the Jesuit Church, but it is now suggested that it was perhaps a sketch of the altar crown for the Carmelite Church, which was demolished in 1798.

important contributions to the design of the magnificent lantern tower and the sculptural decoration of the facade and the interior, but also produced a number of altarpieces and in 1620 painted no fewer than 39 ceiling panels in less than a year, which was only possible with substantial help from Anthony van Dyck. The end result was a church that is now regarded as the high point of the Baroque in the Netherlands. The wood-framed ceiling panels were destroyed by fire in 1718, but Rubens' preliminary oil on panel sketches have survived. They offer us a view from below in a dramatically foreshortened perspective of prophets and saints, doing God's work as they float far above our heads in the celestial spheres. *St. Clare Holding the Saracen Army at Bay with the Blessed Sacrament* (see page 149) is one of the finest examples.

The best pupil in the workshop

From circa 1617 to 1620, the young Anthony van Dyck (1599–1641) was active at the Rubens House in Antwerp, where he was one of the leading assistants. In fact, Rubens called him 'my best pupil' and he was closely involved in work on the cartoons for the tapestry cycle known as *The Life of Decius Mus*, as well as the ceiling decoration in the Jesuit Church. His collaboration with Rubens had a defining effect on his artistic development. He was skilled at copying his master's style, which made him an ideal workshop assistant, but at the same time he gradually evolved towards an immediately recognizable style of his own.

At the end of 1620, Van Dyck left his native city and travelled to London and Anthony, where he discovered the works of Titian, the Venetian artist who, together with Rubens, was his greatest long-term influence. As time passed, Van Dyck moved away from the monumental style of his mentor and eventually acquired fame and fortune as a painter of portraits, in which he combined gracefulness with aristocratic allure, elegant poses and the soft gradations of colour that characterize his oeuvre. In 1632, he was appointed court painter to the king of England and he had a lasting impact on English art.

Anthony van Dyck,
Self-portrait, ca. 1615–1616.
Panel, 36.5 x 25.8 cm.
Antwerp, Rubens House

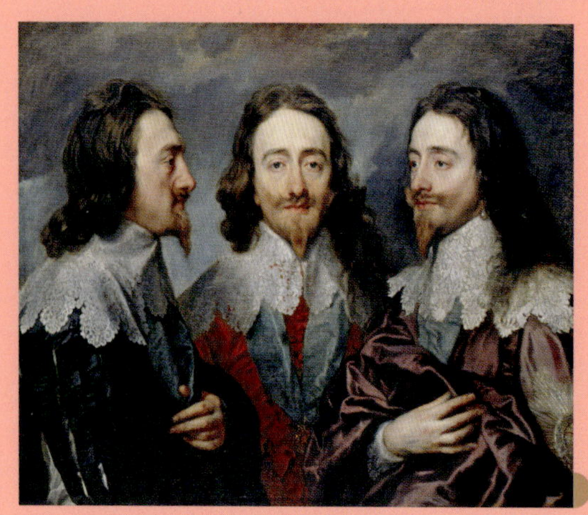

Anthony van Dyck, **King Charles I of England,** 1635-1636. The Royal Collection

Major commissions and international fame

I am the busiest man in the world, and the most under pressure!

P.P. Rubens to Palamède de Valavez, January 1625

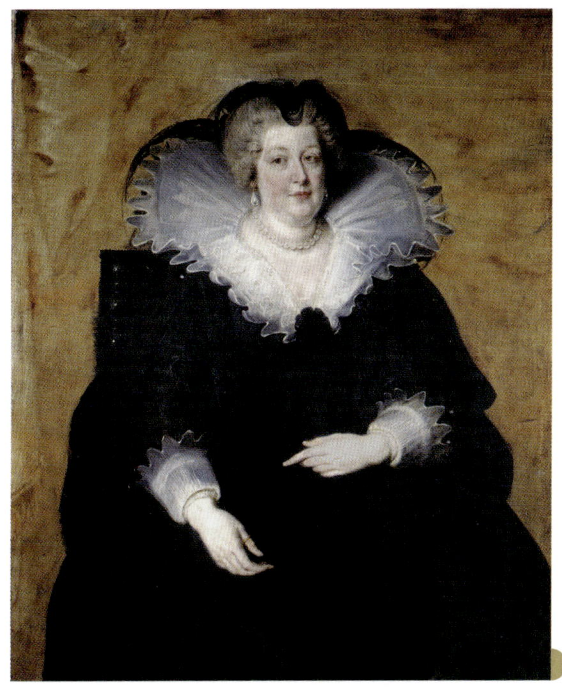

Peter Paul Rubens,
Portrait of Maria de Medici,
1622. Canvas, 130 x 108 cm.
Madrid, Prado Museum

The period of the large-scale series

Rubens' oeuvre shows great variety. His style evolved continually as it followed the various twists and turns of his artistic career. From about 1620 onwards, his brushwork and his technique moved in yet another new direction. He began to use a predominantly bright palette, but toning down the transitions from light to dark and working instead with more gradations and nuances within the same range of colours. As a result, outlines and even the colours themselves seemed to almost dissolve into an endlessly rich pattern of different shadings. This new approach, which was already evident in *The Lance*, was an extension of the technique used for oil sketches, a technique in which Rubens was extremely proficient.

The period starting circa 1620 and ending in 1628 can broadly be described as 'the period of the large-scale series'. One of the earliest precursors of this period was the series of ceiling paintings for the Jesuit Church in Antwerp.

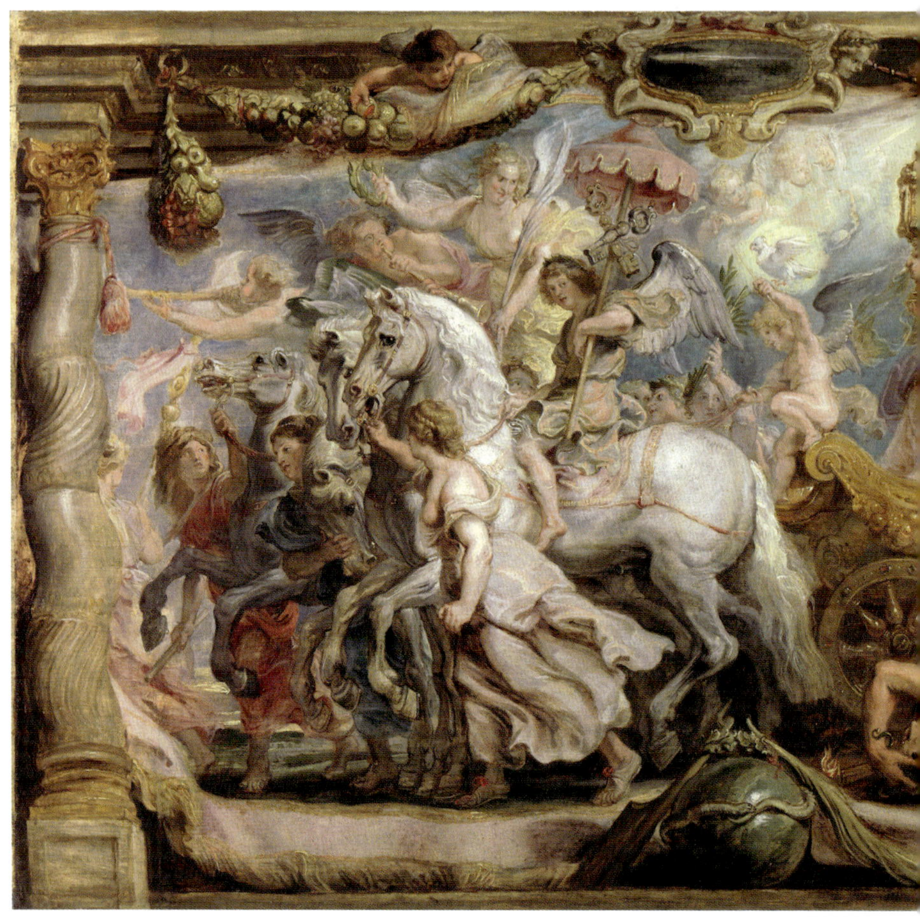

The move towards this type of work signalled Rubens' breakthrough in Europe. Within a relatively short space of time, he received a number of major commissions from foreign courts, either for ensembles of paintings or for the design of tapestry cycles. He had already completed foreign assignments in the past, but nothing on this scale or frequency.

Between 1622 and 1625, he was commissioned by Maria de Medici, the dowager queen of France, to paint a series of 25 canvasses for the decoration of the Luxembourg Palace in Paris (now part of the collection in the Louvre Museum). In this series, he gave the ageing queen's dull and unexciting life a new lustre, surrounding her with gods and heroes from classical antiquity. Impressed with the result, she offered him a second commission, this time for an ensemble about the life of her husband, King Henry IV. The series was never made, but

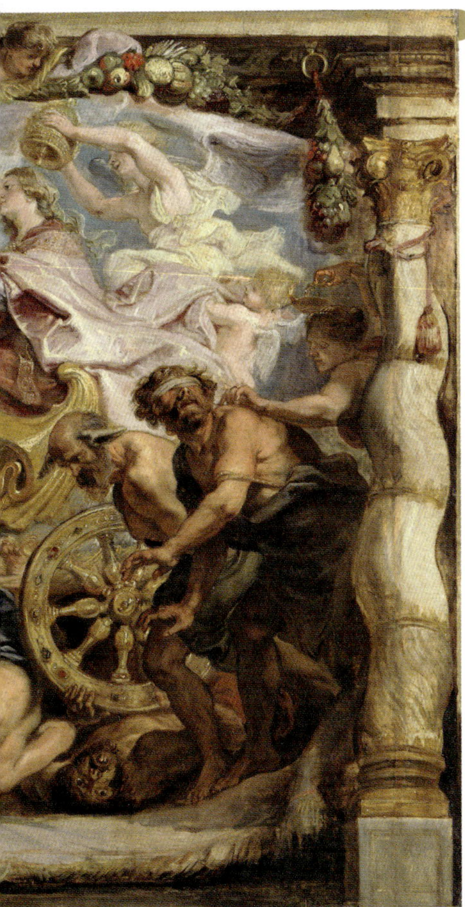

Peter Paul Rubens, **The Triumph of the Catholic Church**, ca. 1626. Oil sketch on panel, 86 x 105 cm. **Modello** for one of the large tapestries in the series **The Triumph of the Eucharist**. Madrid, Prado Museum

later Rubens did design a set of 12 tapestries illustrating *The Life of the Emperor Constantine* for her son, King Louis XIII.

Around 1626-1627, he also designed a series of 20 tapestries for the Infanta Isabella. The theme was *The Triumph of the Eucharist* and the series was intended as a glorification of the Roman Catholic Church. Woven in Brussels, the tapestries were destined for the Descalzas Reales, a convent of the Discalced Carmelites in Madrid, where the archduchess had spent part of her youth.

The pinnacle of High Baroque art

During this same period, Rubens also painted numerous large altarpieces, which were characterized by a breathtakingly beautiful unity of composition. The *perpetuum mobile* generated by the fluctuating movements and counter-movements of the different figures combine to create a graceful synthesis. Rubens achieved this coherence by using an extremely variegated palette. *The Adoration of the Magi* (see page 85), a panel painted by the artist in 1624 for the high altar of the (no longer extant) church at St. Michael's Abbey in Antwerp; *The Assumption of the Blessed Virgin* (see page 109) from 1625-1626, intended for the high altar of the cathedral; and his *Madonna Enthroned with Saints* (see page 86) from 1628, which once graced the high altar of St. Augustine's Church in Antwerp, must be reckoned as three of the most sublime masterpieces of High Baroque art. *The Annunciation* (see page 151), also known as *The Leganés Annunciation*, after the Spanish marquis who purchased the canvas in 1628, was intended for the owner's private chapel and, consequently, was painted in a more intimate, less heroic style, notwithstanding its large format.

In this more pictorial approach that Rubens adopted in his work after 1620, colour and brushwork both played a key role. It is almost as

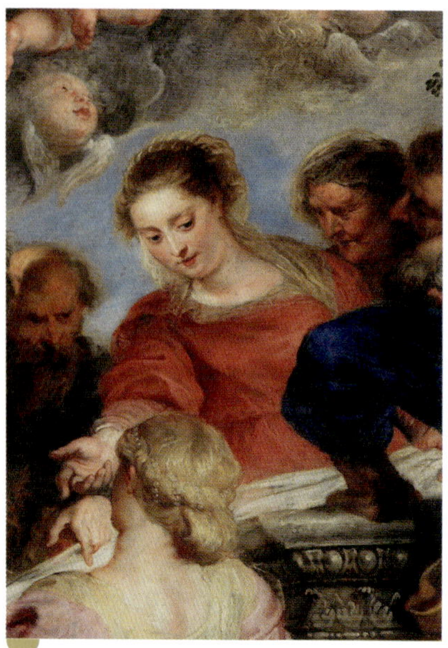

Peter Paul Rubens, **The Assumption of the Blessed Virgin**, 1625–1626. Panel, 490 x 325 cm. Detail of the woman who is pointing at the grave. Antwerp, Cathedral of Our Lady

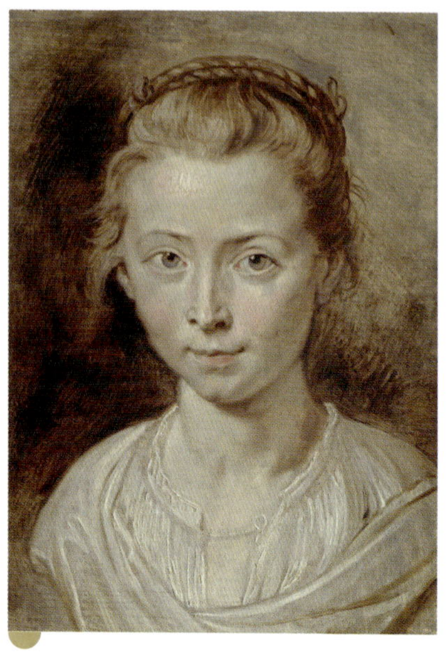

Attributed to P.P. Rubens, **Portrait of Clara Serena Rubens**, ca. 1620-1625 (?). Panel, 35.6 x 26 cm. Antwerp, Rubens House (long-term loan from a private collection, London)

—

Is the girl in this portrait really Clara Serena Rubens? In the past, there was some doubt about this, as there also was about the attribution to Rubens, but now that recent cleaning work has restored the painting's former sheen, both propositions seem more likely to be correct. The depiction of the clever face, the open-necked shirt and the drapery around the shoulders all point in the direction of the master. Clara died when she was just 12 years old. Perhaps Rubens painted her after her death, as a precious reminder of what he had lost.

if this 'material' way of painting expresses the sheer pleasure experienced by the artist when working with his brushes and oils. The dazzling colours, naked bodies, luxuriant fabrics and swirling movements conjure up a picture of a man with a forceful personality and a true lust for life.

Farewell to a wonderful companion

Even so, these years were also years of trial for Rubens and his family. During the early decades of the 17th century, plague killed thousands of people in Antwerp. To avoid one such epidemic, the Rubens household moved to Brussels in 1625, only returning to their home in February 1626. But it was all to no avail. Isabella contracted plague just months later and died on 20 June 1626, at the age of just 34. She left behind two sons, Albert and Nicolas (their oldest child, Clara Serena, died at an early age).

Peter Paul wrote to a friend: 'I have lost a most wonderful companion. It was impossible not to love her, because she had none of the failings that are typical of her sex. She had no capricious moods, no feminine weakness, but was all goodness and honesty, virtues for which she was admired by everyone who knew her during her life and now mourn her in death.'

At the time, Rubens was completing his *Assumption of the Blessed Virgin* for the high altar in Antwerp cathedral, and so he added Isabella's features to the female figure dressed in red in the middle of the composition.

Later that same year, he was troubled by health problems of his own. During a visit to France, he suffered from persistent pain in his foot. This was probably an attack of gout, an affliction that was destined to torment him regularly as he grew older.

The Two Sons of Rubens, burin engraving by J. Daullé of a design by Charles Hutin after P.P. Rubens, 18th century. Antwerp, Plantin-Moretus Museum

—

This print is based on a painting that Rubens made in 1626–1627, shortly after the death of Isabella Brant: **Portrait of Albert and Nicolas Rubens** (Vaduz-Vienna, Liechtenstein, The Princely Collections).

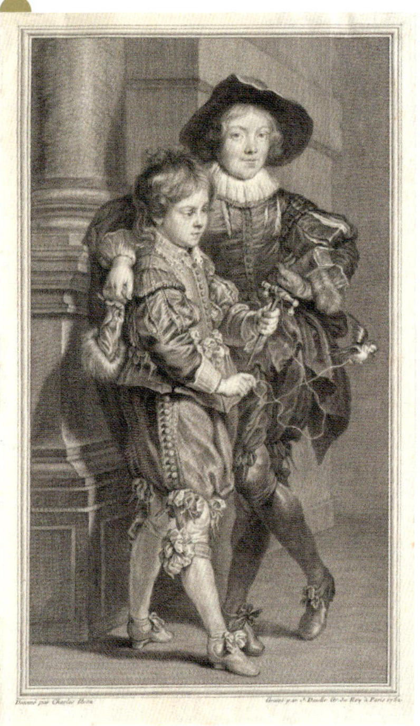

A role in European politics

> For my part, I should like nothing better than that the whole world should live in peace, so that we might experience a golden rather than an iron century.
>
> P.P. Rubens to the French diplomat Pierre Dupuy, April 1627

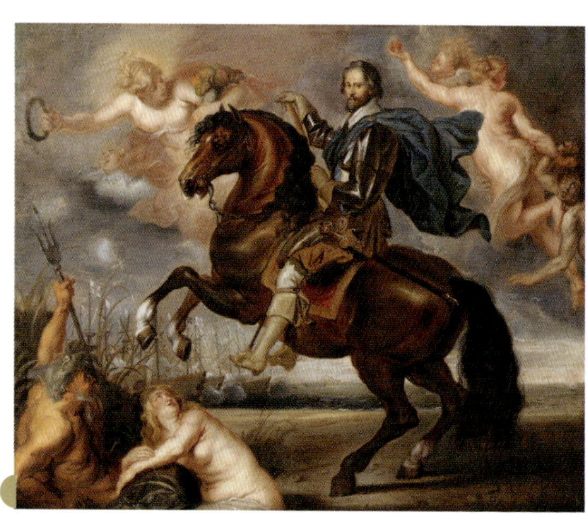

Copy after P.P. Rubens, **Triumph of the Duke of Buckingham**. Canvas, 84.7 x 103.8 cm. Antwerp, Rubens House

—

The original painting that Rubens made for the Duke of Buckingham was destroyed in a fire. An original oil sketch of the painting still survives (in an American museum), which depicts the duke on his magnificent steed in a much more dramatic manner than this copy.

The archduchess's counsellor

After the death of Isabella Brant, Rubens travelled more than ever before. In the first half of the 1620s, he spent a number of months at the French court, in part to complete his commission for Maria de Medici. Moreover, following the death of Archduke Albrecht in 1621, he was appointed as a political counsellor to the Infanta Isabella, who was now sole governess of the Southern Netherlands. The archduchess and her closest adviser, General Ambrogio Spinola, both had great confidence in Rubens and had no hesitation in involving him in the negotiations that followed the expiry of the Twelve Year Truce, also in 1621. Faced with the threat of war and a possible resumption of hostilities, and hampered by the lack of official diplomatic channels and by resistance to further peace initiatives in the highest political circles in both camps, the governess pinned her faith on the use of informal

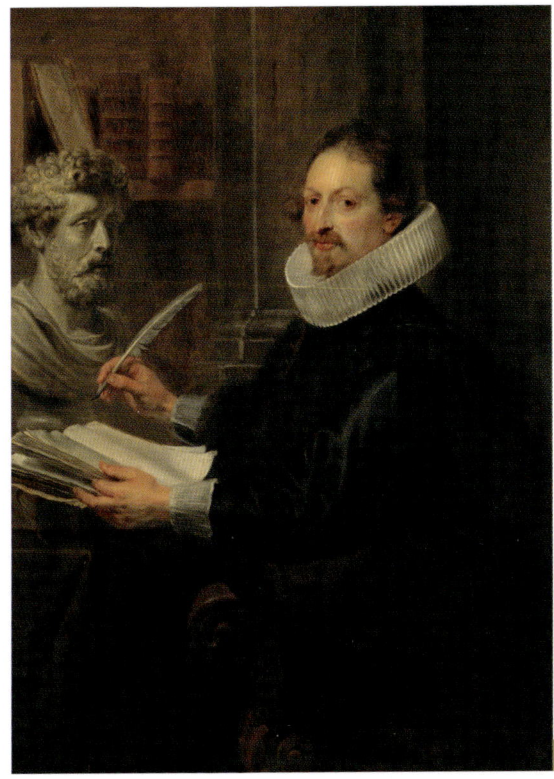

Peter Paul Rubens, **Portrait of Jan Gaspar Gevartius**, ca. 1628. Panel, 119 x 98 cm. Antwerp, Royal Museum of Fine Arts

—

Jan Gaspar Gevartius, or Gevaerts, was the city registrar of Antwerp. Appropriately, he is sitting at a table with a pen and his deed book in front of him. The marble bust in the background depicts the Roman emperor and philosopher Marcus Aurelius, whose works were studied and appraised by Gevartius.

—

The registrar was a good friend of Rubens, a personal connection suggested in the subject's relaxed pose, almost as if he is looking up from his book to address the artist, who has just dropped in to his workroom.

secret negotiators, in the hope of being able to reach a new truce or perhaps even a lasting settlement with the United Provinces. It was a role for which Rubens was ideally suited.

The international situation looked far from promising, since both England and France were intent on interfering in the Low Countries, seeing this as a further step towards breaking Spain as a world power. Even so, after a meeting in Paris in 1625 with the Duke of Buckingham and his emissary Balthasar Gerbier (also a painter), Rubens finally succeeded in opening official diplomatic contacts at a European level. This meant that after 1626, his journeys away from home became even more frequent, although perhaps this offered him some welcome distraction following the death of his wife.

In his absence, he entrusted the running of his workshop to one of his former pupils and the raising of his two sons to a friend, Jan Gaspar Gevartius. In 1628, he travelled to Madrid, where he remained for eight months. From there, he was sent on a new peace mission to London. In the interim, the Duke of Buckingham had been murdered, but Rubens was still able - albeit with great difficulty - to lay the foundations for peace negotiations between Spain and England. As a result, the English king later appointed an ambassador to Madrid and the Spanish king appointed an ambassador to London, bringing Rubens' mission to a successful conclusion.

After he had been knighted by King Charles I of England in recognition of his efforts to bring about peace, he returned to Antwerp in April 1630. It was in this same year that he made a delightful *Self-portrait* (see page 155), which reveals a gentle and expressive face, framed by a white collar (providing contrast to the brown background), a black hat and a dark doublet.

A secret diplomat in the service of peace

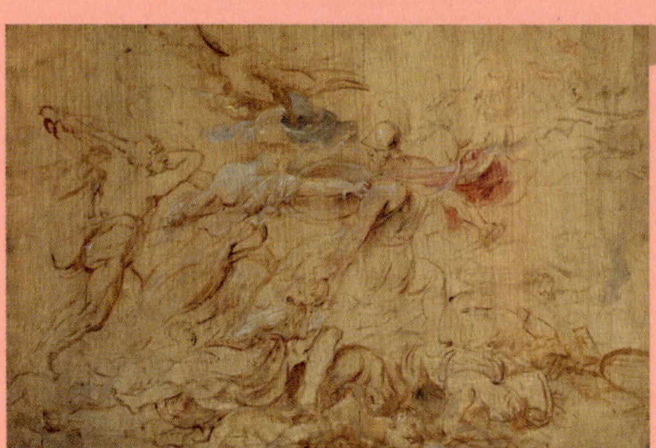

Peter Paul Rubens, **Minerva and Hercules Fighting Mars**, ca. 1630. Oil sketch on panel, 35 x 53 cm. Antwerp, Royal Museum of Fine Arts

—

The postures of Mars and Minerva as each other's opponent are the same as in **The Allegory of Peace** (London, National Gallery). There is no known painting by Rubens based on this preliminary sketch.

The driving force behind Rubens' activities as a secret diplomat and a fundamental theme throughout his artistic oeuvre was a powerful longing for peace and a deep desire for good government that would bring order and prosperity to his troubled land. In July 1625, he wrote in a letter to his father-in-law, Jan Brant: 'The time has come as a good patriot to do everything possible to promote the general good, for which we have worked so hard, in the hope that with God's help our efforts will not be in vain.' And in August 1628, to his friend Pierre Dupuy in Paris: 'Here we find ourselves in a position midway between war and peace, and we are experiencing all the misery caused by the violence of war, but without enjoying any of the benefits of peace. Our city is being pushed slowly towards its ruin.'

Political travels with an artistic impact

Rubens' diplomatic travels were not without significance for his art. In Madrid, he painted a portrait of King Philip IV and other members of the Spanish royal family, and in London he painted, amongst other things, *The Allegory of Peace* (London, National Gallery) for King Charles I. The English monarch also gave him a second major commission to take back to Antwerp: the painting of canvases for the decoration of the ceiling of the Banqueting House in Whitehall Palace, a monumental task that would only be completed in 1634-1635.

During his stay at the courts in Madrid and London, Rubens once again, for the first time in many years, came into contact with the style of Titian (ca. 1488/90-1576), since both royal collections contained numerous works by the Venetian master. This re-acquaintance influenced his painting after 1628 and was much in evidence in his *ultima maniera*, the final phase of his artistic development. From 1628 onwards, his style evolved towards the use of lighter and softer colours that blended subtly into a variety of intermediary tones, combined with the more blurred definition of figures, so that they appeared to be less sharply modelled.

Peter Paul Rubens, **Peasant Dance**, ca. 1635. Panel, 73 x 106 cm. Madrid, Prado Museum

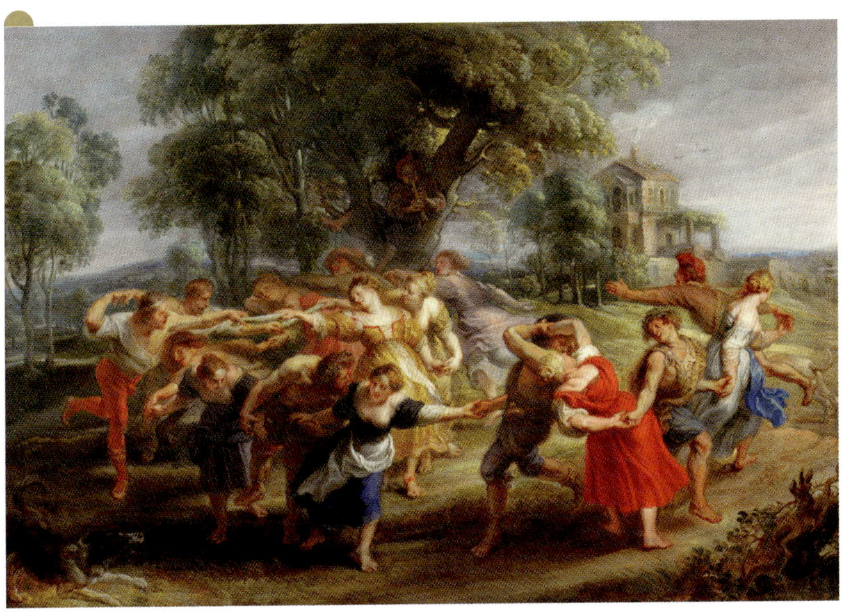

Freer and more fluid brushstrokes than in his earlier career also give these later compositions a spontaneity and directness that is almost 'impressionist' in nature.

The spreading of Rubens' Baroque style

Rubens' artistic activities were not limited to painting. He also had a huge influence on 17th century print-making (both burin engraving and woodcuts). A number of engravers in his entourage were continually occupied in reproducing the master's creations with the burin. Rubens accredited his renown in part to the many prints that were published under his personal supervision and made his style widely known throughout Europe. He controlled the entire production process, retouching the drawings and sometimes even the final proofs. He demanded the highest levels of skill from his engravers, whom

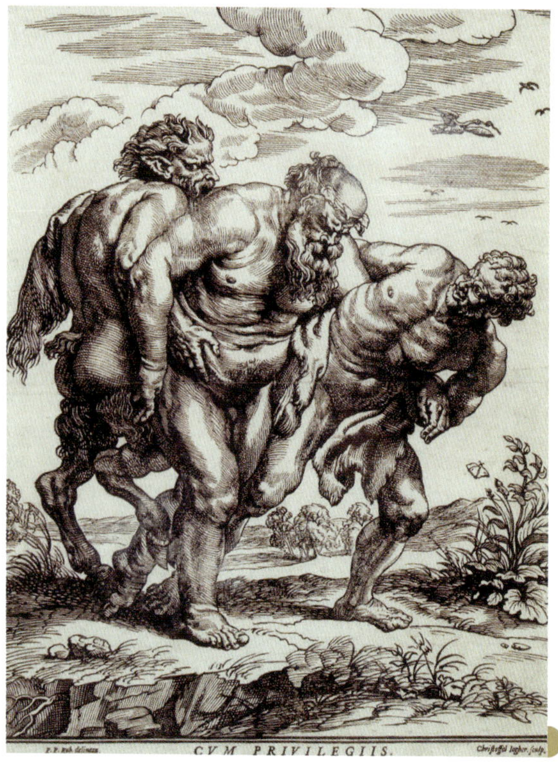

The Drunken Silenus, woodcut by Christoffel Jegher after P.P. Rubens, post 1630. Antwerp, Plantin-Moretus Museum

he trained himself. These graphic reproductions of his paintings and designs are faithful copies of the originals, reflecting both the typical Baroque flamboyance and the characteristic light and colour gradations, translated in the engraving medium into a succession of grey-black nuances.

For Balthasar I Moretus, who was in charge of the Gulden Passer printing workshop (the Officina Plantiniana) in Antwerp, and also occasionally for other publishers, Rubens designed title pages and illustrations, through which he introduced the Baroque style to book illustration. His contribution to the art of tapestry making has already been mentioned. In addition, he also exerted a strong influence on Baroque sculpture, gold and silversmithing, and ivory carving in Flanders. He had a great interest in sculpting in all its forms, counted a number of sculptors among his friends and even drew designs for statuary or precious works in gold and silver. Through Hans van Mildert

Title page of **Mathias Casimir Sarbievski, Lyricorum libri IV**, Antwerp, Officina Plantiniana of Balthasar I Moretus, 1632. Copper engraving by Cornelis I Galle after a design by P.P. Rubens. Antwerp, Plantin-Moretus Museum

—

The Polish Jesuit Mathias Casimir Sarbievski was a well-known composer of Latin verses. Various elements in this title page refer both to the poet's art and to the person to whom Sarbievski dedicated this collection of poems, Pope Urban VIII (Maffeo Barberini). This explains the presence of the papal symbols of office – the tiara and the keys of St. Peter – above the escutcheon.

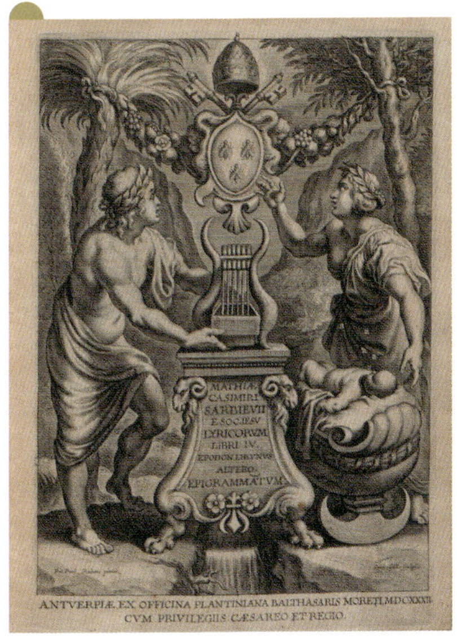

Title page design for **Mathias Casimir Sarbievski, Lyricorum libri IV.** Oil sketch in grisaille on panel, 18.7 x 14.4 cm. Antwerp, Plantin-Moretus Museum

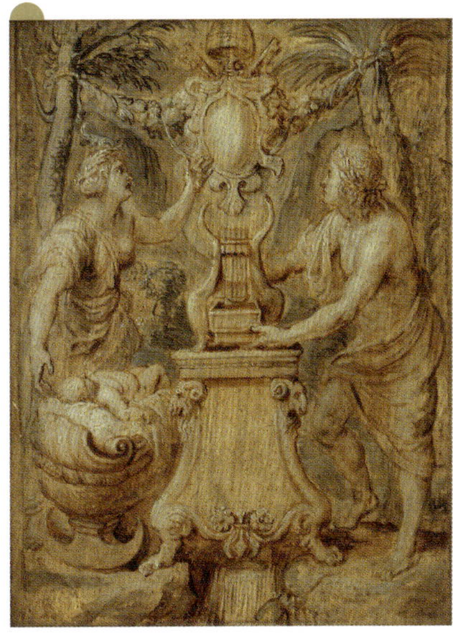

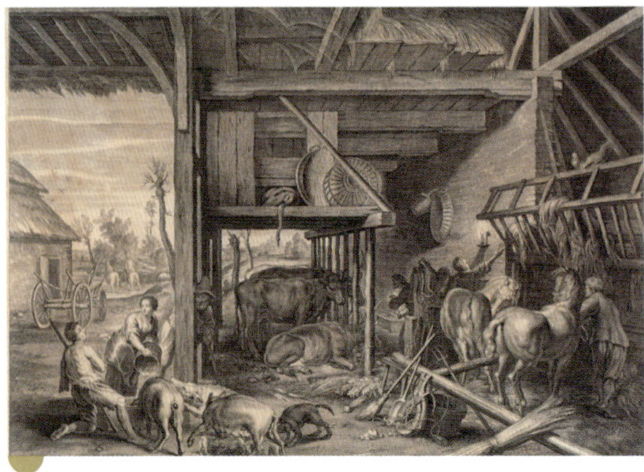

Landscape with Stable, burin engraving by Schelte à Bolswert after P.P. Rubens, 1630s (?). Antwerp, Plantin-Moretus Museum

and many other sculptors, both in Antwerp and elsewhere, the Baroque ornamentation favoured by Rubens also broke through into architecture.

An ordinary girl as his bride

In December 1630, four years after the death of his first wife, Rubens remarried. His bride was the 16-year-old Helena, the daughter of the tapestry merchant Daniël Fourment, a friend of the artist. Some years later, Rubens wrote to Nicolas-Claude Fabri de Peiresc: 'I took a young woman of a worthy but modest family, even though everyone tried to persuade me to marry a lady of the court, but I feared their pride, that inherent vice of the aristocracy, particularly in the female sex, and so I chose instead a woman who would not be ashamed to see me with a paintbrush in my hand. And to be honest, I would have found it difficult to exchange the priceless treasure of freedom for the embraces of an old woman.'

Europe at war

In that same year, the political and military situation in the Netherlands once again became extremely tense. The wars of religion had developed into a general European conflict, involving complex political and economic interests pursued through a series of shifting alliances, so that the possibility of a peaceful solution through diplomatic negotiation seemed almost impossible. Even so, Rubens once again attempted to pave the way for peace between the Republic and the Spanish Netherlands, but

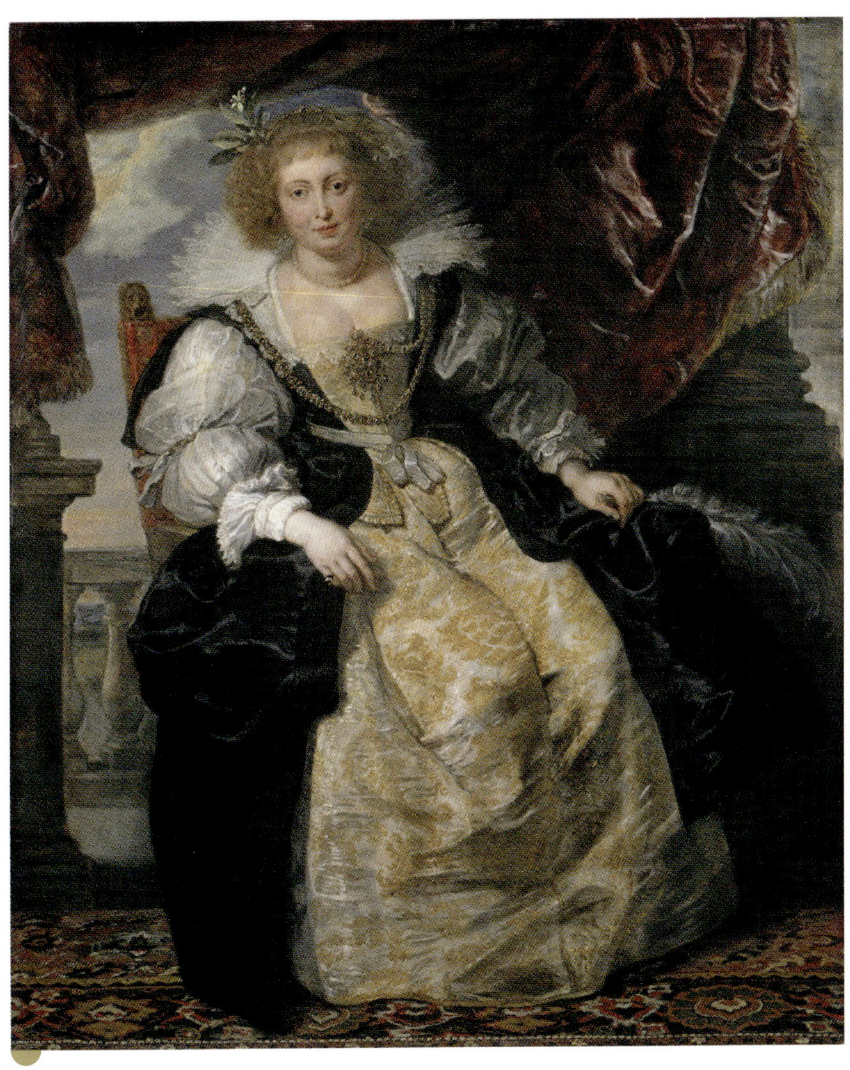

Peter Paul Rubens, **Helena Fourment in Her Wedding Dress**, ca. 1630–1631. Panel, 163.5 x 136.9 cm. Munich, Old Picture Gallery

this time without success. This disappointment, no doubt coupled with his recent marriage and the death of the Archduchess Isabella in 1633, persuaded him to withdraw from diplomacy for good.

The lyrical period

> Now, thank God, [...] I am quietly at home with my wife and children, and my only desire in this world is to live in peace.
>
> P.P. Rubens to Nicolas-Claude Fabri de Peiresc, December 1634

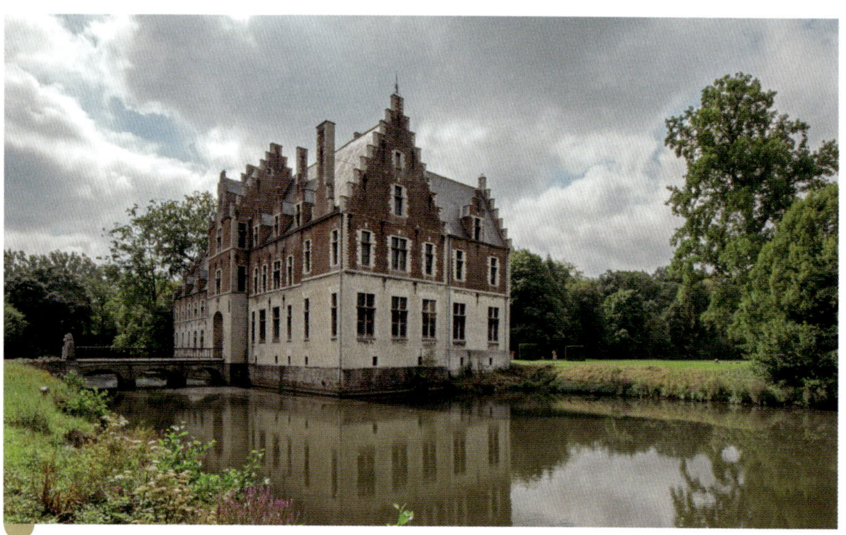

In 1635, Peter Paul Rubens and his young wife Helena Fourment bought the Het Steen at Elewijt as their country estate.

The noble Rubens, Lord of Steen

Now that he no longer needed to travel so much, Rubens' life became calmer. Helena bore him five children. He lived with his family as a wealthy resident of his native city and devoted his inexhaustible energy to his art. His productivity remained high, thanks in part to his smooth-running workshop. After 1630, he was regularly troubled by attacks of gout, sometimes preventing him from working, so that tasks he had previously carried out himself, such as retouching the copper plates of the engravers or the design of book illustrations, he now left to his assistants.

Roger de Piles has given us a description of a typical Rubens day: 'He rose each morning at four o'clock and always began the day by attending mass, unless he was prevented by the gout that troubled him so greatly. Afterwards, he got down to work, but always with a lector close by, whom he paid to read from one or other good book, mainly Plutarch, Livy or Seneca. Because he so enjoyed working, he ordered his life in such a way that he could do it easily and without taxing his health; that is why he ate very little at noon. [...] He worked until five o'clock in the afternoon, following which he went for a ride

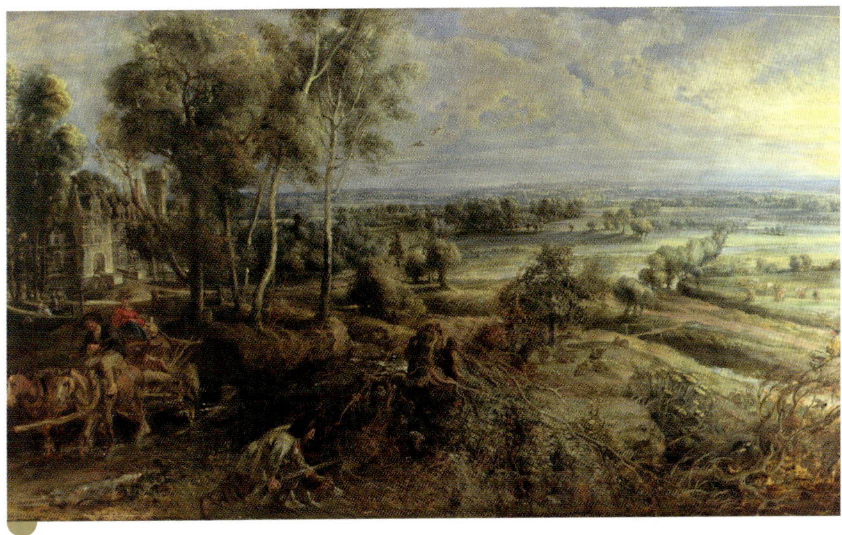

Peter Paul Rubens, **A View of Het Steen in the Early Morning**, ca. 1635–1638. Panel, 131 x 229 cm. London, National Gallery

with his horse outside the city walls or on the ramparts, or did something else that relaxed his mind. When he returned from his ride, he usually found friends waiting for him at his home, with whom he shared his evening meal and the pleasures of his table. That being said, he did not approve of excessive drinking, eating and gambling. The things that gave him most enjoyment were riding a fine Spanish horse, reading a book, or examining his medallions, his agates, carnelians or other cut stones, of which he possessed a fine collection.'

In 1633, Rubens was appointed as dean of the St. Luke's Guild in Antwerp. As was traditional, he received his own leather-covered walnut chair embossed with his name and the guild's coat of arms, but the actual exercising of the dean's function he entrusted to his friend, the sculptor Hans van Mildert.

In 1635, he purchased a country manor house, Het Steen, at Elewijt near Mechelen, where he spent the summer months each year with his family. In 1630, he had been knighted by the English king and in 1631 he had been similarly ennobled by the Spanish king, so he was entitled to call himself the Lord of Steen. He painted the gently rolling Brabant countryside around Het Steen in a series of landscapes that exude something visionary, a kind of cosmic intensity. Ursel Court in Ekeren, which he had purchased earlier in 1627, was also the subject of one of his paintings, *The Castle Grounds at Ekeren*, depicting a carefree group of friends playing in a rural setting with a castle in the background (Vienna, Art History Museum; there is a workshop copy in Antwerp, Rubens House).

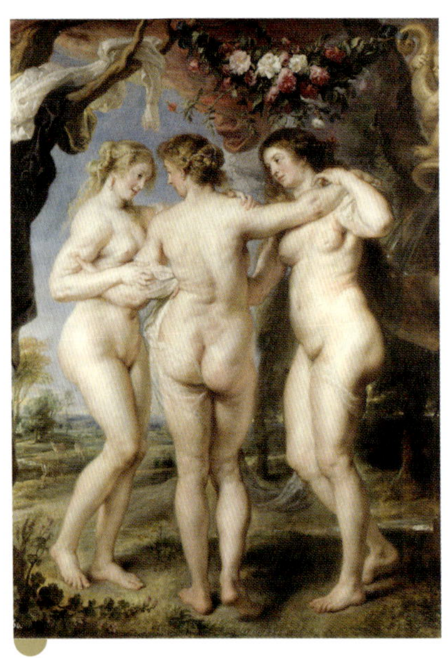

Peter Paul Rubens, **The Three Graces**, 1639. Canvas, 221 x 181 cm. Madrid, Prado Museum

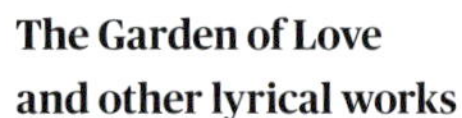

The Garden of Love and other lyrical works

But his most fruitful source of inspiration in these later years was his young wife. With her youthful beauty, she was his favourite model for female figures in his biblical, allegorical and mythological scenes, and he also painted several fine portraits of her. Rubens' final stylistic period, covering the 1630s, is usually referred to as his lyrical period. The number of monumental works and altarpieces gradually diminished. It seemed as though the artist no longer accepted as many commissions as in the past, so that he could concentrate instead on subjects that now interested him more and gave him greater personal enjoyment. He painted not only sensual female nudes with great tenderness, or mythological figures in Arcadian decors, but also magnificent portraits and the previously mentioned rolling landscapes.

The works from this period include: *Portrait of Helena Fourment*, known as *'The Fur'*, *The Three Graces*, *A View of Het Steen in the Early Morning* and *Landscape with a Rainbow* (London, The Wallace Collection), as well as various other portraits of Helena Fourment, sometimes with her children. However, it is the painting entitled *The Garden of Love*, completed in 1631-1632, which

Peter Paul Rubens, **Portrait of Helena Fourment, known as 'The Fur'**, ca. 1638.
Panel, 176 x 83 cm.
Vienna, Art History Museum

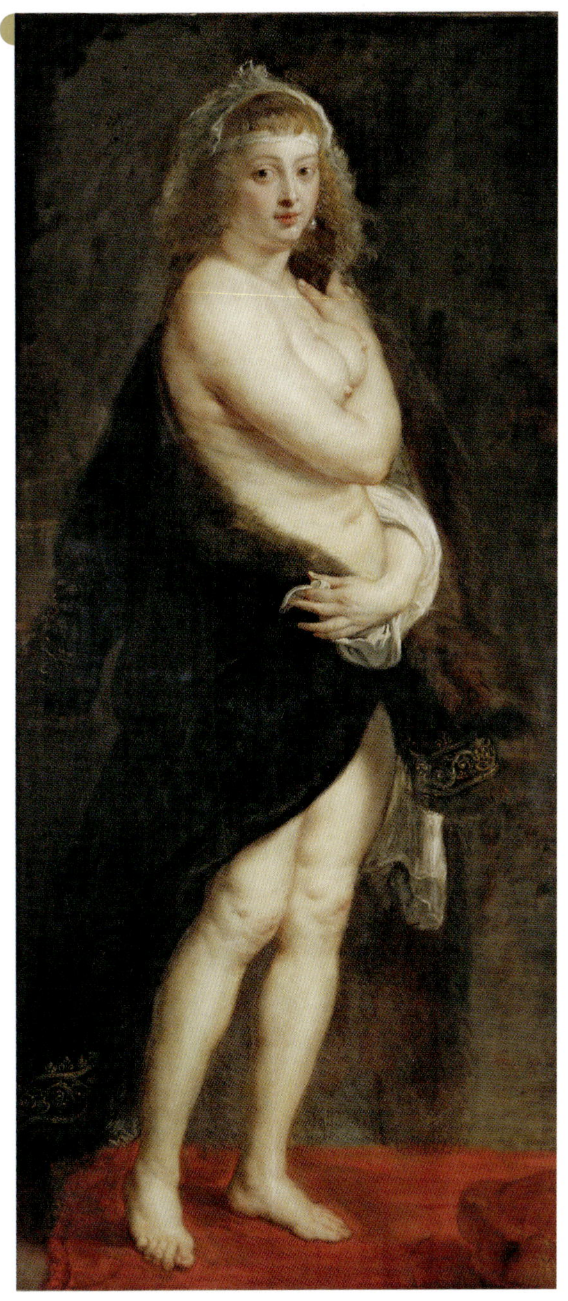

best expresses Rubens' happiness after his second marriage. A group of flirtatious revellers, spurred on by enthusiastic putti, are making merry in a delightful garden close to a fountain of love.

Grandiose commissions

Although their number declined, the artist continued to carry out large-scale commissions. In 1634, the city administration asked him to design the triumphal arches for the Joyous Entry of the new governor of the Southern Netherlands, the Cardinal-Infante Ferdinand, brother of King Philip IV. Rubens made all the necessary oil sketches himself, incorporating ornate and grandiose decorative forms that were in keeping with the nature of the event, but left the execution of the actual canvases for the embellishment of the arches to a group of other Antwerp painters. *The Pompa Introitus Ferdinandi* eventually took place in April 1635. Two of Rubens' original designs are still preserved in Antwerp, those for the front and rear of the Gate of Honour erected at the Mint.

Rubens' greatest undertaking in his final years - in fact, the largest commission he ever accepted - was an ensemble of more

Peter Paul Rubens, **The Garden of Love**, ca. 1631–1632. Canvas, 198 x 283 cm. Madrid, Prado Museum

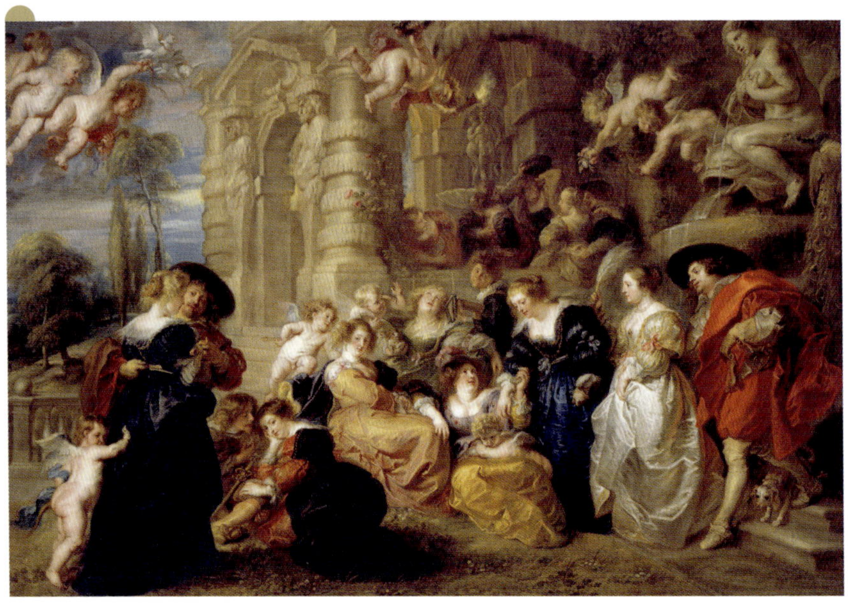

than a hundred mythological and hunting scenes, painted between 1636 and 1638 with the help of assistants, for the decoration of the Torre de la Parada, the King of Spain's new hunting lodge outside Madrid. Rubens made more than fifty oil sketches for the mythological subjects and personally executed four of the finished panels. The remainder were completed by Jacques (alias Jacob) Jordaens, Cornelis de Vos, Theodoor van Thulden, Erasmus Quellinus and other artists from his entourage. The hunting scenes were designed by Frans Snijders and Paul de Vos. Rubens' sketches demonstrate his unparalleled virtuosity, assurance and imagination, allied with a remarkable clarity of vision and a sparing use of resources - just a few brushstrokes and dabs of colour are sufficient to bring out the essence of the entire composition. This same supple technique was also evident in *The Triumphal Chariot of Kallo* (see page 87) from 1638 and in the sketches for *The Rape of the Sabine Women* and *The Reconciliation of the Romans and the Sabines* from 1640.

Rubens executed the commissions for the Joyous Entry and the Torre de la Parada in collaboration with his most able colleagues, a way of working that was not unusual in 17th century Antwerp. This collaboration involved not only his workshop pupils and assistants, but also painters who were masters in their own rights. The sharing of large commissions with other artists was necessary to complete the work on schedule, or at least within an acceptable timeframe. Sometimes, even more intensive forms of collaboration were possible, with two or more artists working on a single canvas, on which both their names appeared.

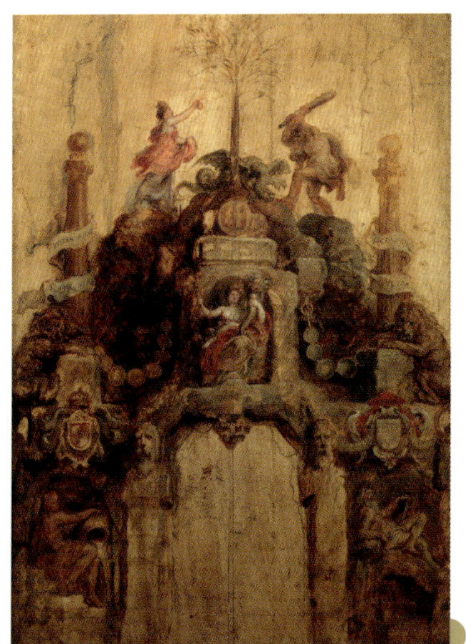

Peter Paul Rubens, **The Gate of Honour at the Mint (front side)**, 1635. Oil sketch on panel, 104 x 71 cm. Antwerp, Royal Museum of Fine Arts

—

The wealthy Guild of Minters paid for the erection of a gate of honour near their mint, at the start of the Kloosterstraat, to celebrate the Joyous Entry of the new governor of the Southern Netherlands, the Cardinal-Infante Ferdinand of Spain, in 1635.

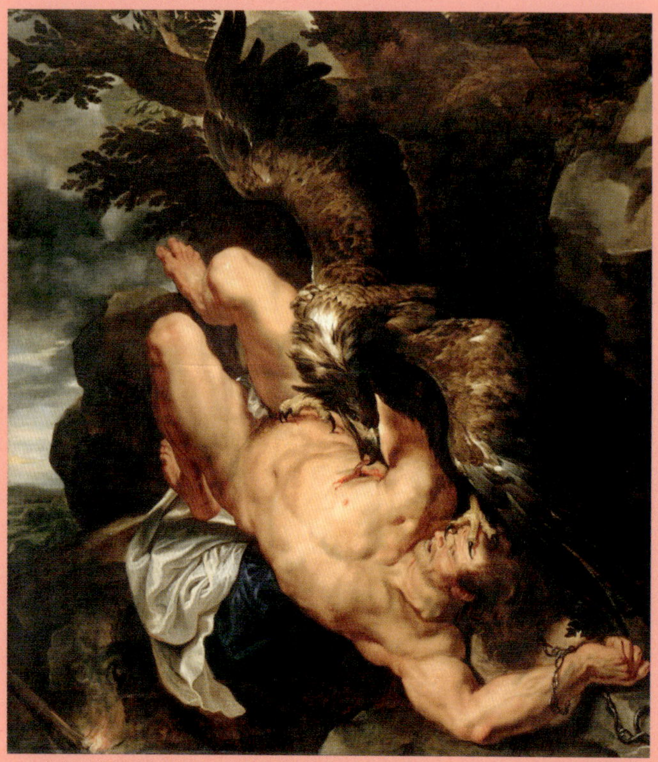

Specialization and collaboration in the Antwerp art world

Most Antwerp artists were specialized in a particular genre, in which they excelled. Throughout his career, Rubens made use of different colleagues – Jan Brueghel I (the Velvet Brueghel), Frans Snyders, Paul de Vos, Jan Wildens and others – to complete under his supervision elements in his paintings that matched their strengths. He always mentioned this in his accreditations: '*Panthers* [...] Original by my hand, apart from the landscape by a specialist in such matters' or '*Prometheus Bound* [...] Original by my hand, with the eagle by Snyders'.

Sometimes, the opposite also happened, with Rubens contributing to the works of his artist friends, usually as the painter of figures. For example, the inventory of his estate listed a number of paintings in his collection that were clearly created in this manner, such as: '*Diana Hunting*; the figures by master Peter Rubens, the landscapes and animals by Brueghel'.

As the Old Sing, So Pipe the Young

Rubens not only collaborated with Anthony van Dyck, but also occasionally with that other great Antwerp painter of the Baroque, Jacques Jordaens (1593-1678). Jordaens was never a pupil of Rubens, but during the early years of his career looked up to the great master and sought to imitate his heroic style. Later, he developed a more personal style that reflected his own temperament and had a less ostentatious, more down-to-earth character, perhaps arising from the fact that he never visited Italy. He is above all known for his genre pieces, like *The King Drinks* and *As the Old Sing, So Pipe the Young*, as well as his mythological scenes, such as *Meleager and Atalanta*, *Satyr and Peasant* and *Homage to Pomona*. His powerfully rendered figures, bathed in a deliciously warm light, radiate sensuality and a lust for life. After the death of Rubens and Van Dyck, Jordaens became the leading painter in the Southern Netherlands.

Peter Paul Rubens, **Prometheus Bound**, ca. 1611–1612, completed after ca. 1618. Canvas, 243 x 210 cm. Detail. Philadelphia Museum of Art

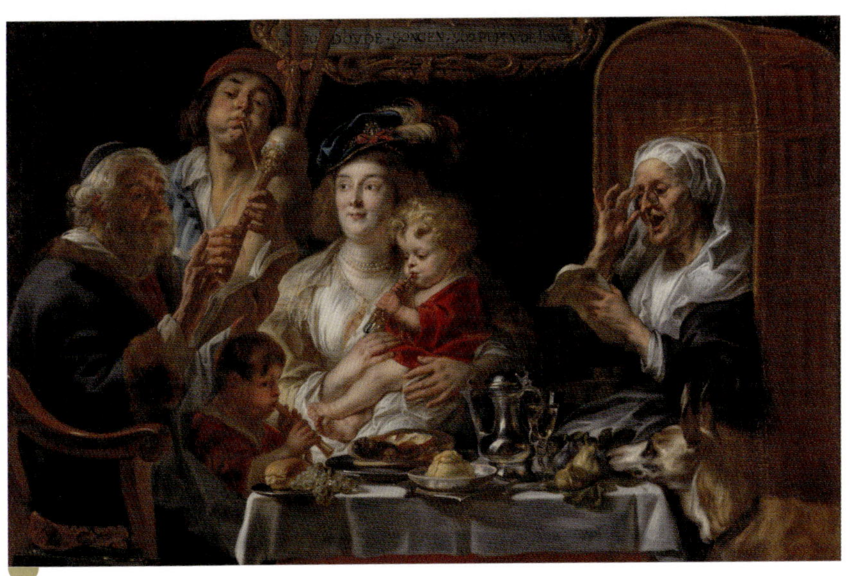

Jacques Jordaens, **As the Old Sing, So Pipe the Young**, 1638. Canvas, 128 x 192 cm. Detail. Antwerp, Royal Museum of Fine Arts

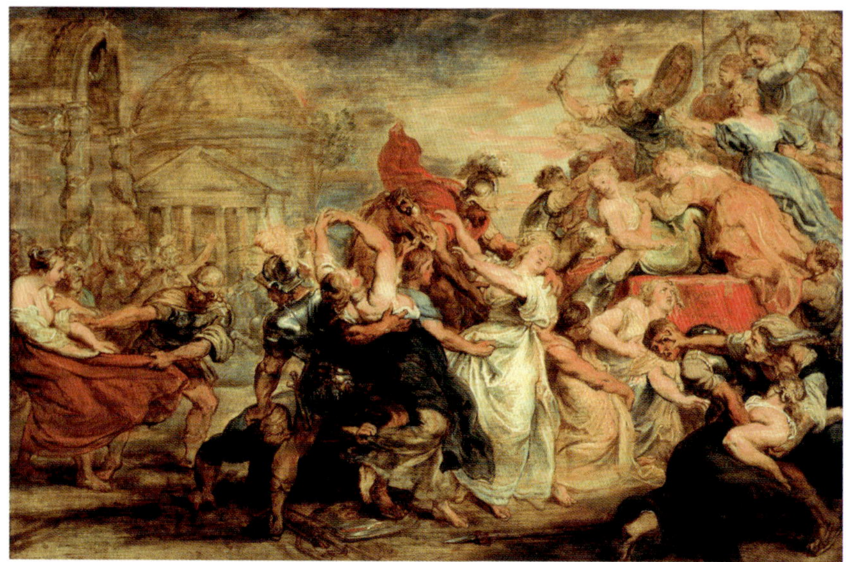

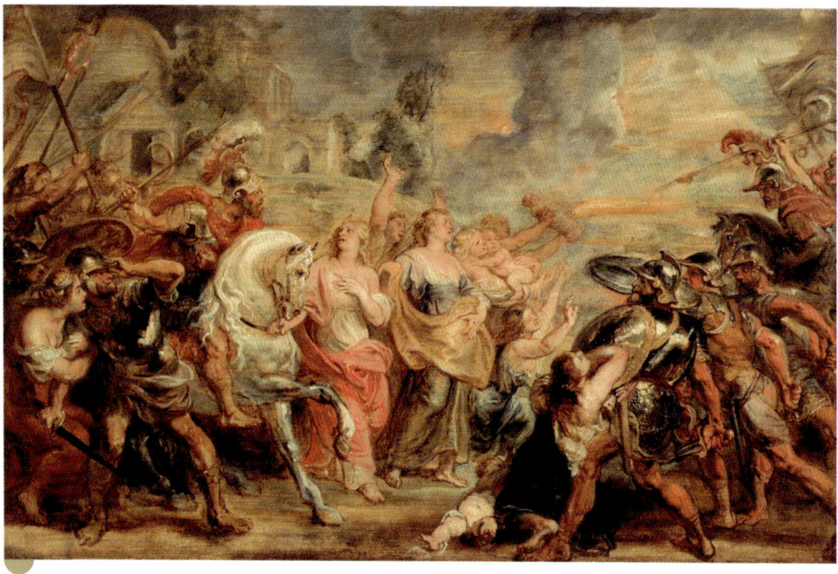

Peter Paul Rubens, **The Rape of the Sabine Women** and **The Reconciliation of the Romans and the Sabines**, 1640. Oil sketches on panel, 56 x 87 cm and 55.5 x 86.5 cm. Brussels, Belfius Collection

—

The paintings based on these oil sketches were later lost in a fire. The underlying themes in these depictions of a well-known Roman saga are fertility and peace, two fundamental concepts in Rubens' art.

Peter Paul Rubens, **Self-portrait**, after 1635. Canvas, 109.5 x 85 cm. Vienna, Art History Museum

—

This final self-portrait of the artist, sometime around his 60th birthday, shows a dignified but tired and ageing man in poor health.

Peter Paul Rubens died at his home in Antwerp on 30 May 1640. In accordance with his wishes, a painting of *The Blessed Virgin and Child Surrounded by Saints* (see page 139), which he had completed during the final years of his life, was hung above the altar of the burial chapel in which his remains were interred in St. James's Church. The painting, which depicts a *sacra conversazione* between the Virgin Mary, bearing the Infant Jesus in her arms, and a group of saints, illustrates the exquisite brushwork and warmth of colour of his lyrical period, bathed as it is in the soft and gentle light that gives so many of his paintings a paradisiacal sheen.

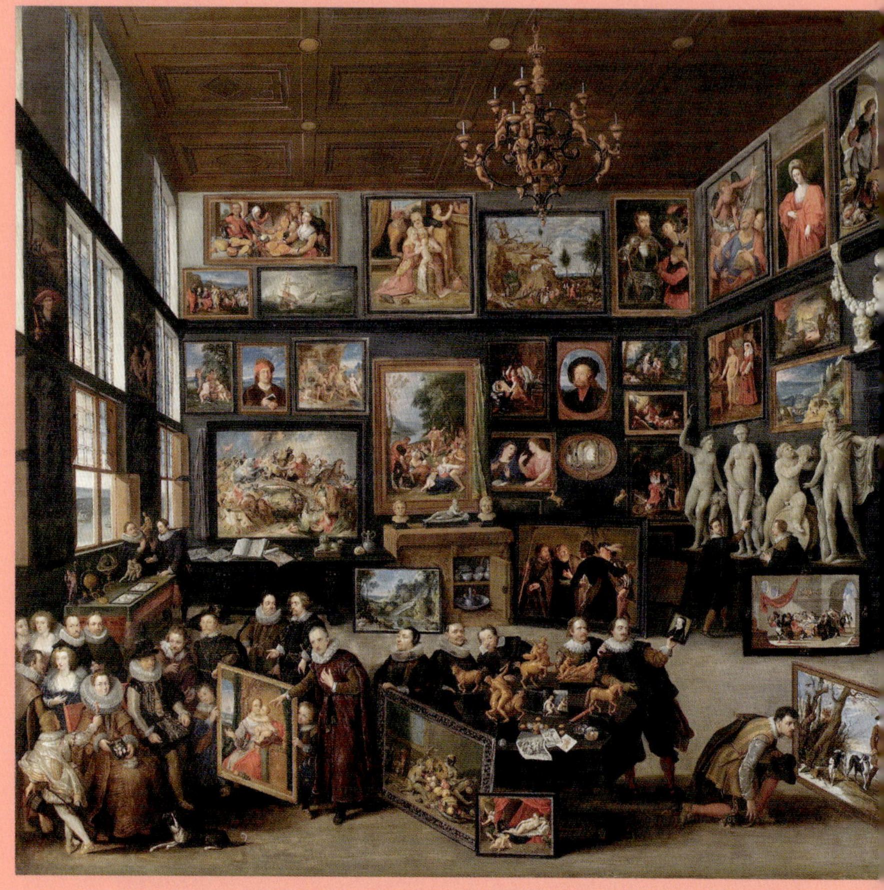

The 'Constkamer' of Cornelis van der Geest

Peter Paul Rubens and the Antwerp of his day are 'commemorated', as it were, in a single canvas: *The picture gallery of Cornelis van der Geest* (now in the Rubens House). This painting depicts the private art collection of the rich Antwerp merchant and art-lover, Cornelis van der Geest. Van der Geest was a friend of Rubens, who once called him 'my constant patron and protector from my youth onwards'. Willem van Haecht, who made the painting, was the son of Rubens' first teacher, Tobias Verhaecht. He worked in Van der Geest's service as the curator of his collection.

Such paintings were common in 17th-century Antwerp. The wealthy owners of art collections were so proud of the treasures they possessed that they wished to have them immortalized in a painting of their own, right down

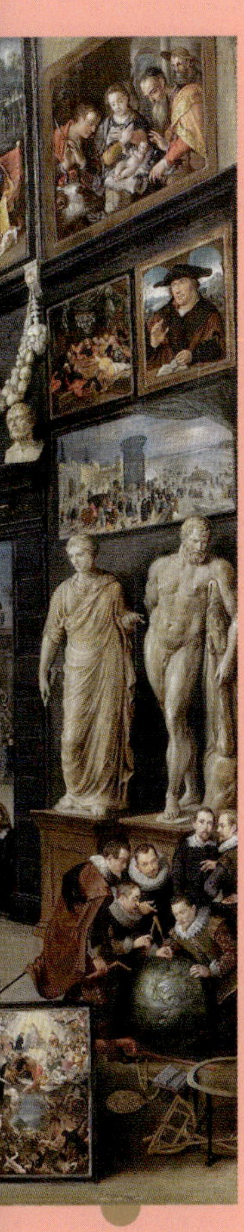

Willem van Haecht, **The Picture Gallery of Cornelis van der Geest**, 1628. Panel, 100 x 130 cm. Antwerp, Rubens House

to the smallest detail. Van der Geest had one of the finest collections in the city. Amongst the famous works depicted in his gallery are a panel by Van Eyck, a number of pieces by Quinten Metsijs, a landscape by Pieter Bruegel the Elder and two major canvases by Rubens (*The Battle of the Amazons* and *Portrait of a Commander with Two Pages*), as well as many other paintings by contemporary artists of note.

But it is not only the works of art on display that make this panel so unique. It also depicts a number of the leading figures in the cultural life of Antwerp and the Southern Netherlands in Rubens' time. Van der Geest stands as the proud owner of the fabulous collection, surrounded by his friends and prominent Antwerp artists of the day, who have joined him to welcome some very high-ranking visitors. The painting records an actual historical event: a visit by Archduke Albrecht and Archduchess Isabella in 1615, on the occasion of a tournament on the waters of the Scheldt, which they were able to view from Van der Geest's mansion overlooking the river. However, some of the details are inaccurate. Van Haecht completed the painting in 1628, but some of the works he shows were not part of the collection in 1615, nor was it possible for some of the people he portrays to have been there. The archducal couple are seated on the left, surrounded by their entourage of courtiers, ladies in waiting and counsellors. Behind them stands burgomaster Rockox. The man leaning over the archduke's left shoulder, seemingly in conversation with him, is Rubens. His position next to Albrecht underlines his close relationship with the court. Anthony van Dyck stands a little further along, to the right of his host, who is showing a painting of Our Lady to the archduchess. The remaining guests are mainly other painters, sculptors and art collectors.

The two views from the room are also interesting. The window on the left looks out over the broad river, with ships sailing under a clear blue sky. The doorway on the right leads to what seems to be a public square with a fountain depicting Laocoön and a Renaissance portico with balustrade, where several local people and halberdiers are enjoying an afternoon stroll. The unassuming figure on the staircase is probably Willem van Haecht, who used a number of Van Dyck portraits to help recreate this scene.

The motto above the door encapsulates the philosophy of life of not only Cornelis van der Geest, but also that of Peter Paul Rubens and many of their contemporaries: 'Vive l'Esprit'.

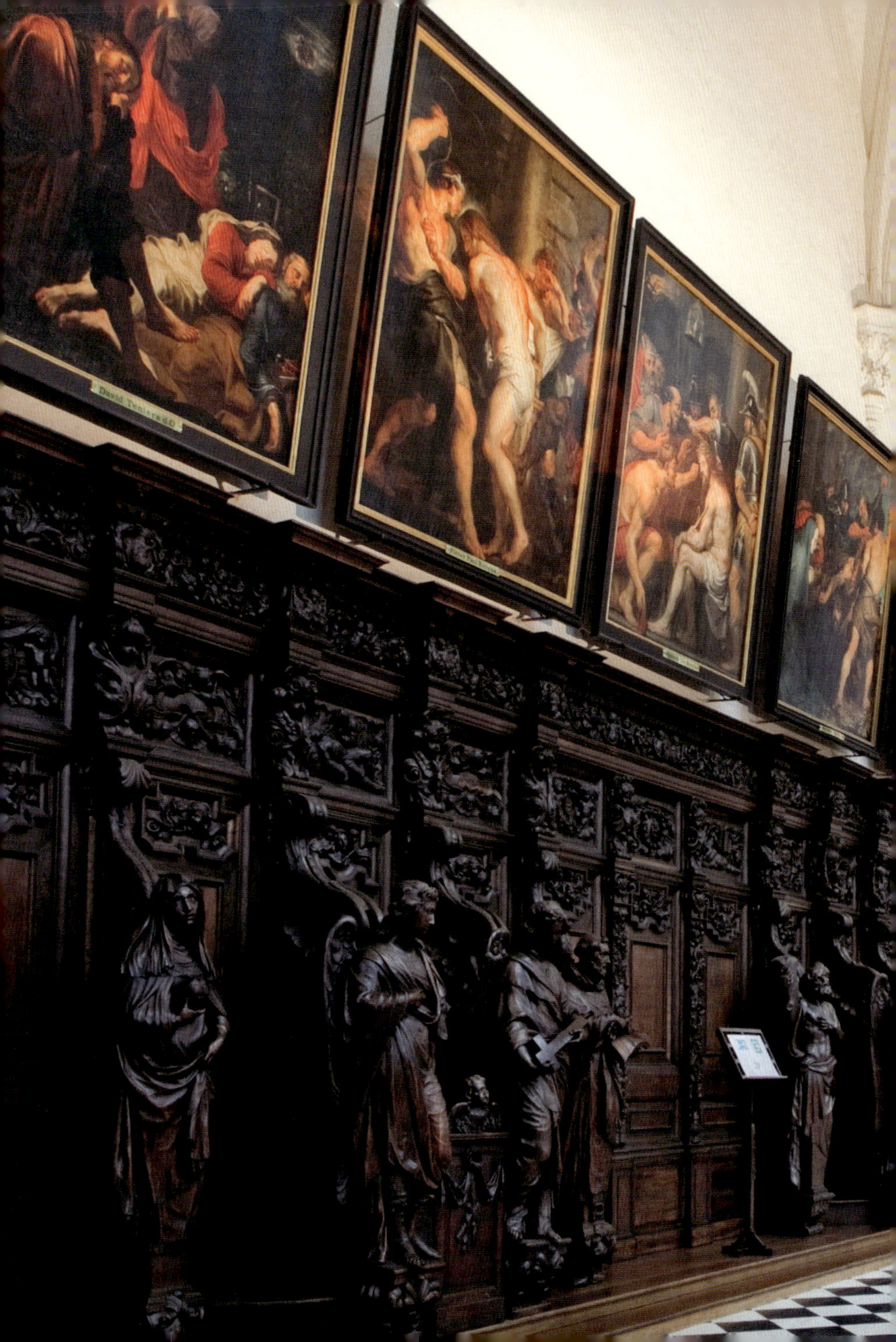
David Teniers d.O.

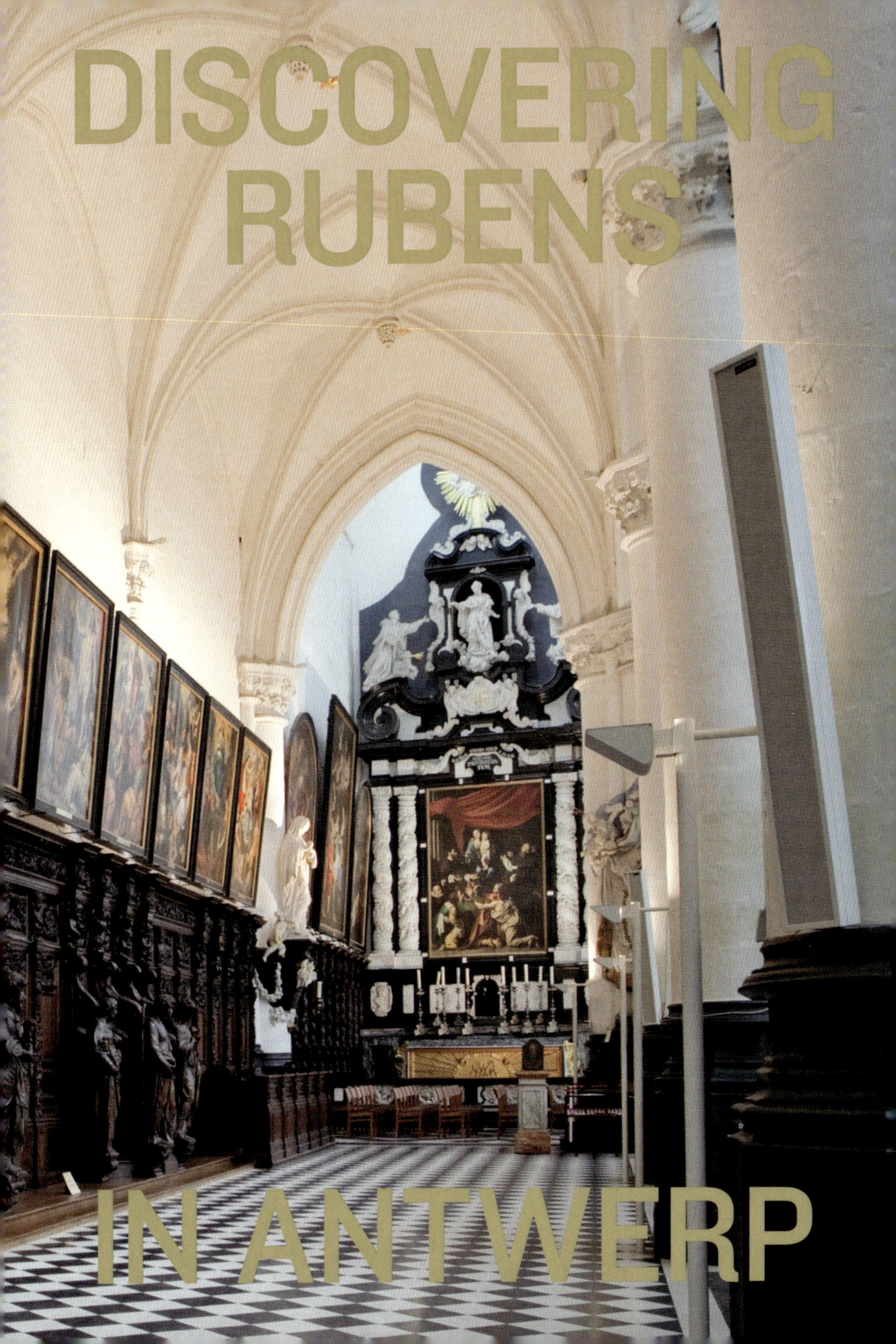
DISCOVERING RUBENS
IN ANTWERP

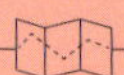

WALK

For your Rubens walk through Antwerp, including the visits to all the listed churches and museums, you will ideally need three days. This will allow you to discover the charms of the different districts of the city at your own pace. What's more, they will be three richly filled days, because in Antwerp there is so much to see and enjoy!

Your walk begins at the Groenplaats in the heart of Antwerp city centre (see page 88). It is probably wisest to plan a separate visit to the Royal Museum of Fine Arts, either before or after your walk, or, better still, on a different day. You need to make sure you have enough time to do justice to the museum's wonderful collection, including numerous masterpieces by Rubens.

Important: please remember to consult websites like www.visitantwerpen.be, www.topa.be and www.mkaweb.be, as well as other relevant channels of information for the current opening times of museums and churches.

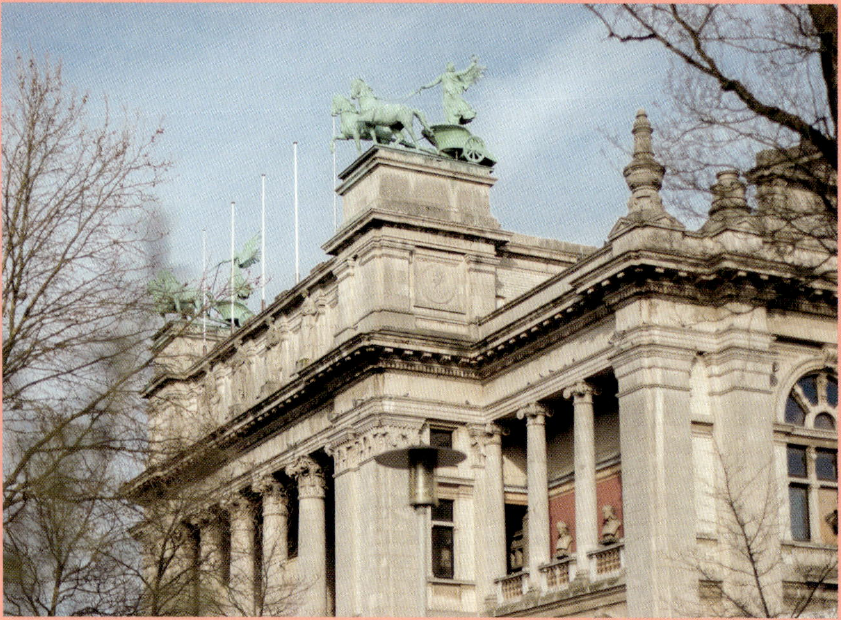

Royal Museum of Fine Arts in Antwerp (KMSKA)

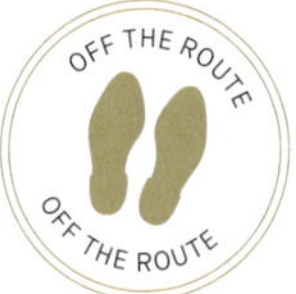

Leopold de Waelplaats
+32 (0)3 238 78 09
www.kmska.be
🕒 The renovated KMSKA reopens in 2020

The Royal Museum of Fine Arts in Antwerp has a large number of paintings and oil sketches by Rubens. Following a spectacular rebuilding and renovation programme, the museum will reopen in 2020, when its magnificent collection will surprise and amaze visitors more than ever before.

The Leopold de Waelplaats, where the museum is situated, is named after an important former burgomaster of the city, under whose administration between 1872 and 1892 Antwerp first became a world city. It was Leopold de Wael who, amongst other things, had major work carried out to expand the harbour and also founded the Royal Museum of Fine Arts. The museum is located in the district of the city known as 'het Zuid' (South), which was largely built at the end of the 19th and the beginning of the 20th century.

In Rubens' time, this area was dominated by a large citadel, which had been built during the period of Spanish rule, partly at the expense of the city. Its purpose was not to protect the city from outside attack, but to protect the Spanish garrison from attack by the local population! These were dangerous and volatile times! The citadel, a much hated symbol of foreign oppression, was finally demolished around 1875.

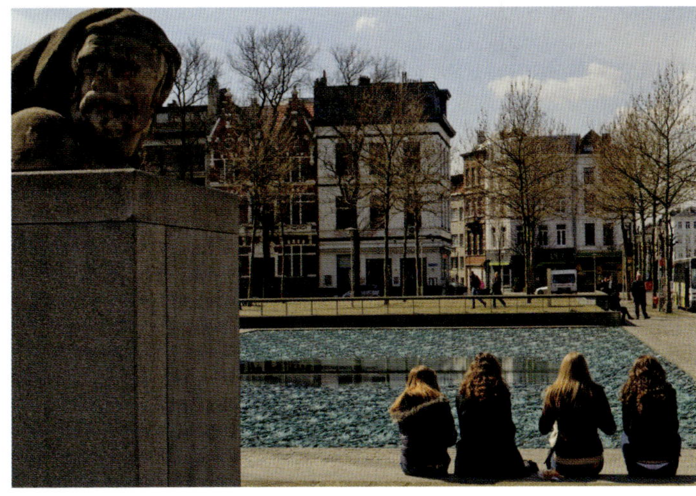

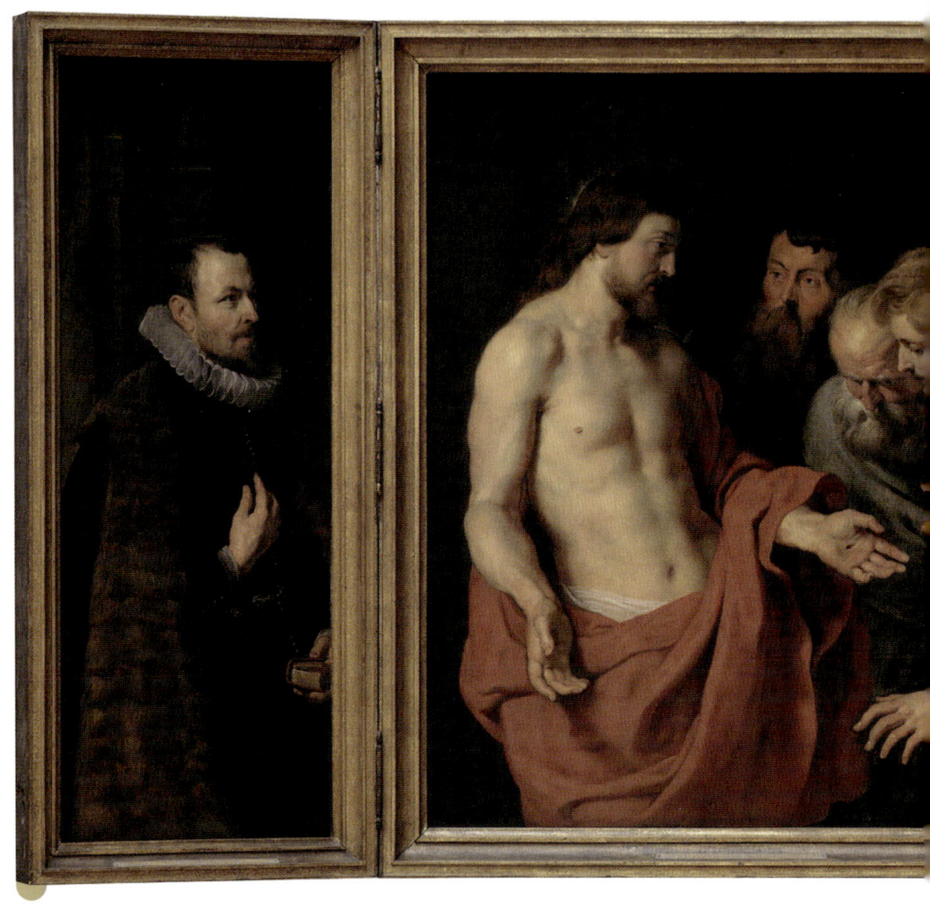

Panel, 143 x 123 cm (central panel), 146 x 55 cm (side panels)
An epitaph triptych for the Rockox couple in the Church of the Friars Minor in Antwerp

Epitaph for Nicolaas Rockox and his wife Adriana Perez 1613-1615

Rubens was commissioned to paint this triptych by his friend Nicolaas Rockox, who in 1615 was appointed as burgomaster of Antwerp for the fifth (but not final) time. Rockox is depicted in the left-hand panel and his wife, Adriana Perez, in the right-hand panel. The work, which took as its theme *The Doubting of St. Thomas*, was intended

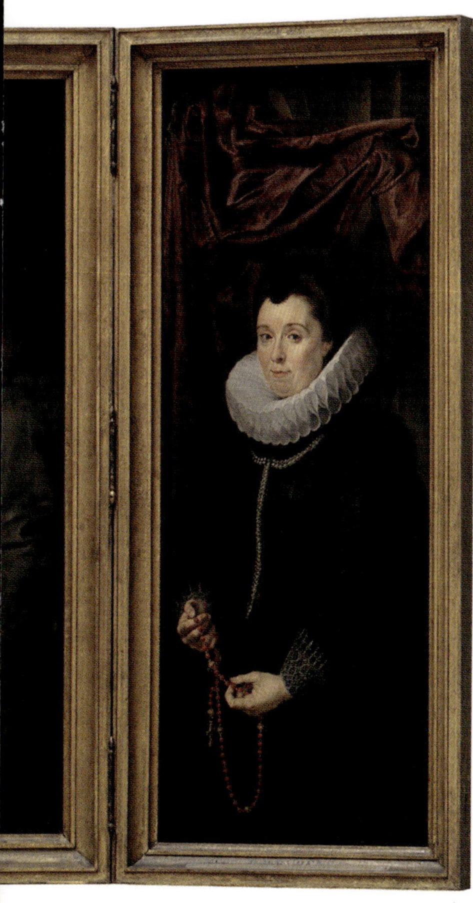

for the couple's future burial place in a chapel of the Church of the Friars Minor, which was also their parish church. At that time, the monastery of the Friars Minor was situated at the corner of the Mutsaardstraat and the Minderbroedersstraat, where the Royal Academy of Fine Arts now stands.

In the central panel, Rubens portrays an episode from the New Testament. The resurrected Jesus appears to his disciples and shows them the wounds in his hands as proof that he has truly risen from the dead - a subject that was appropriate for a burial chapel.

The triptych belongs to the artist's classical period between 1612 and 1615. His works in this period were characterized by a clear and controlled style, with restrained poses, an even distribution of light devoid of heavy shadowing, and a silvery 'glow' superimposed on the other colours. The figures in these compositions are often represented half-length.

Venus Frigida 1614

For this interpretation of the quotation *Sine Cerere et Libero friget Venus* ('Without Ceres and Bacchus, Venus freezes', meaning that without food and wine, love dies) by the Roman comic playwright Terence, the artist drew his inspiration from an ancient marble statue of the goddess he had once seen in Rome. An apathetic Venus is accompanied by her son Amor, who is shivering from the cold. A satyr tries to attract their attention with a horn of plenty, overflowing with wheat, grapes and other fruits.

This is a work typical of the artist's classical period. It is possible that the painting was already enlarged during Rubens' lifetime, with the addition of a broad panel on the left and smaller strips on the right and at the top. The landscape background was then painted in its entirety by a second artist.

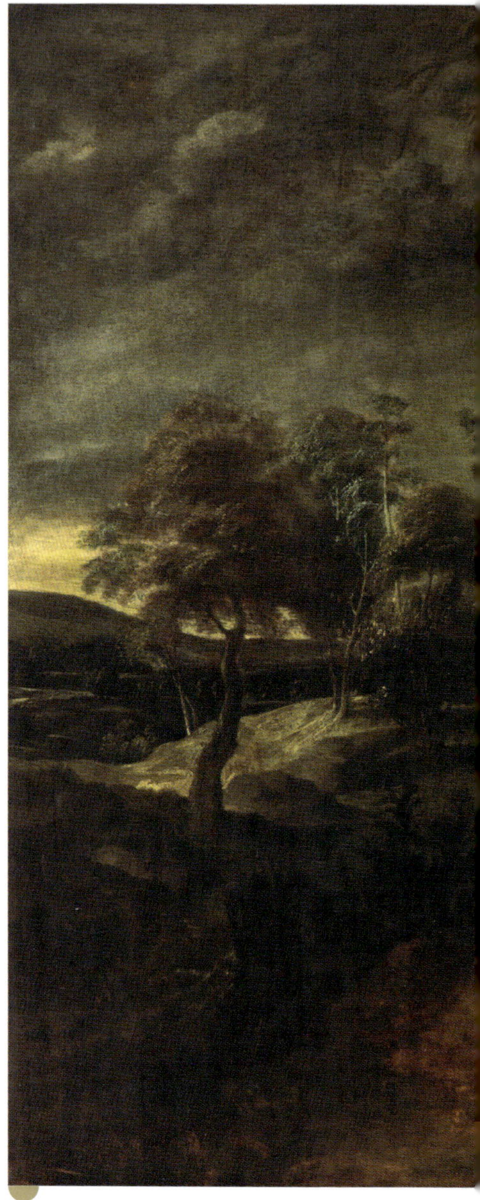

Panel, originally 121 x 95 cm, enlarged to 142 x 184 cm (first half of the 17th century?) The landscape was painted by another artist

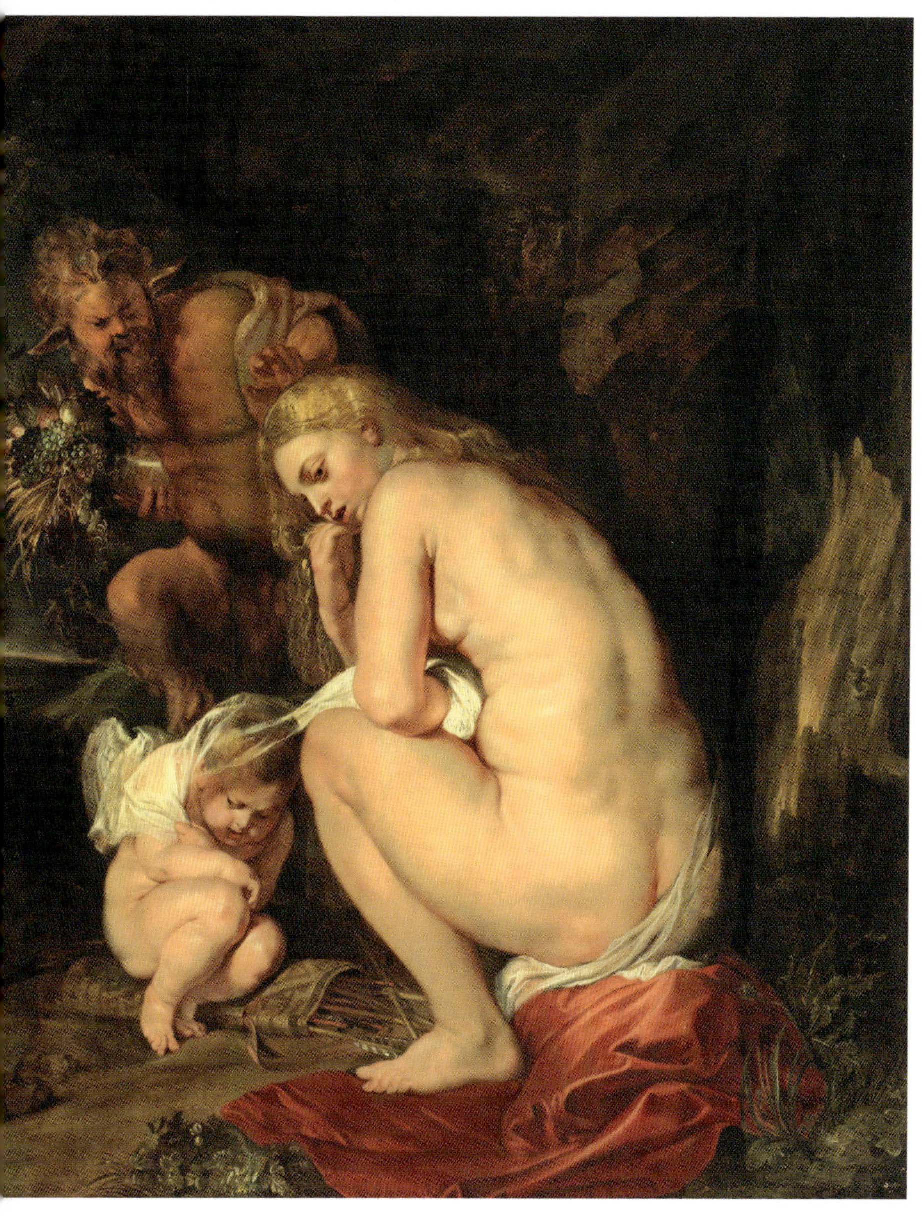

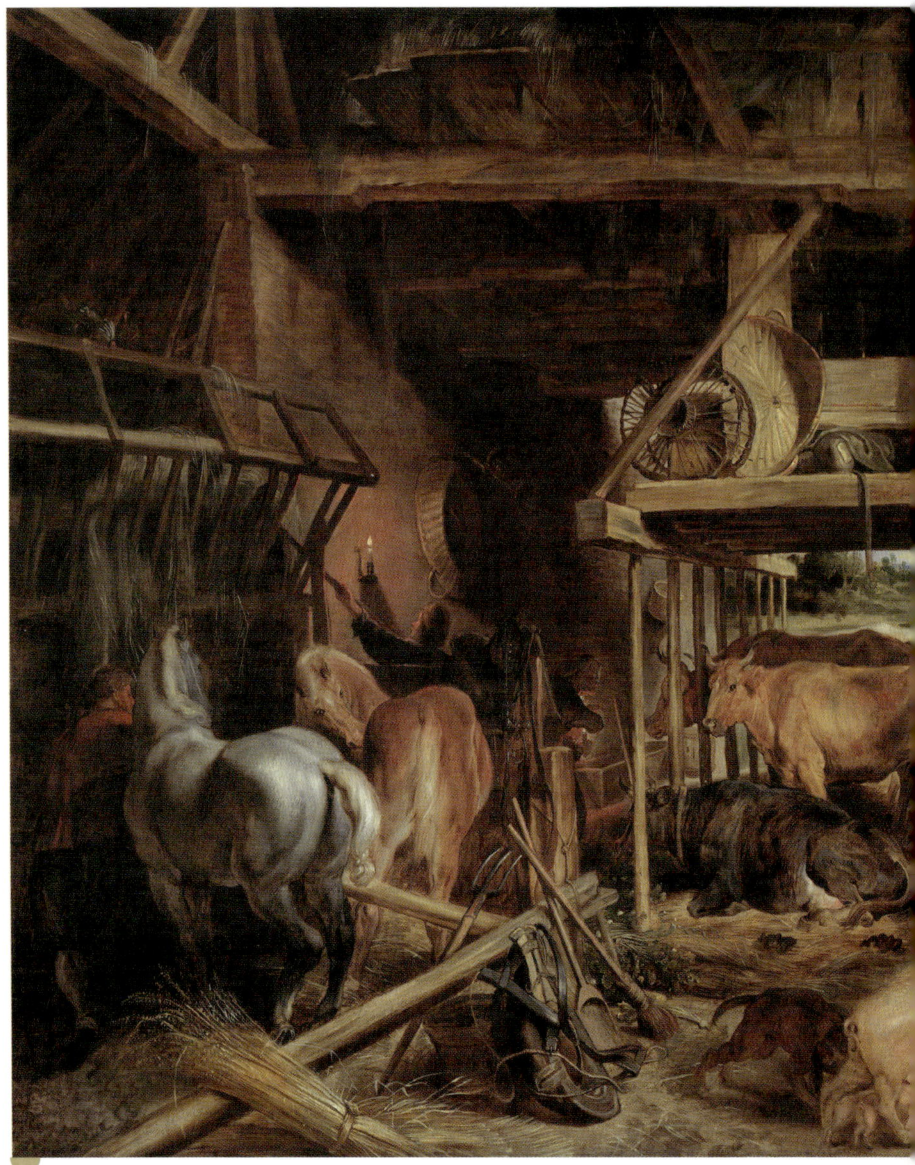

Panel, 107 x 155 cm

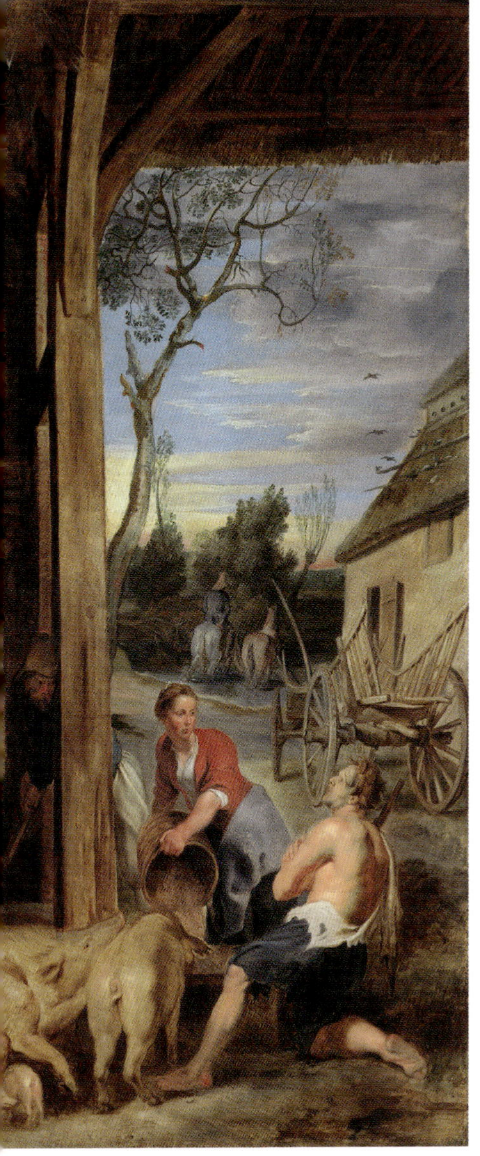

The Prodigal Son 1618

In a corner, almost as a detail in the whole, the prodigal son sits forlornly on the ground, begging for food, while a young farm girl fills up a trough for the animals. The religious theme - a story from the New Testament about a loose-living young man who leaves home and falls into abject poverty before coming to his senses - is almost incidental. Rubens used it as an excuse to paint one of his finest depictions of country life.

Powerful horizontal and vertical lines give structure to the composition. Most of the viewer's attention is drawn to the stable, the farming implements and the animals. It is evening. The cattle have been brought in from the fields, the horses are pawing impatiently in their stalls and the pigs are being fed. The farmhands are completing the final tasks of the day by candlelight. In the distance, we can also see a wide, tree-filled landscape, in which two horses are quenching their thirst in a nearby pond under the last rays of the setting sun.

This was not a scene painted from real life. In Rubens' time, this kind of landscape painting was made in the artist's workshop, using preliminary sketches from nature. This meant that a single composition might contain figures, animals, trees, stables, implements, etc. that were drawn at different times and in different places. In other words, the completed painting was not the result of direct observation, but was a recreation based on the artist's visual memories, imaginative powers and compositional talent. *The Prodigal Son* must have meant something special to Rubens; the panel was still in his possession at the time of his death.

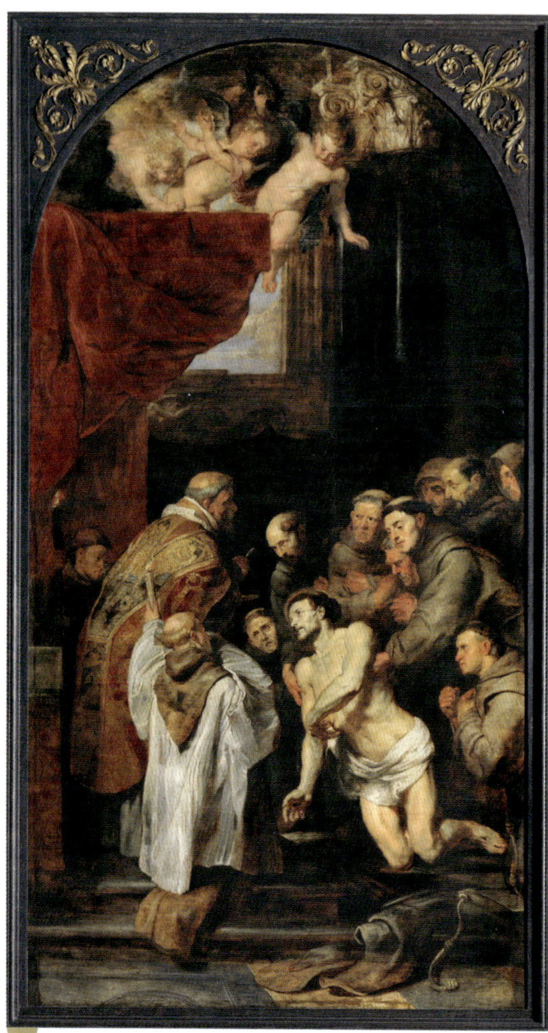

Panel, 422 x 266 cm
Altarpiece for the Church
of the Friars Minor in Antwerp

The Last Communion of St. Francis of Assisi
1618-1619

This painting was commissioned by a rich merchant for donation to the Church of the Friars Minor (a brotherhood in the Franciscan Order) in Antwerp. Consequently, it illustrates an episode from the life of St. Francis of Assisi. The work, which was intended to hang above one of the side altars, also depicts a small altar in a dimly-lit church, in front of which a dramatic scene is being played out, as the saint receives the sacrament for the final time before his death. Rubens renders the subject in a series of soft transitions from light to dark, whilst at the same time imparting intense feeling to the gestures and facial expressions of the monks. The dying saint is surrounded by 12 of his companions, perhaps as a way of emphasizing his close union with Christ, who also had 12 disciples. The open window behind the canopy reveals a glimpse of heaven, for which Francis is soon destined.

Panel, 429 x 311 cm
Altarpiece for the high altar
of the Church of the Friars Minor
in Antwerp

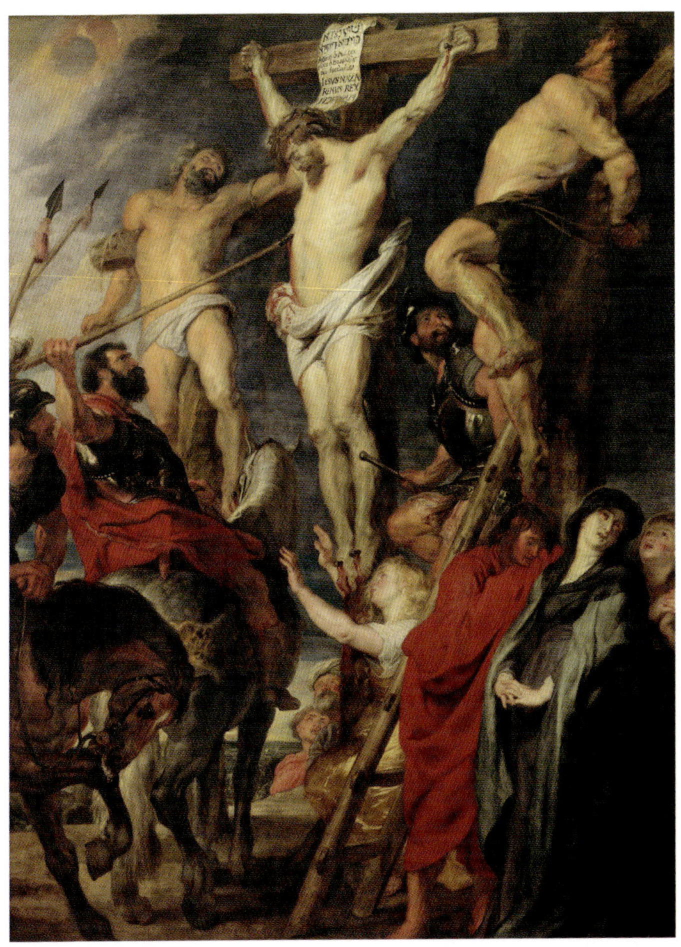

The Lance ca. 1619-1620

Thanks to the generosity of several wealthy local citizens, the Church of the Friars Minor possessed a number of Rubens masterpieces. *The Lance* (or *Christ on the Cross*) was commissioned by Nicolaas Rockox. The central theme of this dramatic composition draws a clear parallel with the spiritual world and the beliefs of the Friars Minor, whose founder, St. Francis, had also miraculously received the five stigmata of Christ (the wounds made by the nails in his hands and feet and by the piercing of his side with the lance). Stylistically, the painting belongs to the transitional phase between Rubens' classical period and his new style during the years after 1620, with more refined gradations of colour and more softly delineated contours.

Panel, 447 x 336 cm
Altarpiece for the high altar in the church
of St. Michael's Abbey in Antwerp

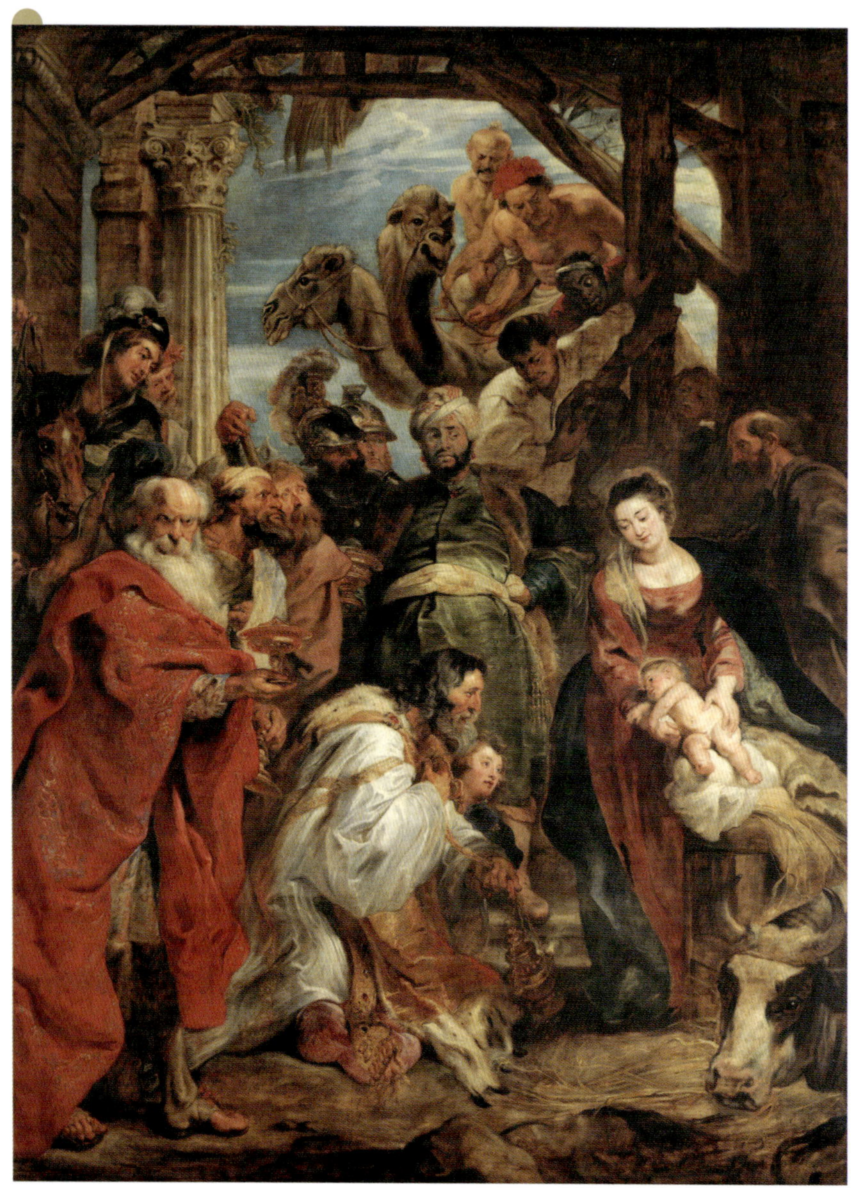

The Adoration of the Magi 1624

This panel is now regarded as one of Rubens' finest altarpieces and was originally displayed in the church of the once powerful St. Michael's Abbey, which was decommissioned and demolished at the start of the 19th century. The painting is also one of the most sublime expressions of the High Baroque. It creates a powerful impression through the dynamism of its asymmetric composition, the richly nuanced colouring, the expressiveness of the figures and the sureness of the execution. The highly differentiated and restless group is held together, as it were, by a few strong vertical architectural elements, like the column, a horizontal beam at the top of the stable and a number of diagonal roof beams that follow the main lines of the composition.
This monumental panel also displays a number of remarkable painting techniques. For example, in some parts of the composition, Rubens conjures up figures on an ochre background with just a few strokes of the brush, as is the case in the bottom right corner with the head of the ox and the straw on the floor. This is essentially the technique for making small oil sketches, which he here applies in a large-scale format.

According to tradition, Rubens completed this work in just two weeks. The deftness of the virtuoso brushwork and the sparing use of paint make this story credible.

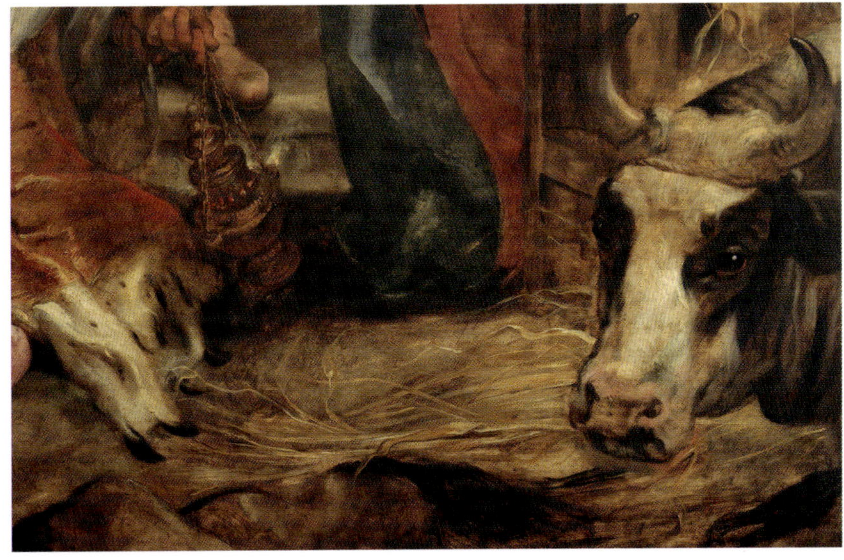

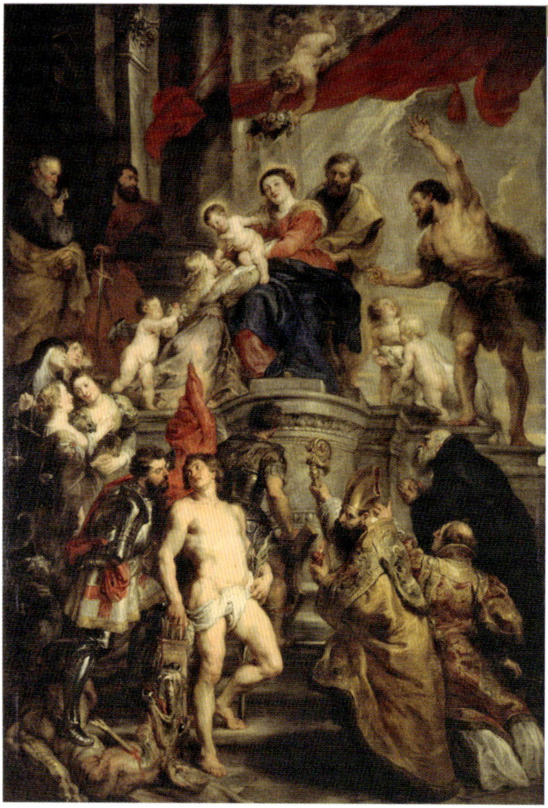

Canvas, 564 x 401 cm
Altarpiece for the high altar of
St. Augustine's Church in Antwerp

Madonna Enthroned with Saints 1628

A company of male and female saints is gathered around the Holy Family. Only two figures look towards the viewer: Our Lady, who is the ultimate goal of this saintly procession, and the imposing bishop figure at the foot of the stairs, who is holding a crosier and a burning heart. This is St. Augustine. It seems as if he is beckoning the faithful, asking them to focus their attention on the Blessed Virgin, who is about to be crowned Queen of Heaven by the angel hovering above her head. Because this painting was intended for the Church of St. Augustine, Rubens decided to place a clear and unmistakeable emphasis on this venerable Father of the Church.

The composition displays a strong dynamism, created by a succession of spiral movements that seem to draw the figures upwards towards the Madonna and Child, with an inconspicuous St Joseph half-hidden behind them. This massive painting, with its swirling energy and its warm glows of light, supplemented by deeper reds and golds, is one of the high points of Rubens' religious art during this period.

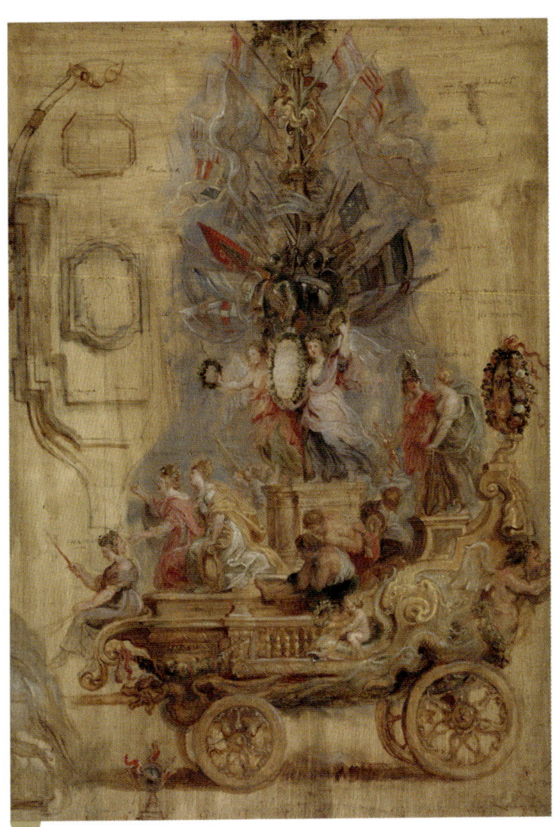

Panel, 103 x 71 cm
Oil sketch

The Triumphal Chariot of Kallo 1638

After the Spanish governor of the Netherlands, the Cardinal-Infante Don Ferdinand, had defeated the Dutch and French in battle at Kallo and Saint-Omer in 1638, the city administration in Antwerp decided to honour the victorious general by commissioning Rubens to design a triumphal chariot for him.

The chariot was conceived as a kind of wheeled ship, decorated with different allegorical figures, including Prosperity, Providence, Courage, the city virgins of Antwerp and Saint-Omer, and, on a socle, Victory in the shape of two further winged virgins holding aloft floral garlands and an inscribed medallion. This rapidly executed design in oils highlights the virtuosity and surety of Rubens' sketching technique.

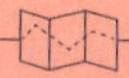

WALK

A good place to start your Rubens walk through Antwerp is the statue of the great master on the Groenplaats, in the centre of the city.

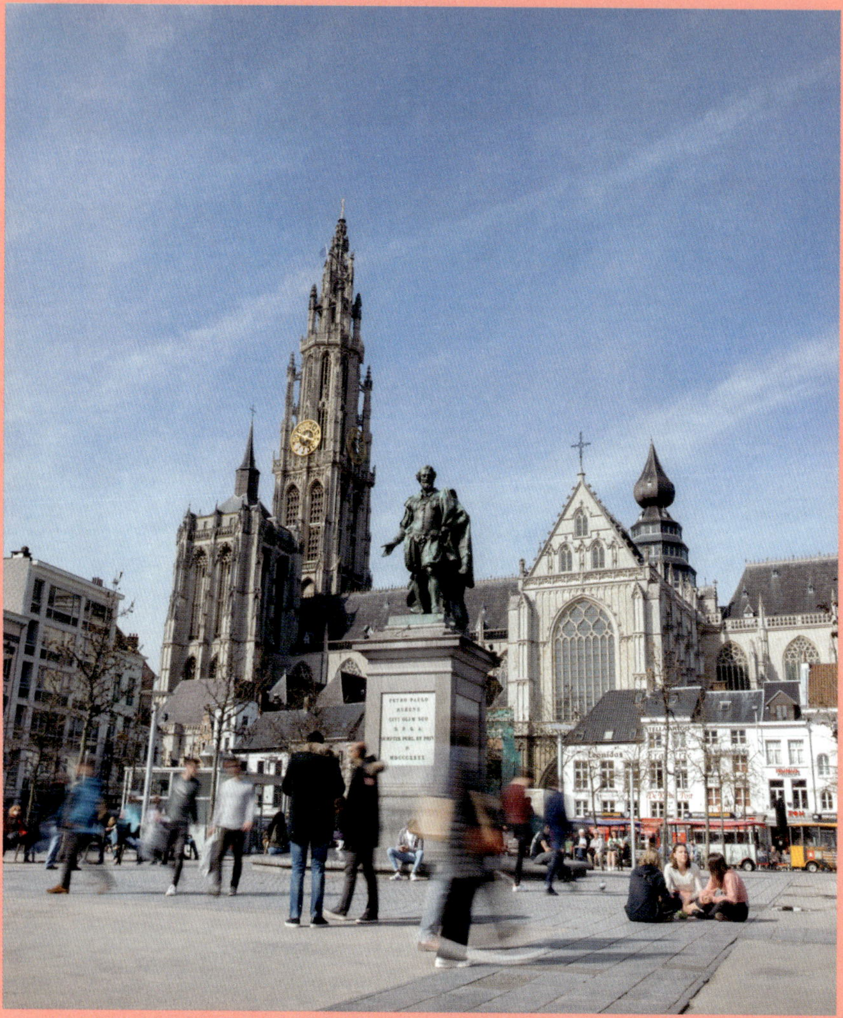

2

Groenplaats

In Rubens' time, this large city square was a cemetery close to the cathedral, known as the Groot Kerkhof (Great Cemetery) or Groen Kerkhof (Green Cemetery). The current square was only created around 1800. It was first known as Place de l'Egalité (Liberty Square), in keeping with the spirit of the French Revolution, whose armies had overrun the Southern Netherlands and annexed the region to France. Just a few years later, when Napoleon Bonaparte came to power, the name was changed to Place Bonaparte. It was only when the Southern Netherlands became part of the Kingdom of the Netherlands after 1815 that the square was given its definitive name: the Groenplaats.

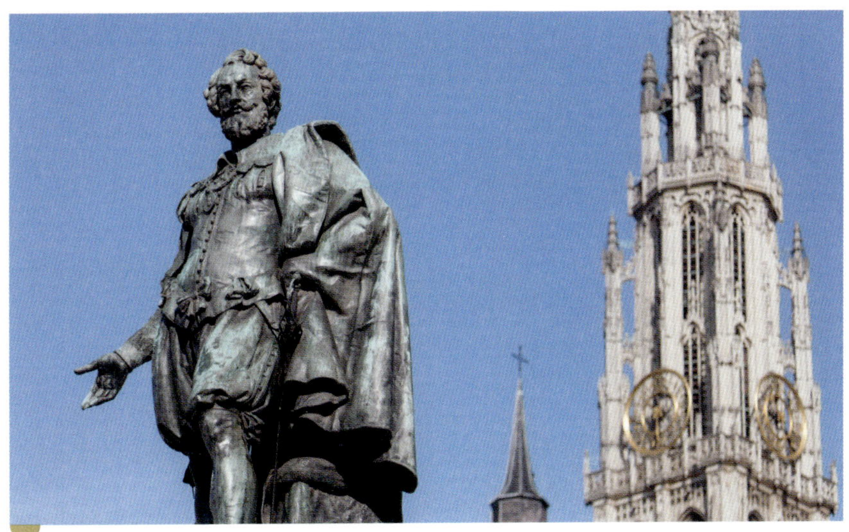

Willem Geefs, cast in bronze in 1843 by J.G. Buckens

Statue of Peter Paul Rubens 1840

This likeness of Rubens was made in 1840 to mark the 200th anniversary of the painter's death. Crafted by the Belgian sculptor Willem Geefs (1805-1883), it was originally conceived as a plaster statue and stood not in the Groenplaats but on the banks of the Scheldt. It was cast in bronze in 1843 and was erected in the centre of the Groenplaats, on the precise spot where the large central crucifix of the old cemetery once stood.

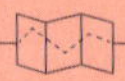

WALK

From the Groenplaats, it is just a stone's throw to the cathedral, whose elegant tower - and perhaps even its melodious bells - seem to pull you magnetically in that direction. But you must resist, since our Rubens' walk first takes us in the opposite direction! Passing first through the Groenkerkhofstraat (which, in view of its ugliness, is fortunately short) and then along the Reyndersstraat and the Leeuwenstraat, you will soon arrive at the Vrijdagmarkt, where you will discover a unique historical museum.

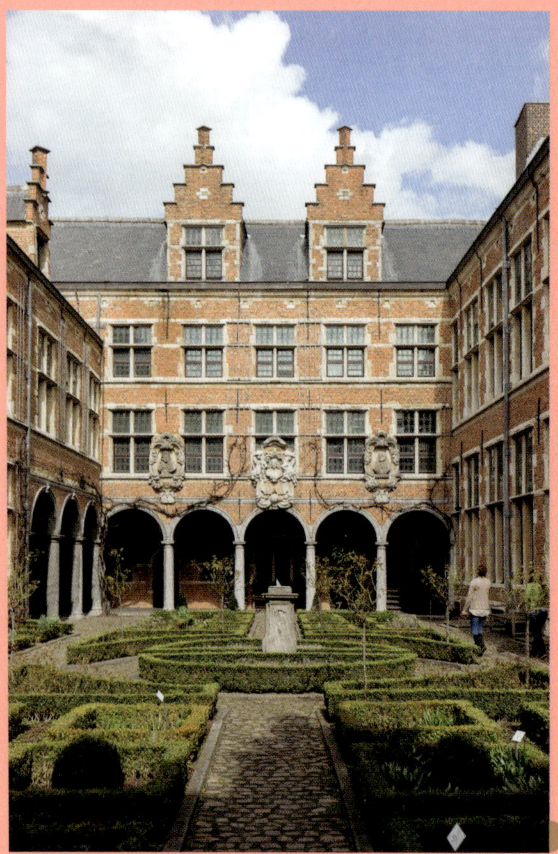

Antwerp, Officina Plantiniana of Balthasar I Moretus
Copper engravings by, amongst others, Theodoor Galle, partly to his own design and partly to designs by P.P. Rubens.
Page with **The Adoration of the Magi**, a copper engraving by Theodoor Galle to a design by P.P. Rubens.

In 1992, the courtyard of the Plantin-Moretus Museum was laid out as a garden from the late-16th, early-17th century. The tight symmetrical forms separated by paths is typical of garden designs in Rubens' time. The garden also contains many of the plants that were popular in those days. The quiet of the courtyard and its perfect harmony with the Renaissance galleries and gables make it a wonderful place to sit and dream.

Plantin-Moretus Museum

Vrijdagmarkt 22-23
+32 (0)3 221 14 50
www.museumplantinmoretus.be
Tues-Sun 10:00-17:00, closed 1 Jan, 1 May, Ascension Day, 1 Nov, 25 Dec

From 1555 onwards, the house known as 'De Gulden Passer' (Golden Compass) was home to a famous printing workshop. It now houses the Plantin-Moretus Museum and Print Cabinet. The workshop was originally founded by Christoffel Plantin, but by Rubens' time it was run by the founder's grandsons, Jan II and Balthasar I Moretus. The family Plantin-Moretus also lived here, occupying a magnificent mansion with an equally magnificent courtyard and garden. Rubens was a friend of Balthasar I Moretus and regularly did work for his printing business.
The workshop buildings and the mansion, dating from the 16th and 17th centuries, have been perfectly preserved and now form the core of the only museum in the world that has been included twice in the UNESCO list of world heritage sites. Its rich art collection includes paintings, drawings and print designs by Rubens.

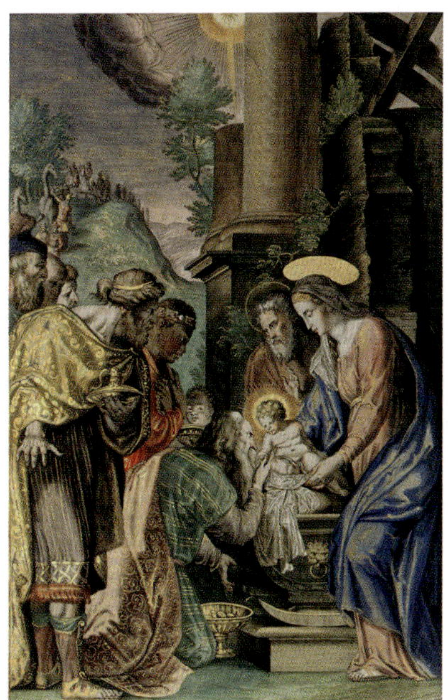

Missale Romanum 1613 (reissued 1616 and 1618)

Printer Balthasar I Moretus frequently made use of his childhood friend Rubens as a designer for book illustrations and title pages. Rubens' drawings were engraved on copper plates by highly skilled craftsmen like Theodoor Galle (1571-1633) and his brother, Cornelis. Under Balthasar's expert guidance, the richly illustrated books of the Baroque reached a new and unparalleled high point of opulence and excellence.
The first edition (1613) of the *Missale Romanum*, a book detailing the liturgy for the entire religious year, contained two engravings from designs by Rubens: *The Adoration of the Magi* and *The Ascension of Christ*. For later editions of this missal, and for other liturgical and religious books, such as breviaries, Balthasar systematically replaced the older illustrations with new designs by Rubens.

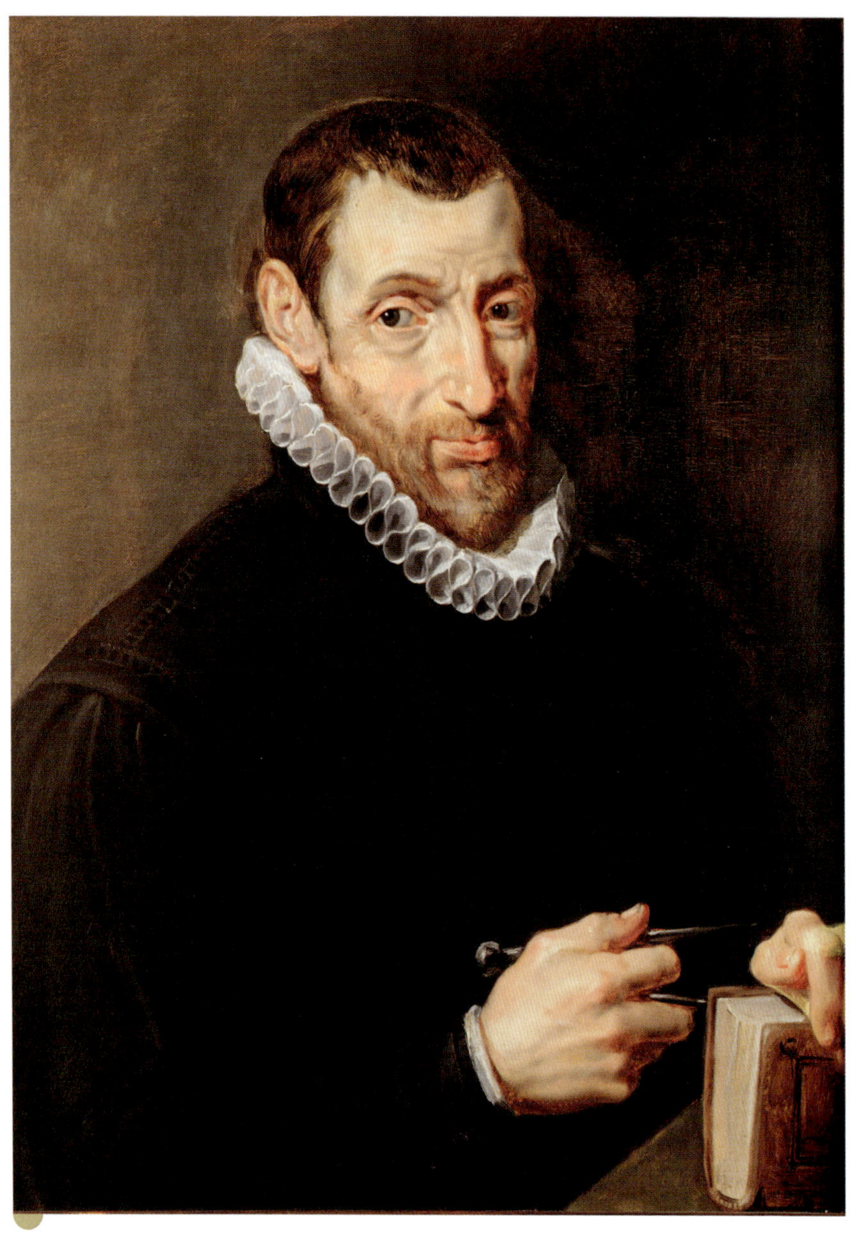

Portrait of Christoffel Plantin,
between 1612 and 1616, panel, 65.9 x 50.7 cm

Portrait of Christoffel Plantin

Rubens made this portrait of the founder of the Gulden Passer printing house on the basis of a late 16th-century painting made by an unknown artist during Christoffel Plantin's lifetime. It shows him as a man in his 64th year. Rubens carried out numerous commissions for Balthasar I Moretus over a 30-year period, not only as a designer of book illustrations and title pages, but also for a series of painted portraits, including Balthasar's parents and grandparents, as well as several good friends of the family, such as Justus Lipsius. These portraits were intended as decoration for the Moretus mansion, where they still hang today.

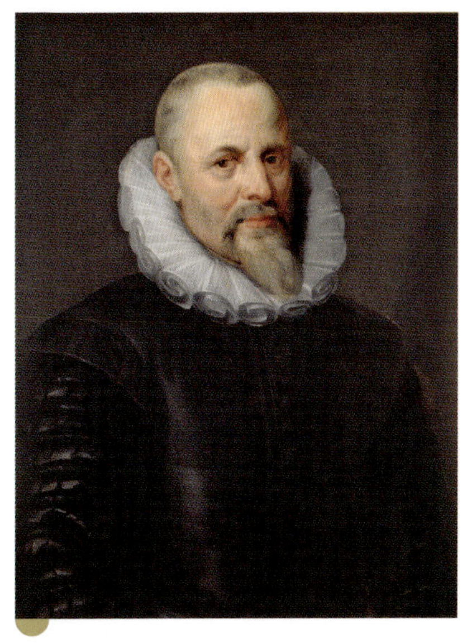

Portrait of Jan I Moretus,
between 1612 and 1616, panel, 66.4 x 51 cm

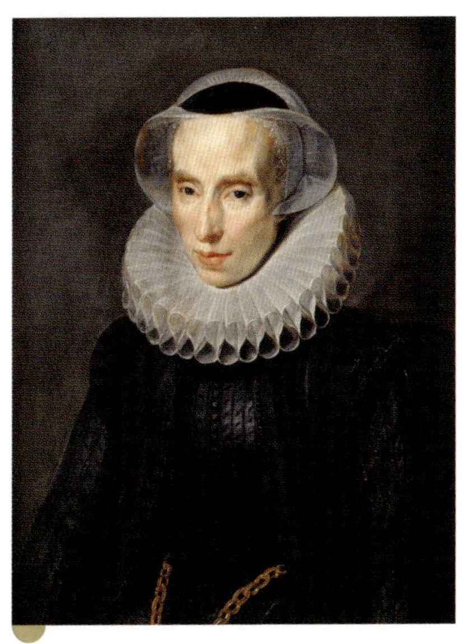

Portrait of Martina Plantin, Wife of Jan I Moretus,
ca. 1633, panel, 65.5 x 50.5 cm

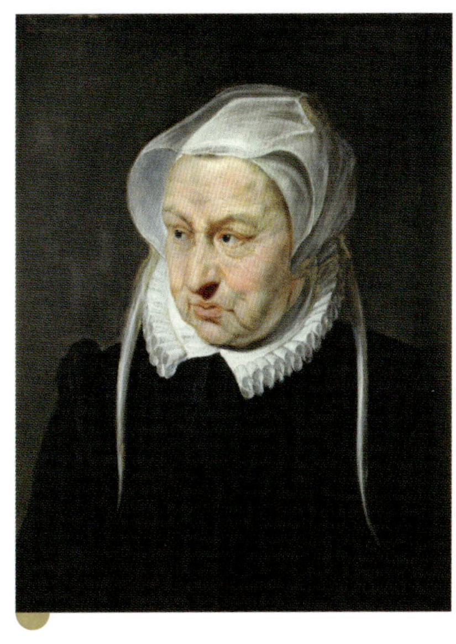

Jeanne Rivière, Wife of Christoffel Plantin,
ca. 1633, panel, 64.6 x 50.1 cm

The dying Seneca between 1612 and 1616

Rubens and Balthasar I Moretus were both true humanists. They were avid readers, loved art and had a great interest in classical antiquity. They were also adherents of Stoicism, an ancient Greek philosophy that was translated into a practical moral code for living in the first century A.D. by the Roman writer and thinker, Seneca. Typical stoic qualities include self-control, spiritual balance, reasonableness, a love of peace, a rejection of violence and cruelty, and a benevolent attitude towards others. Seneca was forced by the Emperor Nero to commit suicide in 65 A.D., a fate he met with dignity and characteristic fortitude.

This outstanding 'portrait' of the dying Seneca was commissioned from Rubens by Balthasar I Moretus and it testifies to their close intellectual affinity and their shared humanist ideals.

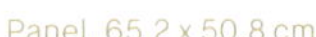
Panel, 65.2 x 50.8 cm

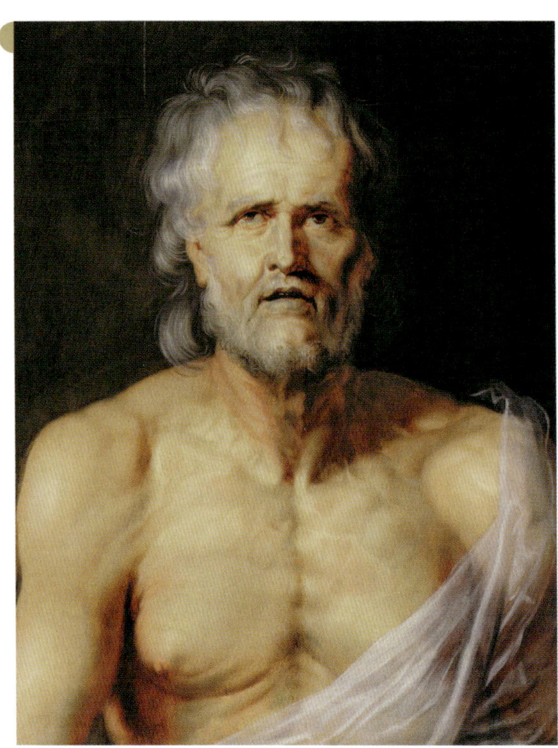

The Moorish King ca. 1618

This portrait is probably a representation of Balthasar, one of the three kings in the nativity story.

As early as the Middle Ages, it was believed that one of the three kings who had followed the star to Bethlehem to find the birthplace of Jesus was a Moor. In the art of the 16th century, it was common practice for King Balthasar to be depicted as the Moor and also as the youngest of the three. Melchior brought gold as a gift for the Christ Child, Gaspar brought incense and Balthasar myrrh. This choice of gift for the Moorish king was no coincidence, since myrrh is a fragrant resin derived from trees that grow, amongst other places, in North Africa.

Around 1618, Balthasar I Moretus asked Rubens to paint three lifelike 'portraits' of the three kings. He had been named after the Moorish king and the other brothers in the Moretus family also included a Melchior and a Gaspar. These were not portraits in the normal sense of the word, but personifications that were intended to underline the symbolic importance of the names. At the same time, they were also a valuable addition to Balthasar's private art collection.

While the Melchior and Gaspar figures were created entirely from his own imagination, Rubens used an existing 15th-century painting of a Tunisian prince as the basis for his Balthasar. It had been painted by an unknown Low Countries artist during a visit to North Africa and Rubens must have seen it somewhere, because he had already made a copy for use as a model by 1609. He later worked the same figure into a number of his compositions.

King Balthasar is holding the casket of costly myrrh in his hands (based on the painting below). The casket lid is open and the myrrh seems to emit a radiant light. It is possible that the casket was intended to symbolize the crib of Jesus, who was the Light of the World. As well as the obvious allusion to the first name of Balthasar, the portrait is also a veiled reference to the Moretus family name, by virtue of its similarity to the word 'Moor'. It was the custom in Rubens' time for hidden meanings of this kind to be included in paintings. These double meanings would usually be immediately recognizable to the patron and to others who viewed the finished work, although more complex symbolism sometimes needed to be explained or could only be divined after a degree of thought.

Panel, 64.8 x 50 cm

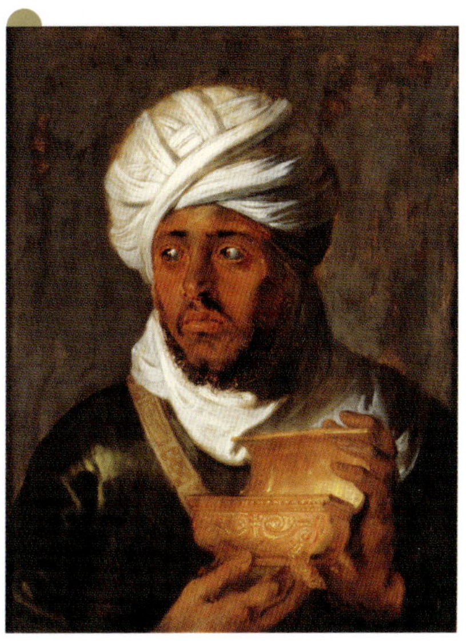

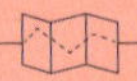

WALK

Were you impressed by the Plantin-Moretus Museum? Stay with your thoughts in Rubens' time and wander at your leisure through Old Antwerp, back towards the cathedral, via, for example, the Heilige Geeststraat, Hoogstraat, Reyndersstraat and Pelgrimstraat. You are now walking through one of the most delightful parts of the city, with numerous 17th-century houses.
So why not have a good look around while you are here? No. 6 Reyndersstraat is the site of the former home and workshop of Jacques Jordaens, one of Rubens' artistic contemporaries. The uninspiring facade conceals a charming historical complex of buildings that runs through to no. 43 Hoogstraat on the other side. Also take a look - or have a breather - in the courtyard of De Groote Witte Arend (Great White Eagle) at no. 18 Reyndersstraat. In fact, the entire neighbourhood - from the Vlasmarkt, through the Hoogstraat with its famous Vlaaikensgang alleys, to the Pelgrimstraat - is well worth a detour.
And don't worry about getting lost. Wherever you are in the city centre, sooner or later you will always be able to find your bearings from the tower of Our Lady's Cathedral, rising majestically above you as a perfect orientation point. Sometimes it will surprise you, as you turn the corner of an old street, sometimes, you can admire it in all its glory as you cross a spacious city square. But one thing is certain: you can't miss it for long!

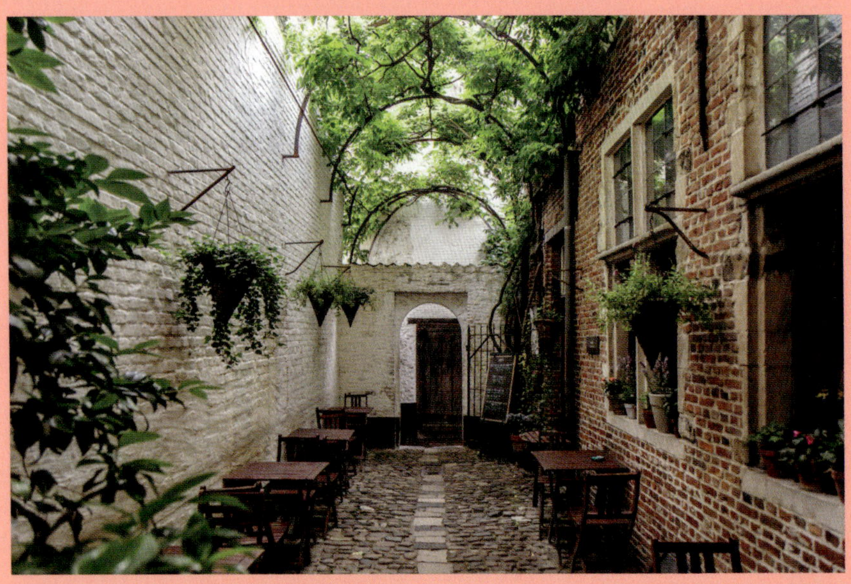

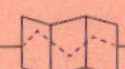

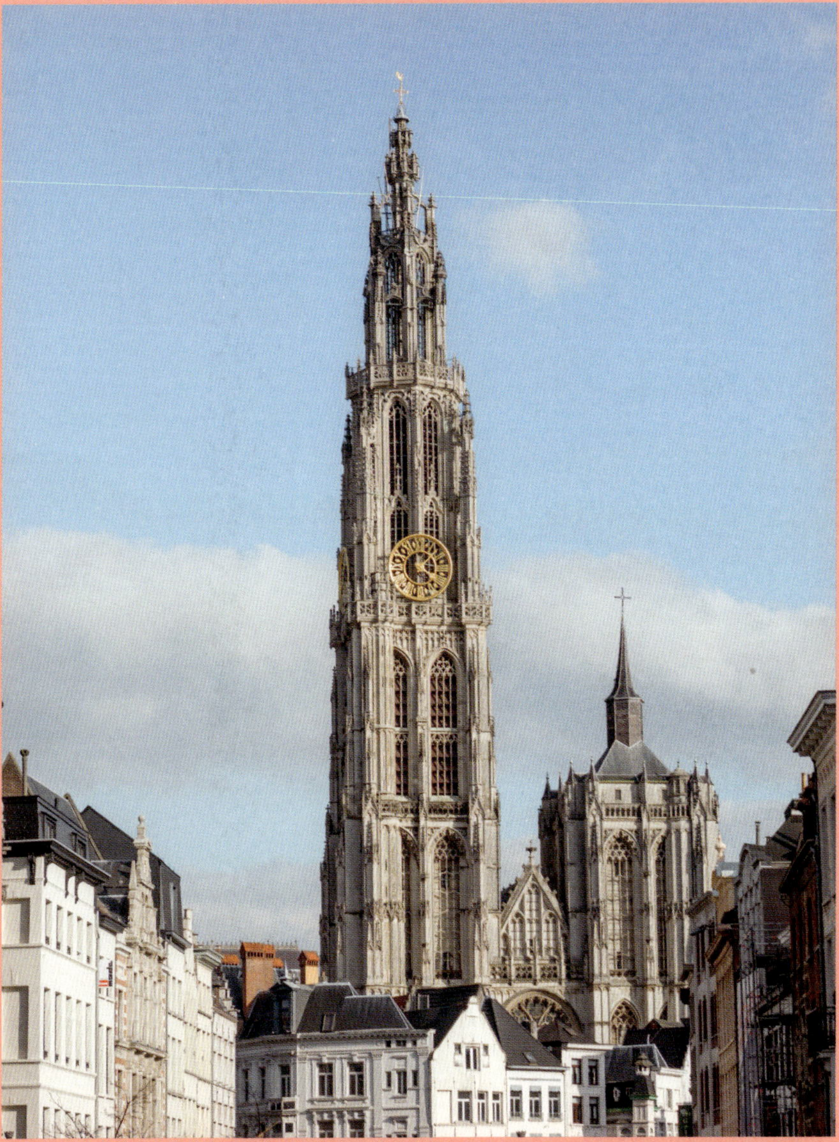

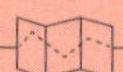

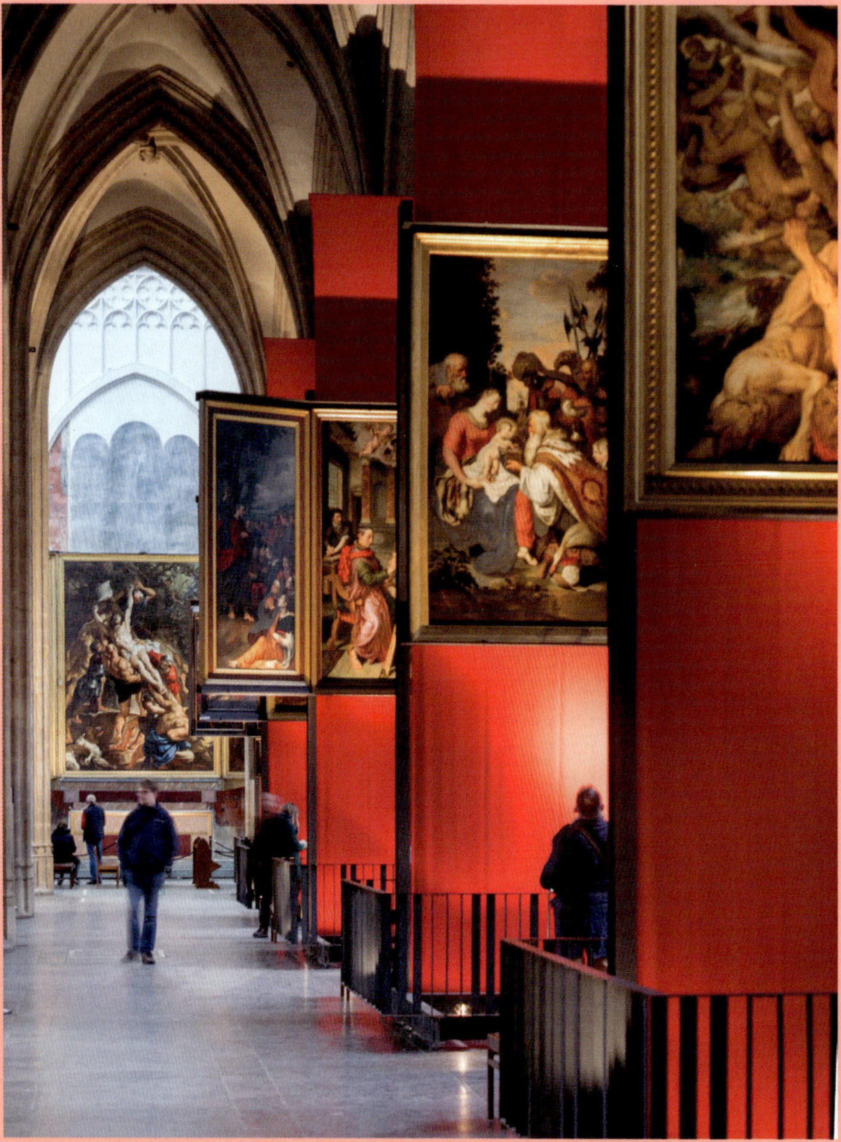

WALK

Cathedral of Our Lady

Handschoenmarkt
+32 (0)3 213 99 51
www.dekathedraal.be
Mon-Fri 10:00-17:00, Sat 10:00-15:00, Sun 13:00-16:00, closed 1 Jan and during religious services

On the Handschoenmarkt you will find yourself standing in front of the main doors of the magnificent Gothic cathedral, the oldest extant church in Antwerp. Whether for its history, its architecture or its artistic treasures, there can be no doubt that the Cathedral of Our Lady is a monument of outstanding importance.

In the Middle Ages, this was the site of the Klein Kerkhof (Small Cemetery), but by Rubens' time it had become a place for the glove-sellers and their stalls during the city's frequent markets and fairs. Admire the ornate wrought-iron cage above the stone well. The intertwined tendrils are surmounted by the legendary Roman soldier Brabo, a symbol of the city of Antwerp. This fine example of the smith's art was made in the 16th century and has been attributed to Quinten Matsijs. Until 1900, the well was still used to draw water, but nowadays its function is purely decorative. Against the west wall, there is a monument to the memory of the architects and craftsmen who built the north tower and the church. The statue group was made by the Belgian sculptor Jef Lambeaux and dates from 1914.

A relatively recent attraction on the square is the poignant statue of the orphan Nello and his dog Patrasche, the main characters in a 19th-century novel in which the cathedral and the paintings of Rubens also play a leading role.

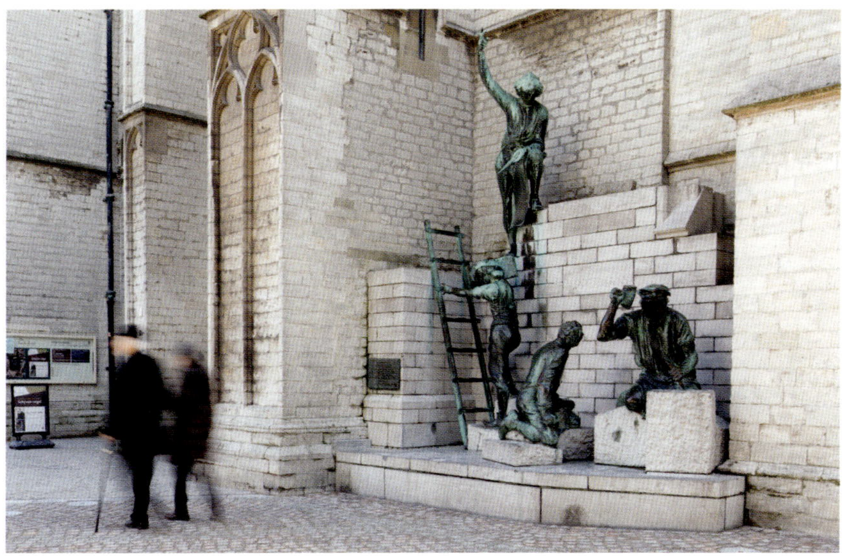

Panel, 460 x 340 cm
(central panel), 460 x 150 cm
(side panels)
Altarpiece for the high alter
of St. Walburga's Church
in Antwerp

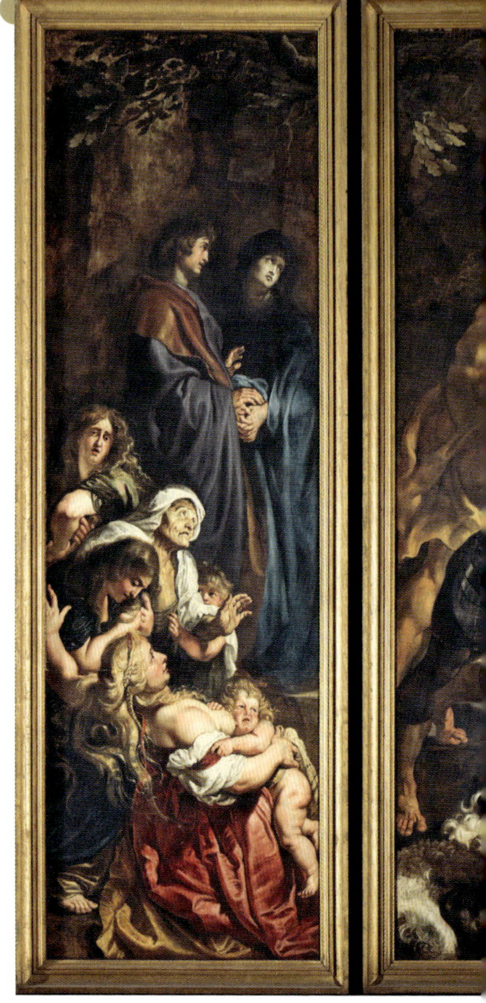

The Elevation of the Cross 1609-1610

Nine of the executioner's assistants strain with all their might to pull upright the cross on which hangs the pallid body of Jesus. On the left stand a group of witnesses: St. John the Evangelist, the Blessed Virgin and several distraught women and children. On the right, a Roman commander on horseback supervises the proceedings, while the soldiers in the background prepare to crucify the two criminals. This is a single composition, spread over three panels.

Rubens painted this work for the high altar in the Church of St. Walburga (demolished in 1817). According to tradition, Bishop Amand founded the church - the first in Antwerp - around the year 650. He is depicted on the back of the left-hand panel, in the company of Walburga, a saint from the 8th century. She is reputed to have spent several years in the vaults of the church, before becoming the abbess of a convent she founded in Bavaria.

On the back of the right-hand panel we can see the saintly smith and later bishop, Eligius. He was the patron saint of the Antwerp blacksmiths' guild, which had its altar in St. Walburga's Church. In front of Eligius stands St. Catherine of Alexandria, with the palm branch and sword as symbols of her martyrdom. Her prominence in this piece suggests a specific devotional cult in her honour associated with the church, but there is no evidence to confirm this supposition.

With this triptych, Rubens introduced the Baroque style north of the Alps in spectacular fashion. The diagonal composition resonates

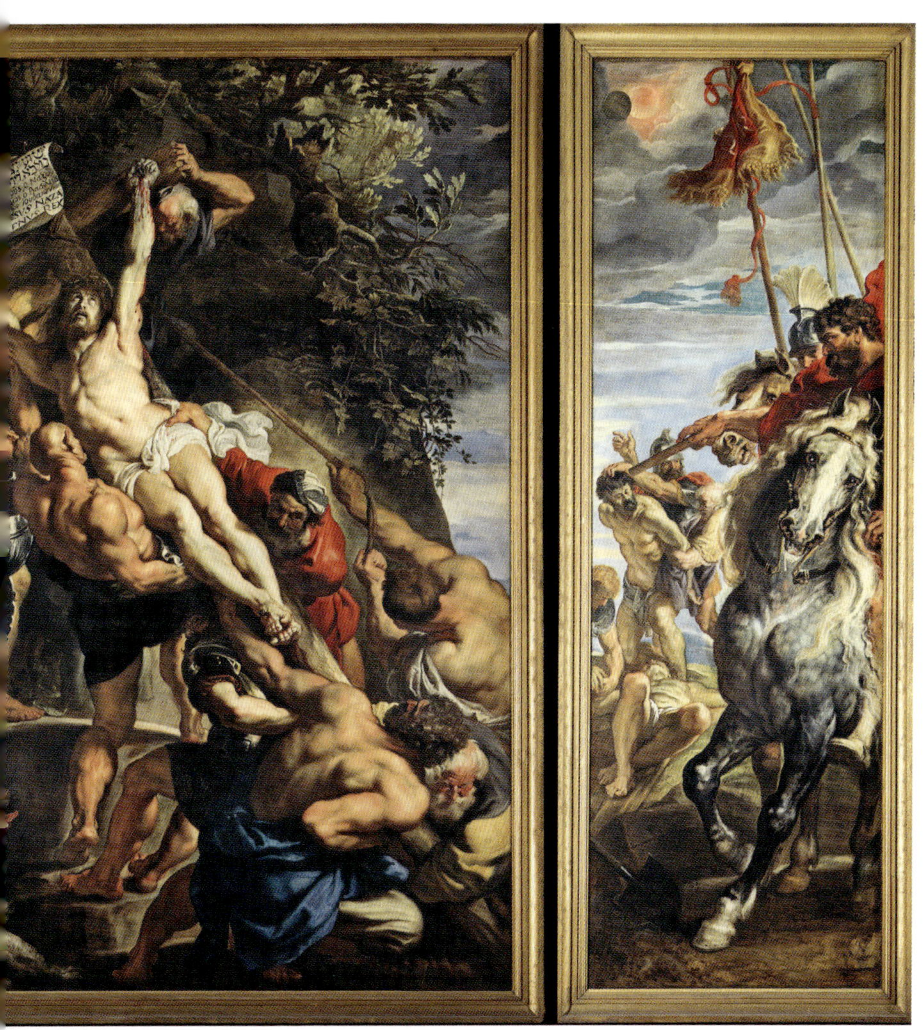

with dynamism and a vibrant interplay of colours. The artist had just returned from Italy, his mind full of the works of Michelangelo, Caravaggio and the great Venetian masters. The vigorous movements of the figures, the contrast-rich fall of light, the glow of the toiling bodies, the shimmer of the harness and the sheen of the luxurious garments all reveal a true talent in the making.

The painting was taken to Paris by the invading French in 1794, but was returned to Antwerp after the fall of Napoleon and the end of French rule in 1815, when it was decided to install it in the cathedral.

The Resurrection of Christ 1611-1612

Rubens painted this 'Moretus' triptych shortly after completing his *Elevation of the Cross*. It was commissioned by Martina Plantin, the widow of the printer Jan I Moretus.

Christ steps resolutely from an open tomb in a rock, and not from a sarcophagus, as had been traditional in the treatment of this subject up to this time. The supernatural radiance of his body contrasts with the darkness in which the terrified soldiers wait to see what will happen next.

The left-hand panel depicts St. John the Baptist, the patron saint of Jan I Moretus, dressed in his 'raiment of camel hair' as he stands on the banks of the River Jordan. The sword at his feet is a reference to his beheading. The right-hand panel portrays St. Martina, the patron saint of the Moretus widow, carrying the palm branch signifying martyrdom. According to tradition, the temple of the sun god Apollo collapsed when she made the sign of the cross in front of it, a legend which is reflected in the decor behind her.

The rear panels are equally magnificent. The two angels in light brown grisaille are reminiscent of classical statues. Perhaps they are the angels who stood by Christ's open grave on the morning of the resurrection? Or maybe they are waiting to open the gates of eternal life for the patrons?

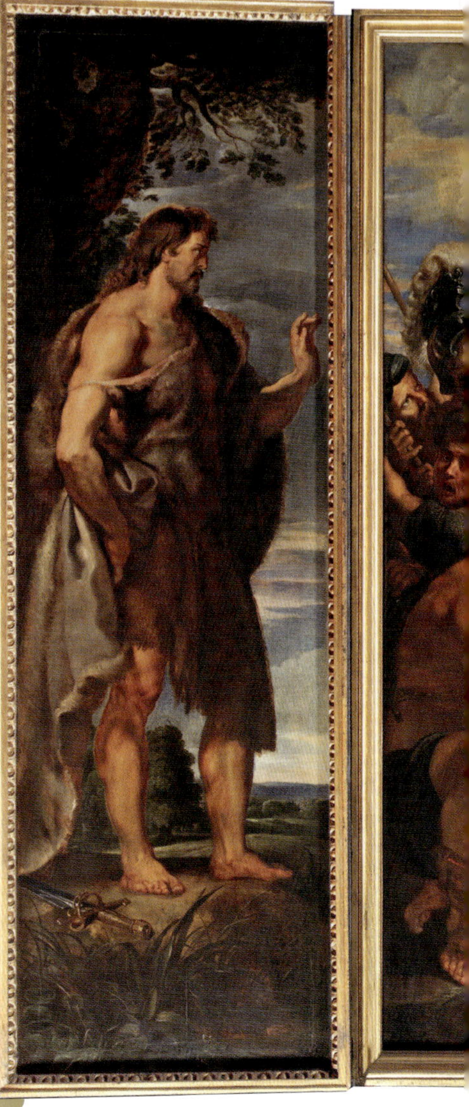

Panel, 138 x 98 cm (central panel), 136 x 40 cm (side panels)
Epitaph triptych of Jan I Moretus and Martina Plantin in the Cathedral of Our Lady in Antwerp

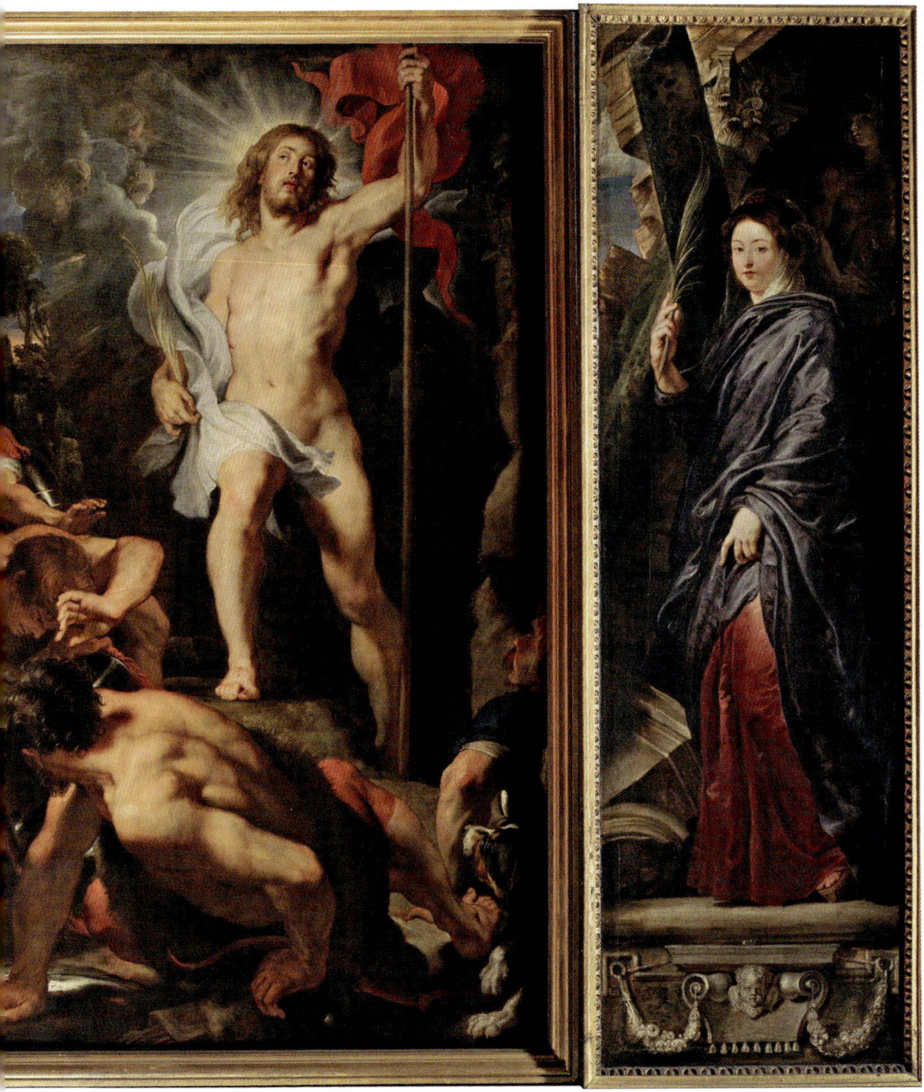

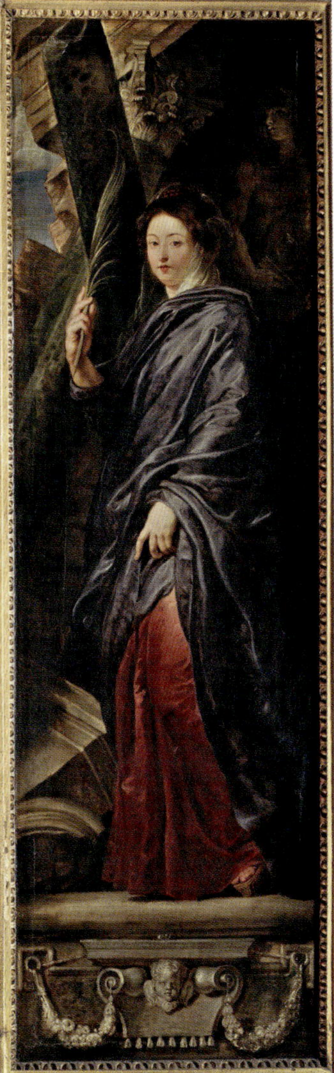

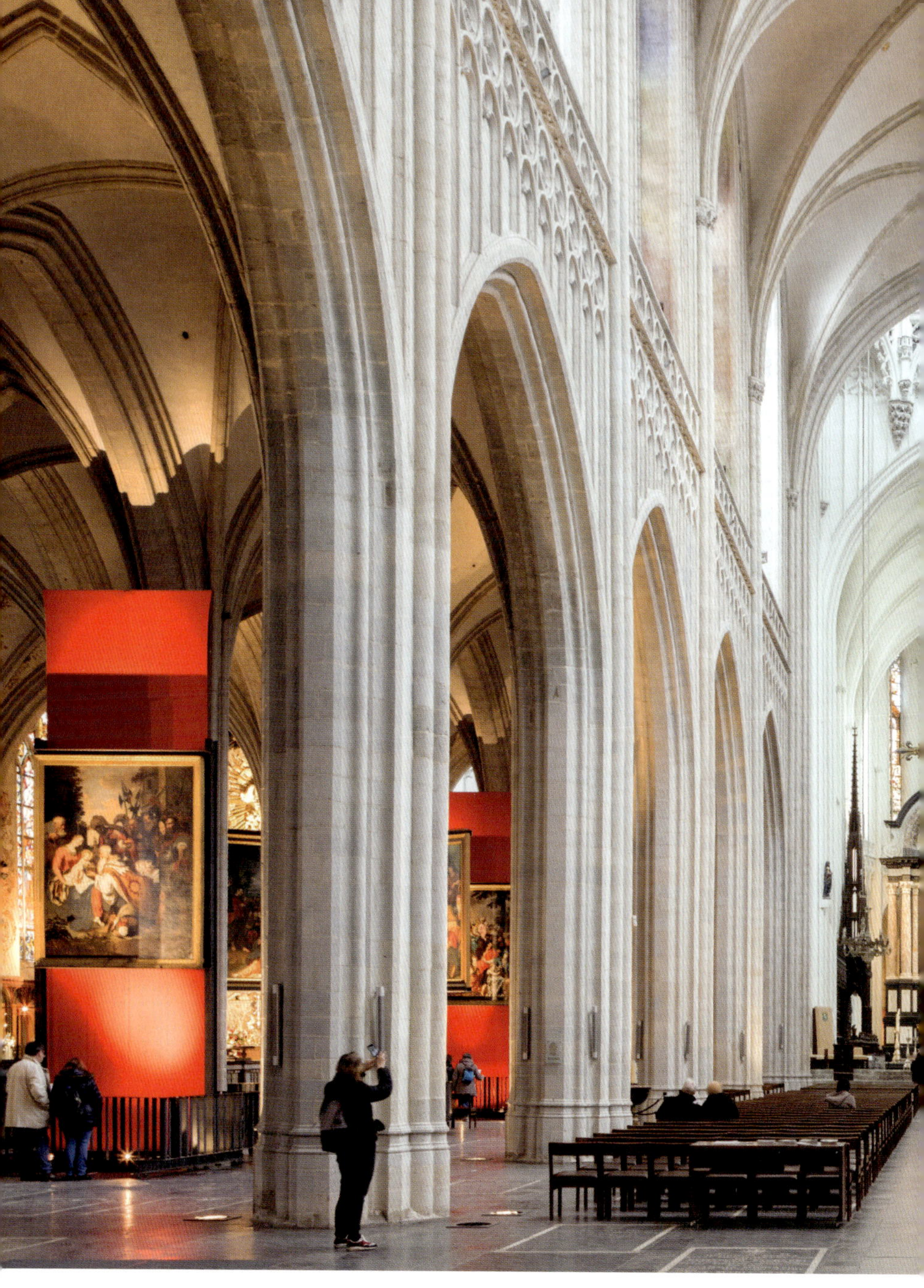

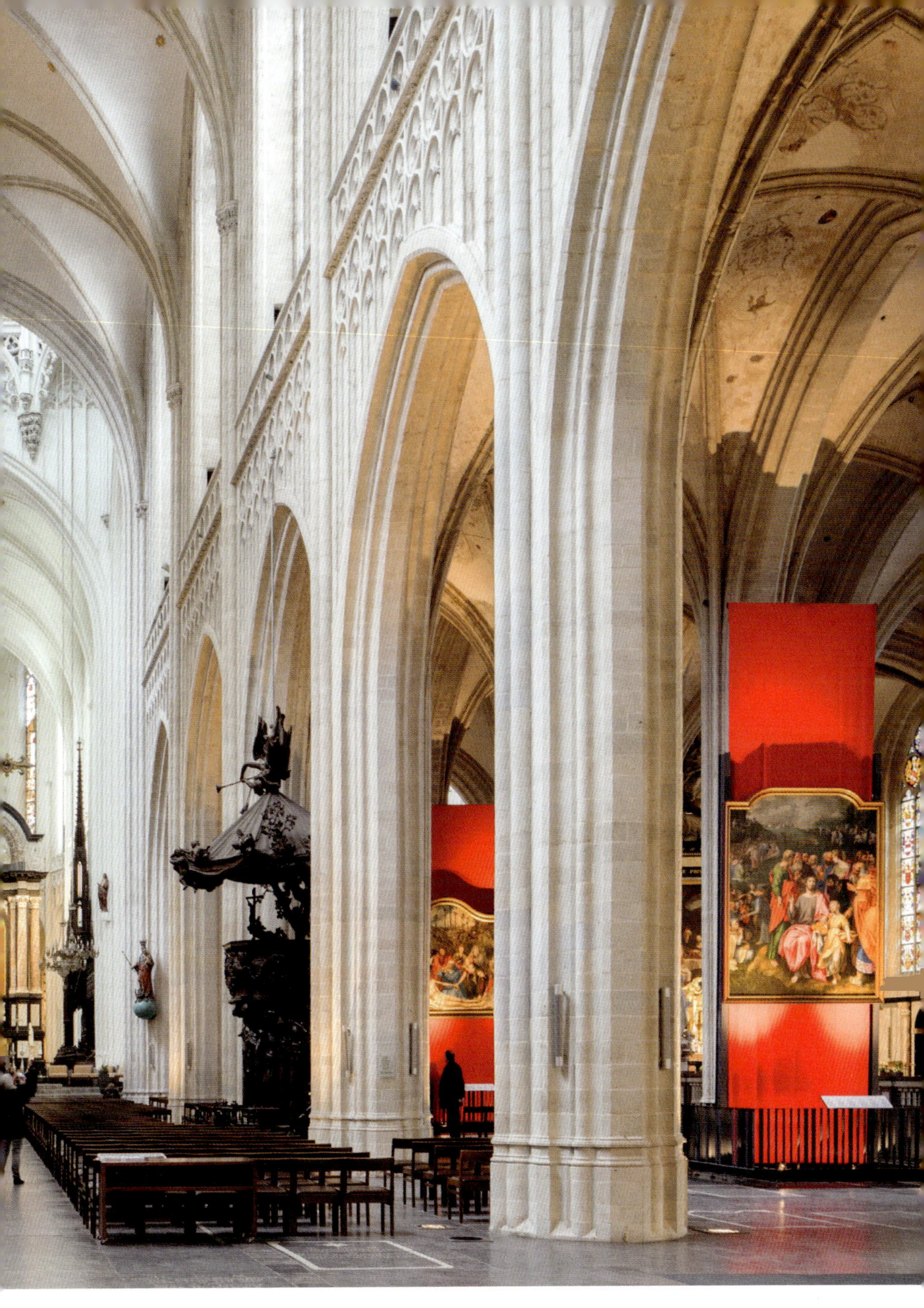

Panel, 421 x 311 cm (central panel), 421 x 153 cm (side panels)
Triptych for the altar of the Harquebusiers in the Cathedral of Our Lady in Antwerp

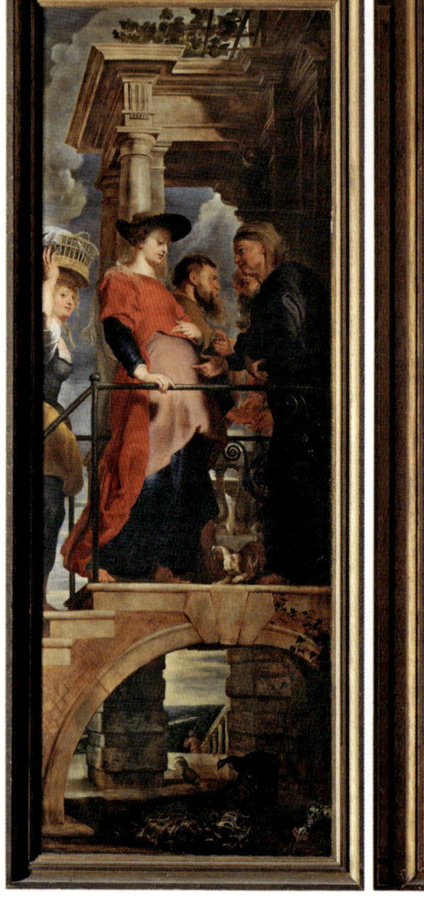

The Descent from the Cross 1611-1614

In 1611, the Antwerp Guild of Harquebusiers commissioned a 'descent from the Cross' for their altar in the city's cathedral from their celebrated fellow citizen, Peter Paul Rubens. The captain of the guild at that time was burgomaster Nicolaas Rockox, who is shown in profile on the far left of the right-hand panel.

The central panel depicts Christ's descent from the cross against the background of a louring sky. With great care, a number of men - Joseph of Arimathea, Nicodemus, St. John the Evangelist and two helpers - are lowering the body of Jesus onto a shroud. Several women, including the Virgin Mary, are helping them. Jesus' left foot rests on the shoulder of Mary Magdalene, who once dried his feet with her hair. The left-hand panel illustrates the Blessed Virgin's visit to her cousin, Elisabeth. Mary is pregnant with Jesus, and Elisabeth with John the Baptist. The women and their husbands, Joseph and Zacharias, greet each other under a portico. Behind them, on the stairs, a serving girl carries a basket with their travel belongings. The right-hand panel shows Jesus' presentation in the temple in Jerusalem. The ageing Simeon holds the Christ Child in his arms, while in the background, between the priest and the Virgin, the prophetess Anne looks on with joy. Joseph, who has brought two sacrificial doves with him, is kneeling at Simeon's feet.

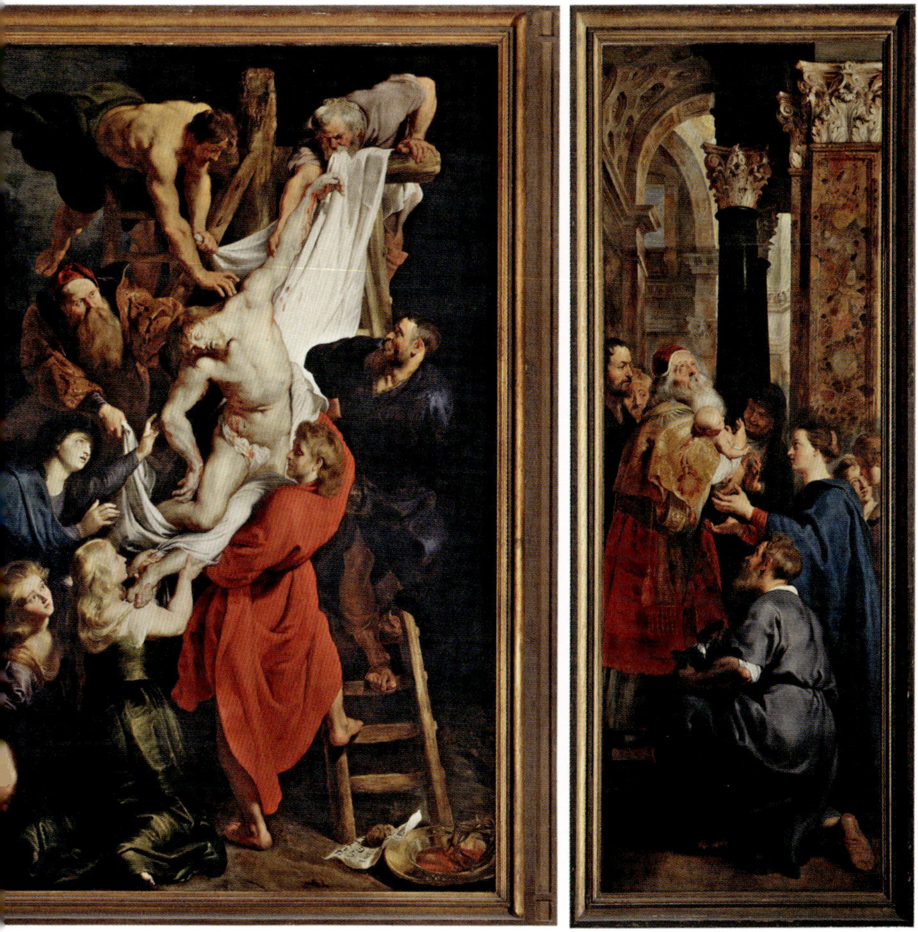

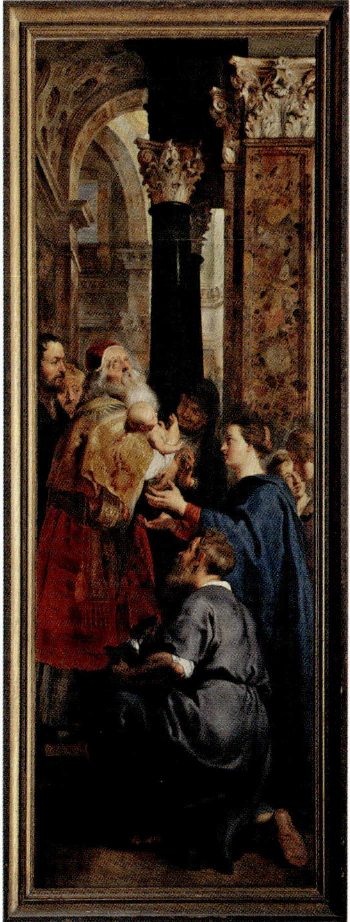

At first sight, this triptych contains three highly divergent subjects, but there is, in fact, a connection between them. Rubens painted the legend of St. Christopher, the patron saint of the Harquebusiers, on the rear panels. According to medieval tradition, this saint once carried the Infant Jesus on his shoulders across a river, finding his way by a light shone by a hermit. When the triptych was closed, the depiction of this legend was all that was visible. However, the symbolism becomes clear when you know that the saint's name in Greek, Christophorus, means 'bearer of Christ'. This explains the key to the entire composition: the friends and holy women in the central panels and Mary and Simeon in the side panels are all 'bearers of Christ'.

The Descent from the Cross was Rubens' first masterpiece - and also the first Baroque painting - to be installed in the cathedral.

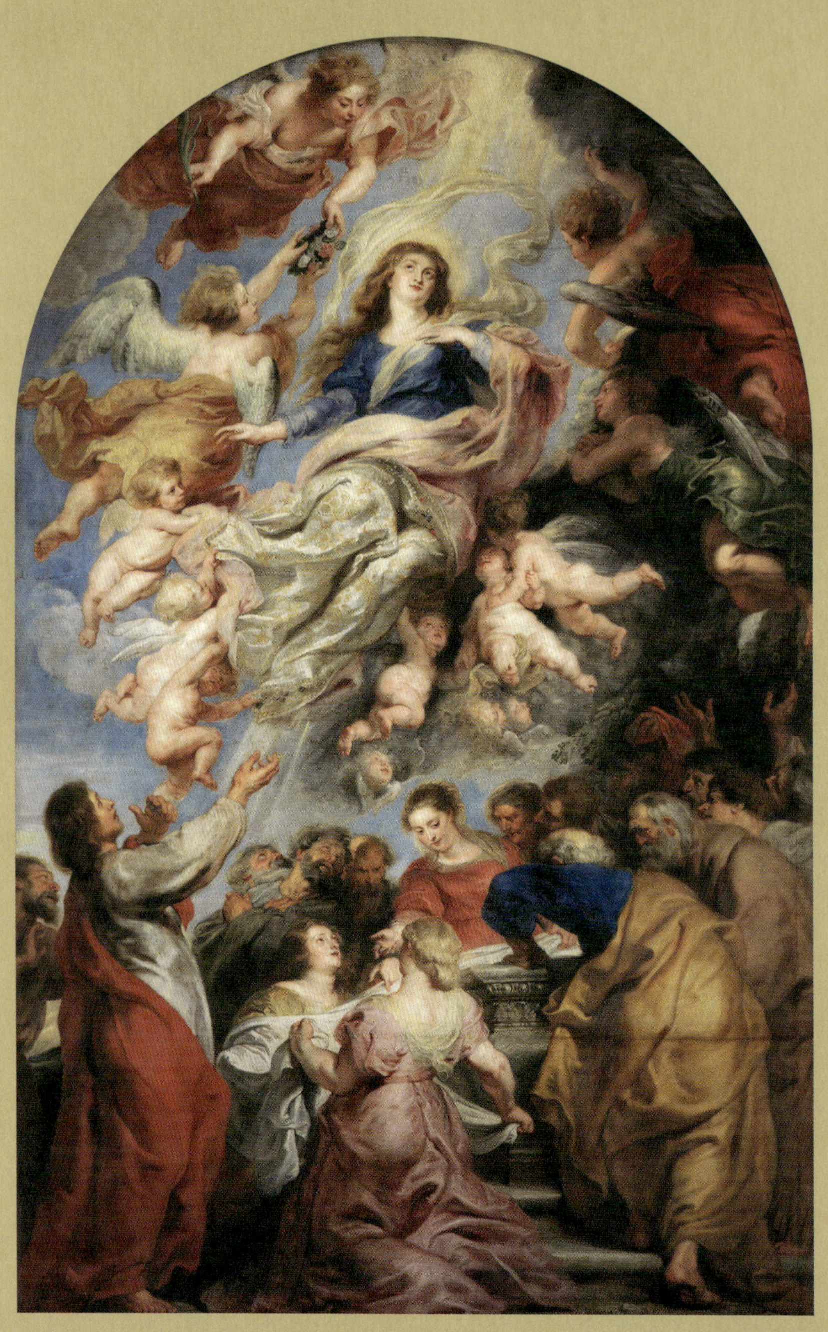

The Assumption of the Blessed Virgin 1625-1626

As part of a Baroque renovation that took place during the early years of the 17th century, a new high altar in marble was installed in the cathedral. Rubens was commissioned to paint the altarpiece, paid for by the deacon, Johannes del Rio, who in return received permission from the cathedral chapter to later be buried in the northern aisle of the choir.

The tradition relating to the ascension of the Virgin Mary into heaven was first developed during the Early Middle Ages and was a popular theme in the art of the 16th century.

The Virgin is rendered graciously, almost animatedly, with her flowing robes and her diaphanous shawl blowing in the celestial wind. She is borne upwards into the clouds by a group of frolicsome *putti*. Higher up on the left, two angels are preparing to crown her with a rosary. Back on earth, the twelve apostles are standing around her sarcophagus. The three women who, according to medieval tradition, were also with the Virgin at the time of her death and laid out her body are also depicted. The pretty woman in the middle wearing the red dress is more strikingly presented than the others. She has the features of Rubens' first wife, Isabella Brant, who died in June 1626 while the artist was working on this painting.

Panel, 490 x 325 cm
Altarpiece for the high altar in the Cathedral of Our Lady in Antwerp

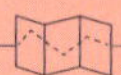

WALK

The Hendrik Conscienceplein and the St. Charles Borromeo Church are only a short walk from the cathedral. There are different ways to get there: for example, via the Blauwmoezelstraat, the Melkmarkt and the Jezuïetenrui, or else via the Korte Nieuwstraat. Whichever way you

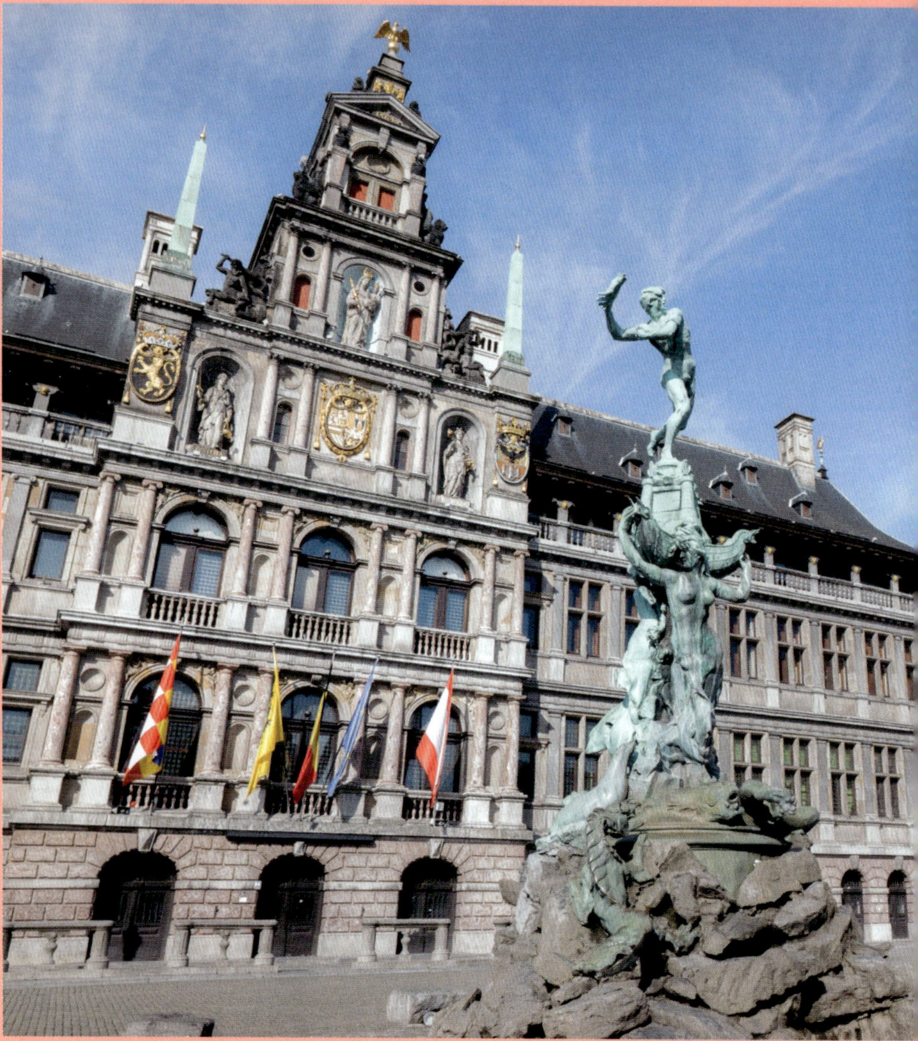

choose makes no difference, but while you are so close by it is well worth the effort to first make a short detour to admire the 16th-century town hall on the Grote Markt. If you wish to do this, take the Maalderijstraat exit when you leave the Handschoenmarkt.

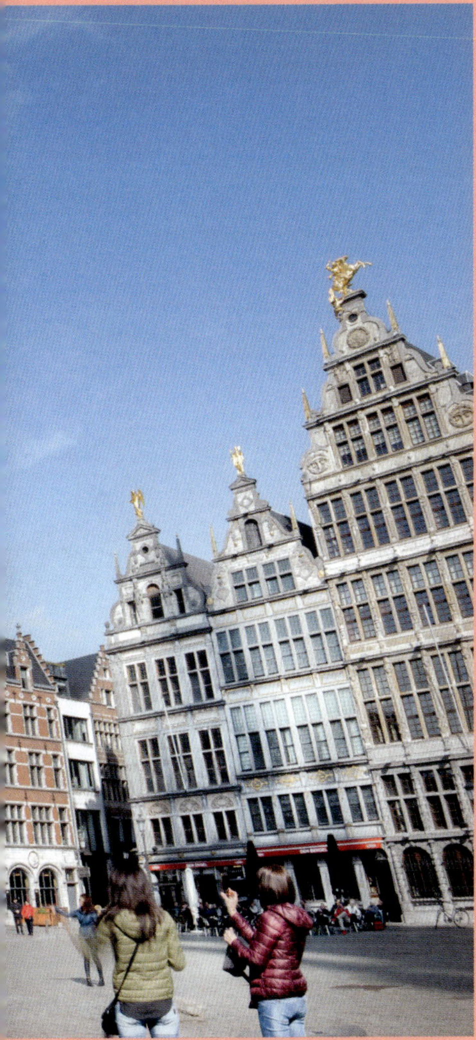

Grote Markt

The magnificent Antwerp town hall is a UNESCO world heritage site. It was designed around 1560 by the architect Cornelis Floris de Vriendt in what was then the 'modern' Renaissance style, and was completed in 1564. Since 1587, a Madonna statue, known as the Madonna of Loretto, has watched over the city from her position high on the front gable. In Rubens' time, the town hall made a powerful impression on all who saw it, which is what the city fathers intended; they saw the building as a way to express the glory of one of Europe's leading trading metropolises. The entire structure, both inside and out, will be thoroughly restored during the period between 2018 and the autumn of 2020. The Brabo fountain that stands in front of the town hall dates from 1887 and was made by Jef Lambeaux. You are now quite close to the River Scheldt and to the old fortress known as the Steen, a place popular with both tourists and local people.

Grote Markt

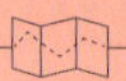

WALK

From the Grote Markt, the Kaasrui and the Wijngaardstraat bring you directly to the Conscienceplein. The word 'rui', as in the street names Suikerrui, Kaasrui and Jezuïetenrui, denotes the site of a watercourse or canal (similar to the famous 'reien' in Bruges). In Antwerp, you will search for these watercourses – 'ruien', 'vesten' and 'vlieten' – in vain: they were all vaulted hundreds of years ago and now flow underground, though they can still be visited with a trained guide. In Rubens' time, there were dozens of these inner city waterways, but they were gradually filled in to eliminate the stench and the pollution they caused. The Church of St. Charles is built on one of these covered 'ruien'.

The atmospheric Conscienceplein, named after a popular Flemish author of the 19th century, displays a clear harmonic unity in the Baroque style. The church and the surrounding buildings date from the first quarter of the 17th century, and were built by and for the Jesuit community. As a result, the square was first known as the Jezuïetenplein. It was renamed in 1883, when the statue of Hendrik Conscience was added.

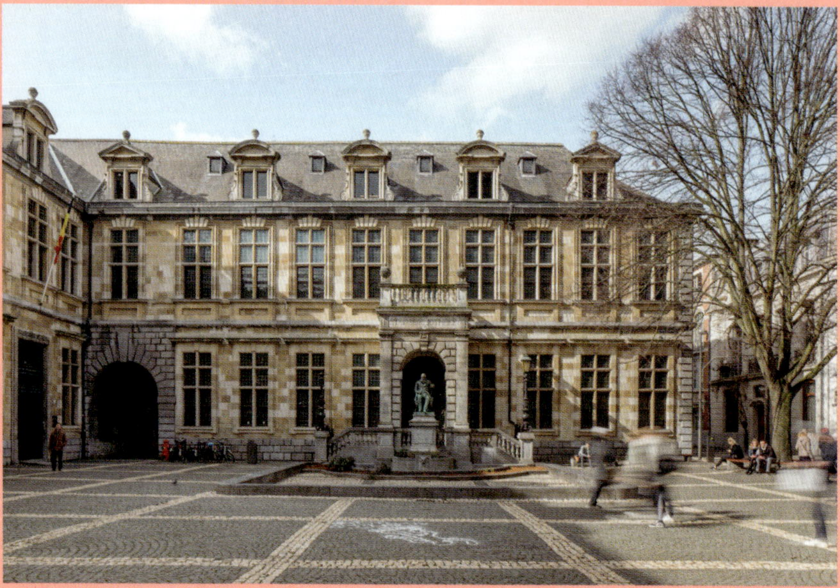

St. Charles Borromeo Church

Hendrik Conscienceplein
+32 (0)3 231 37 51
www.carolusborromeus.com, www.topa.be
Mon-Sat 10:00-12:30 and 14:00-17:00, closed during religious services

The Jesuit Order flourished in Antwerp at the start of the 17th century, a success that was reflected in a large-scale programme of building. The order bought land, demolished houses and filled in ditches and canals, using the resulting space to construct extensive complexes of buildings in the popular architectural style of the day.

The magnificent facade of the church dominates the Conscienceplein. On the other side of the square stands the Sodaliteit. In Rubens' time, this was the meeting house of a pious brotherhood of leading Antwerp citizens. The building on the south side of the square, next to the church, is the former Jesuit monastery, known as the Professenhuis. The Sodaliteit and the Professenhuis were both put to new uses from the end of the 18th century onwards.

The church is sixty metres long and divided into three naves, with two separate side chapels: the St. Ignatius Chapel and the Chapel of Our Lady. The side aisles are surmounted by a broad gallery. The interior is lavishly furnished and richly decorated with works of fine art.

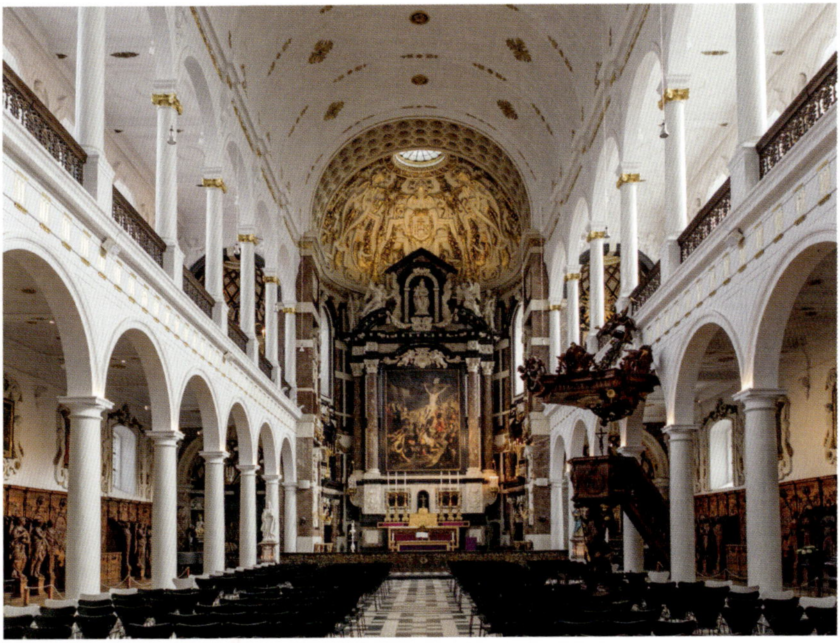

Sculpture work on the front gable of the Jesuit Church (now the St. Charles Borromeo Church) in Antwerp

ca. 1620

The St. Charles Borromeo Church was built between 1615 and 1621. It was originally known as the St. Ignatius Church - the first church in the world dedicated to Ignatius of Loyola, the founder of the Jesuit Order - and was part of the adjacent Jesuit monastery. The rector of the Antwerp College of Jesuits, the mathematician François Aguilon, drew the ground plan. The rest of the building and its decoration were designed by Peter Huyssens, a Jesuit lay brother, with the help of Rubens. The artist made design drawings for the majestic front gable and was also responsible for a number of interior elements, such as the high altar and the ceiling of the Chapel of Our Lady. It seems likely that he was also involved in the design of the elegant lantern tower. The sculpture work for the high altar and the front gable was carved by Hans van Mildert (1585-1638).

For the alcove-shaped choir, Rubens made two paintings depicting scenes from the life of Ignatius of Loyola and another Jesuit saint, St. Francis Xavier. For the Chapel of Our Lady, which was decorated at a later stage, he provided a previously painted *Assumption* from his 'reserve'. All three of these paintings are now part of the collection at the Art History Museum in Vienna. He also made a fourth painting, *The Return of the Holy Family from Jerusalem*, for the altar in the St. Joseph Chapel. However, his most important contribution to the artistic embellishment of the church was unquestionably the ensemble of 39 ceiling paintings that he completed in 1620 with the help of his workshop assistants.

Sadly, much of the magnificence of this 'marble temple' was lost in a fire on 18 July 1718. The nave and the side aisles, together with their ceilings, were completely destroyed. Restoration work was begun immediately under the guidance of Jan Pieter van Baurscheit the Elder and was completed a year later.

Hans van Mildert, to designs by P.P. Rubens

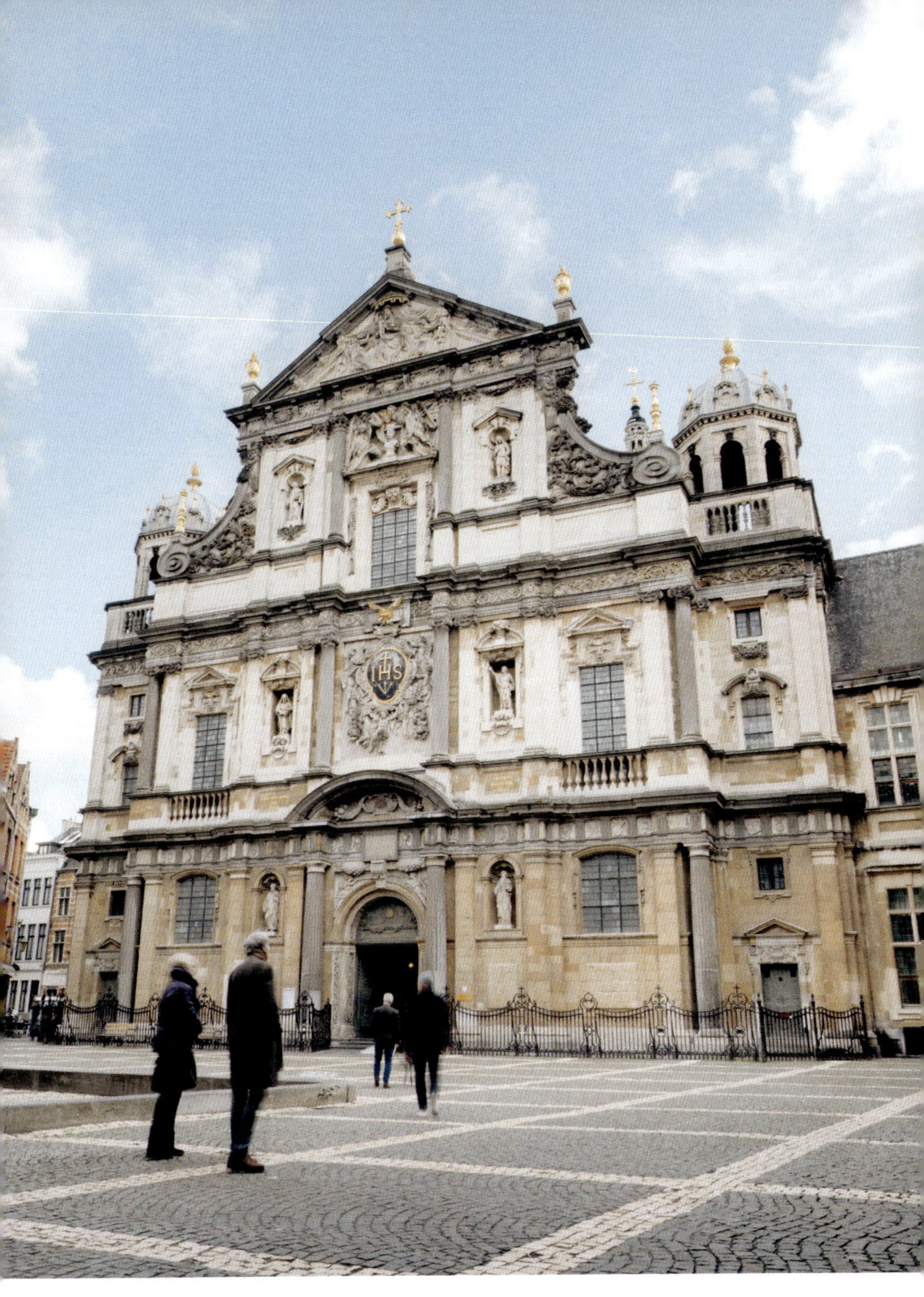

St. Charles Borromeo Church

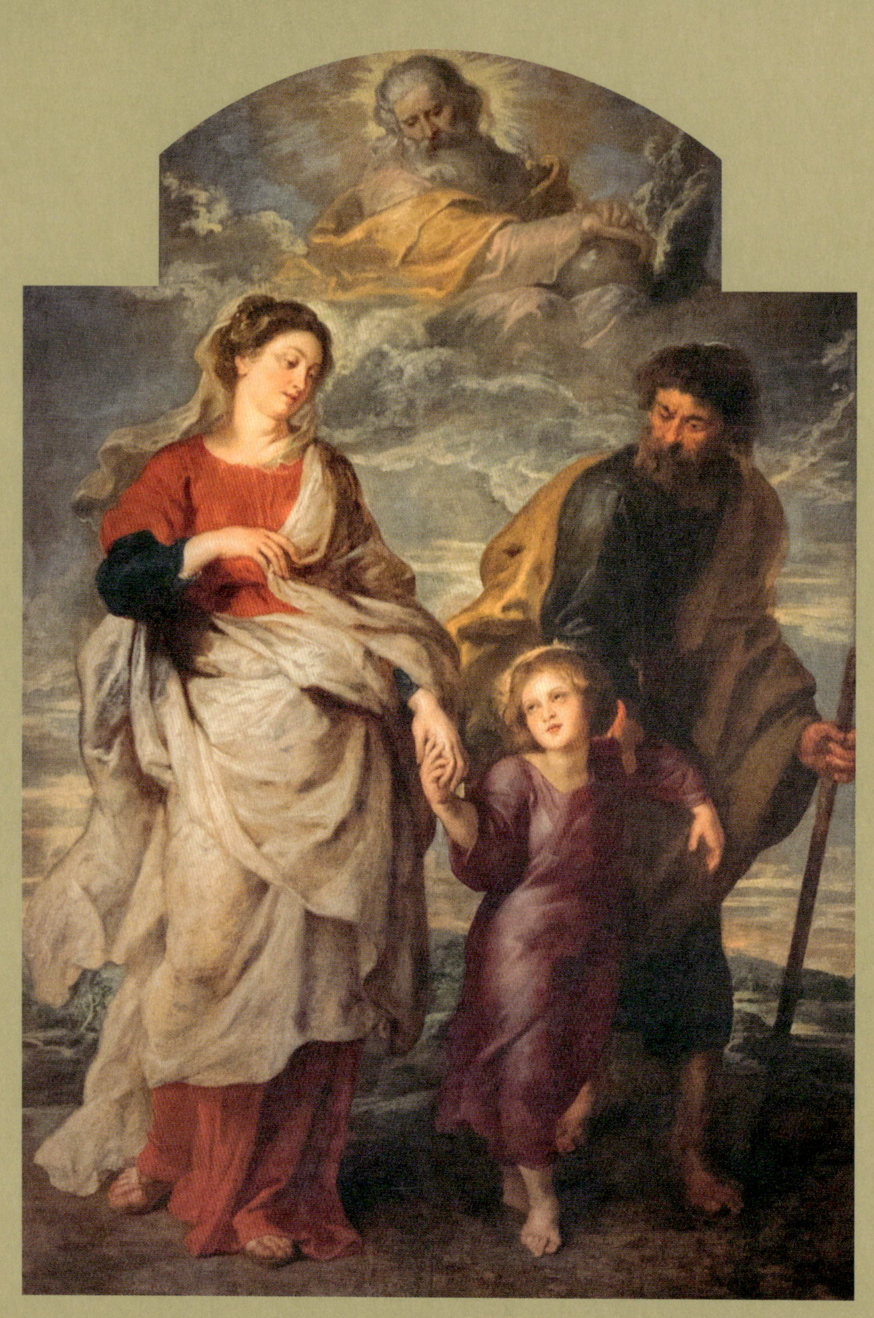

The Return of the Holy Family from Jerusalem 1620-1621

Transferred from panel to canvas,
259 x 177 cm
Workshop of P.P. Rubens,
with alterations and additions
by the master.
Altarpiece for the St. Joseph
altar in the St. Charles Borromeo
Church in Antwerp

In 1620, when the church was almost completed, Nicolaas Rockox commissioned an altarpiece from Rubens for the St. Joseph Chapel. Most of the painting was done by assistants in Rubens' workshop, and it was installed above the altar in 1621.
The panel (it was only transferred to canvas later on) survived the 1718 fire but was badly damaged in the process. When the Jesuit Order was dissolved at the end of the 18th century, Rubens' painting was sold at public auction. After a number of temporary homes, it eventually found its way in 1871 into the collection of the Metropolitan Museum of New York, though a hundred years later it was back on the art market. It was purchased by the St. Charles Borromeo Church in 2011 from an auction in Cologne. By then, the canvas was in very poor condition and in the subsequent years underwent large-scale restoration. In 2017 it was returned to its original position in the church.
The Return of the Holy Family from Jerusalem is ascribed to Rubens' workshop, though cleaning and restoration have revealed several elements that clearly betray the hand of the master, such as the face of the Virgin Mary and the figure of God the Father.

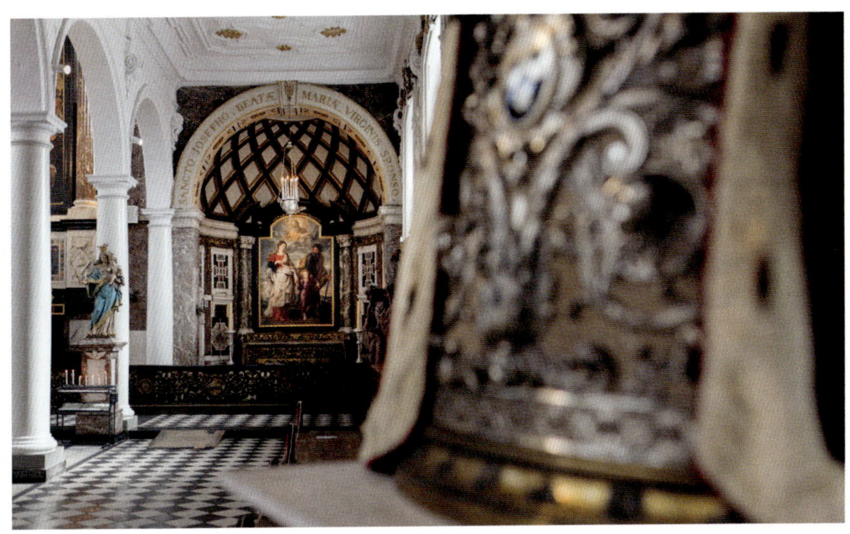

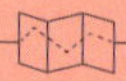

WALK

From the Conscienceplein, walk the short distance to the Minderbroedersrui and turn first left and then right into the Keizerstraat. This will quickly bring you to the Snijders & Rockox House.

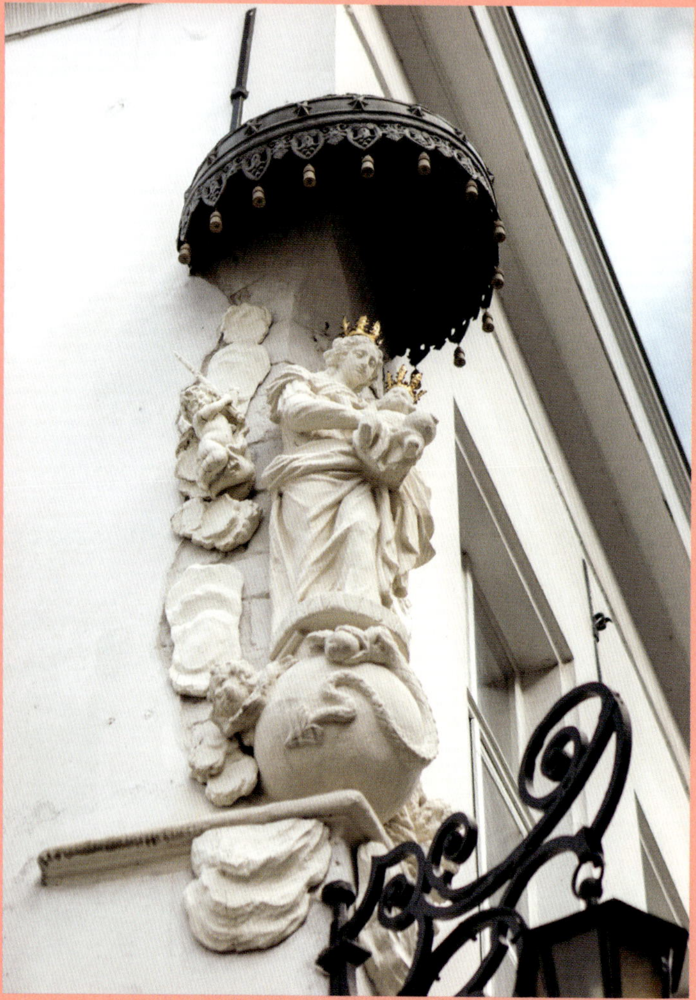

Snijders & Rockox House

Keizerstraat 8-10-12
+32 (0)3 201 92 50
www.rockoxhuis.be
Tue-Sun 10:00-17:00, closed 1 Jan, 1 May, Ascension Day, 1 Nov, 25-26 Dec

This house at nos. 10-12 Keizerstraat, with its fine interiors, its rich collection of art (including several works by Rubens) and its garden, was once the home of Nicolaas Rockox, one of Antwerp's leading figures and a noted humanist and art lover. Rockox was also burgomaster of the city for many years, as well as being a friend and important patron of Rubens.
The house next door at no. 8, with its double stepped gable, belonged to the well-known painter of still lifes and animals, Frans Snijders, who regularly collaborated with Rubens.
On the corner of the Ambtmanstraat, opposite the Snijders and Rockox House, you can see a fine Baroque statue of the Virgin Mary under a canopy. Many of the street corners in Antwerp are graced by elegant Madonna statues of this kind.

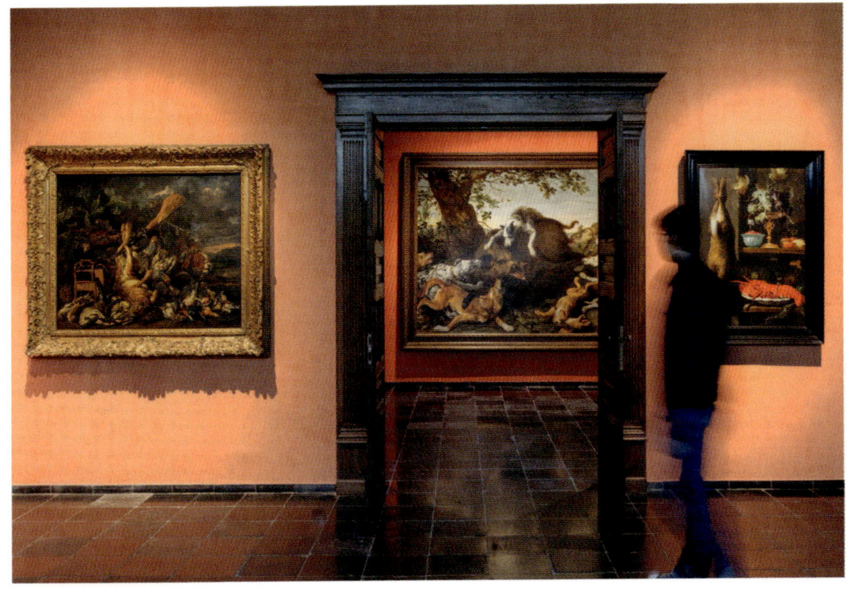

The Blessed Virgin in Adoration Before the Sleeping Infant Jesus ca. 1615

The small format and the intimate nature of the subject suggest that this work was intended for a small room. It probably served as a devotional object in a quiet corner of a house, or in a bedroom, or above the home altar used for private prayer and contemplation. The painting brings together all the main stylistic characteristics of Rubens' classical period (the years between 1612 and 1615); a peaceful composition with sculpturally painted figures in cool colours, but suffused with a silvery sheen.

Panel, 65 x 50 cm

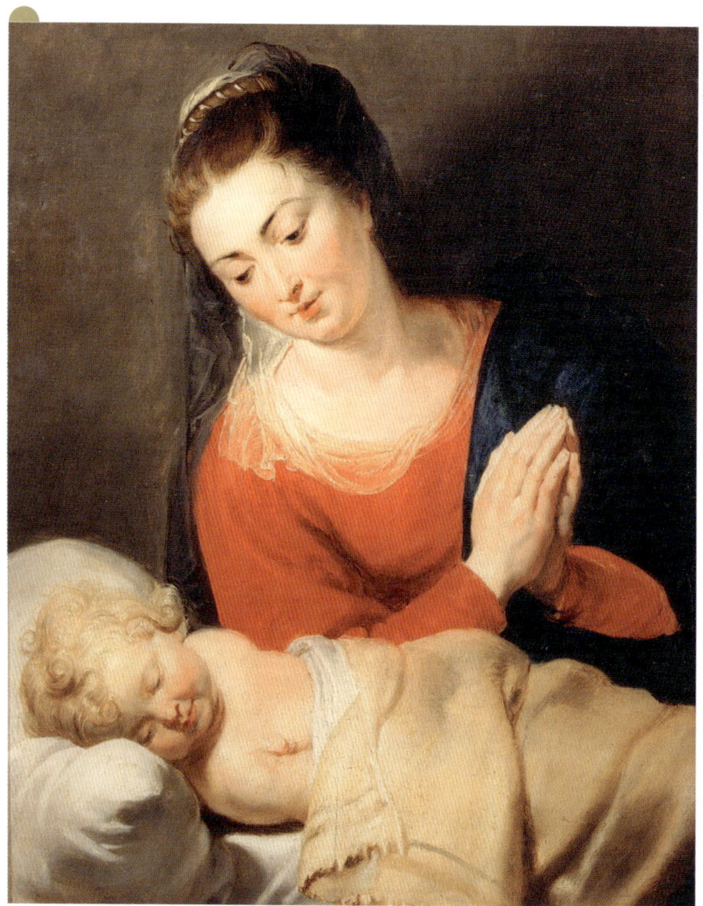

Christ on the Cross ca. 1627

Rubens made this oil sketch in preparation for an altarpiece for St. Michael's Church in Ghent, but the work was never executed - the commission was instead given to Anthony van Dyck. In addition to its vibrant style, the painting is remarkable for the balanced distribution of colour and the fine gradations in the tonality, with different nuances of ochre, red and pink in the central space, set against the blue of the Virgin Mary's cloak in the bottom left foreground and the darker blue of the sky and the background figures in the top right.

Panel, 51 x 38 cm
Oil sketch

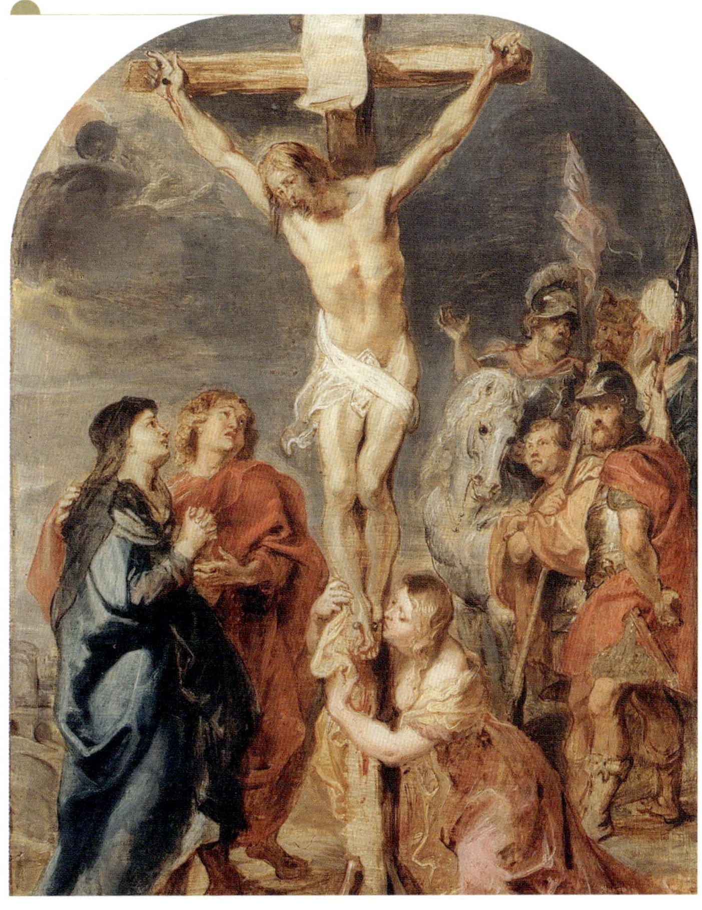

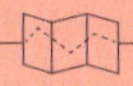

WALK

Further along the Keizerstraat lies another hidden gem of the Baroque period. The exceptionally beautiful portico at no. 23, crowned by an elegant Madonna statue, is the entrance to a chapel that has been preserved in its original 17th-century condition.

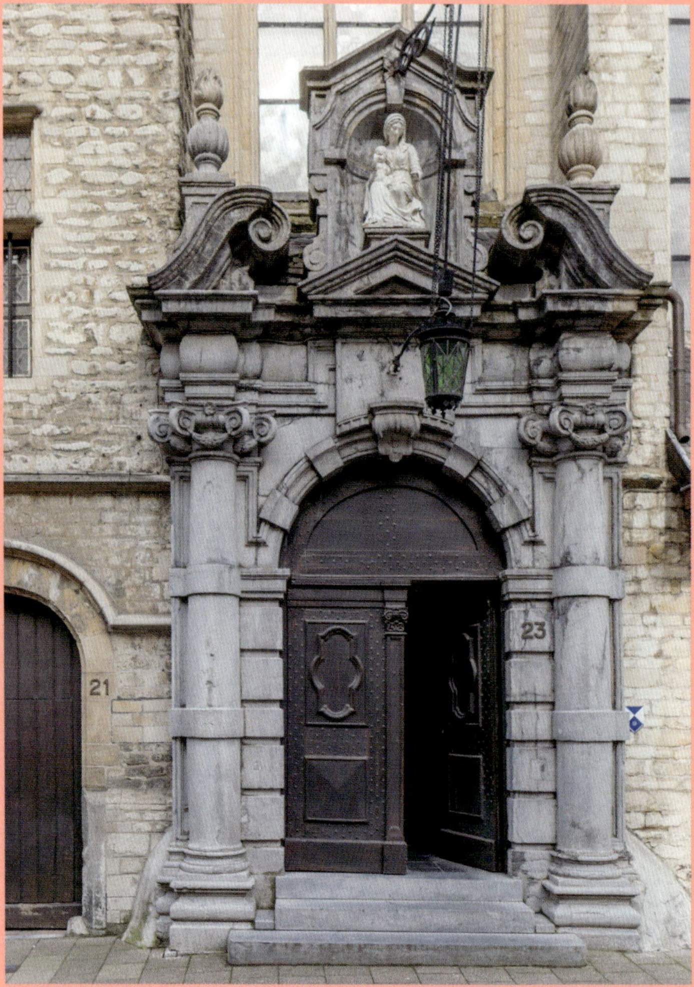

The Emperor's Chapel

Keizerstraat 21-23
info@keizerskapel.com
www.keizerskapel.com
Mon and Wed 10:00-15:00, Sat and Sun 13:00-18:00
(these opening hours are subject to change)

The Emperor's Chapel ('keizer' is the Dutch word for 'emperor'), also known as the Chapel of St. Anne, was originally the chapel of the city's burlers. Burling was one of the processes involved in the making of cloth: any extraneous fibres were cut off with large scissors to give a smooth surface to the finished fabric. The Gothic chapel was built at the start of the 16th century. From 1625 to 1648 it served as the church for the parish of St. Willibrord, which lay outside the city walls and was at risk from the frequent outbreaks of violence associated with the Eighty Years' War. The treasures from the original St. Willibrord's Church, including a much-venerated statue of Our Lady, were brought to the burlers' chapel for safekeeping. In 1648, when the war finally came to an end, everything was returned to the church in the Kerkstraat, amongst which was an altarpiece painted by Rubens.

Between 1650 and 1700, the chapel was renovated in the Baroque style, complete with an imposing high altar, a new vault, marble floors, statues of saints on pedestals, beautifully sculpted church furniture and a portico with a seated Madonna in a recess.

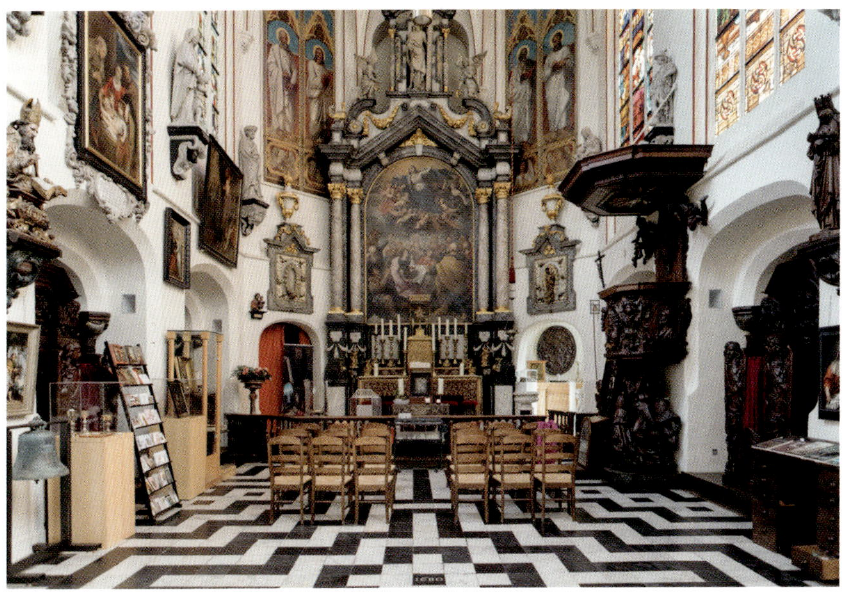

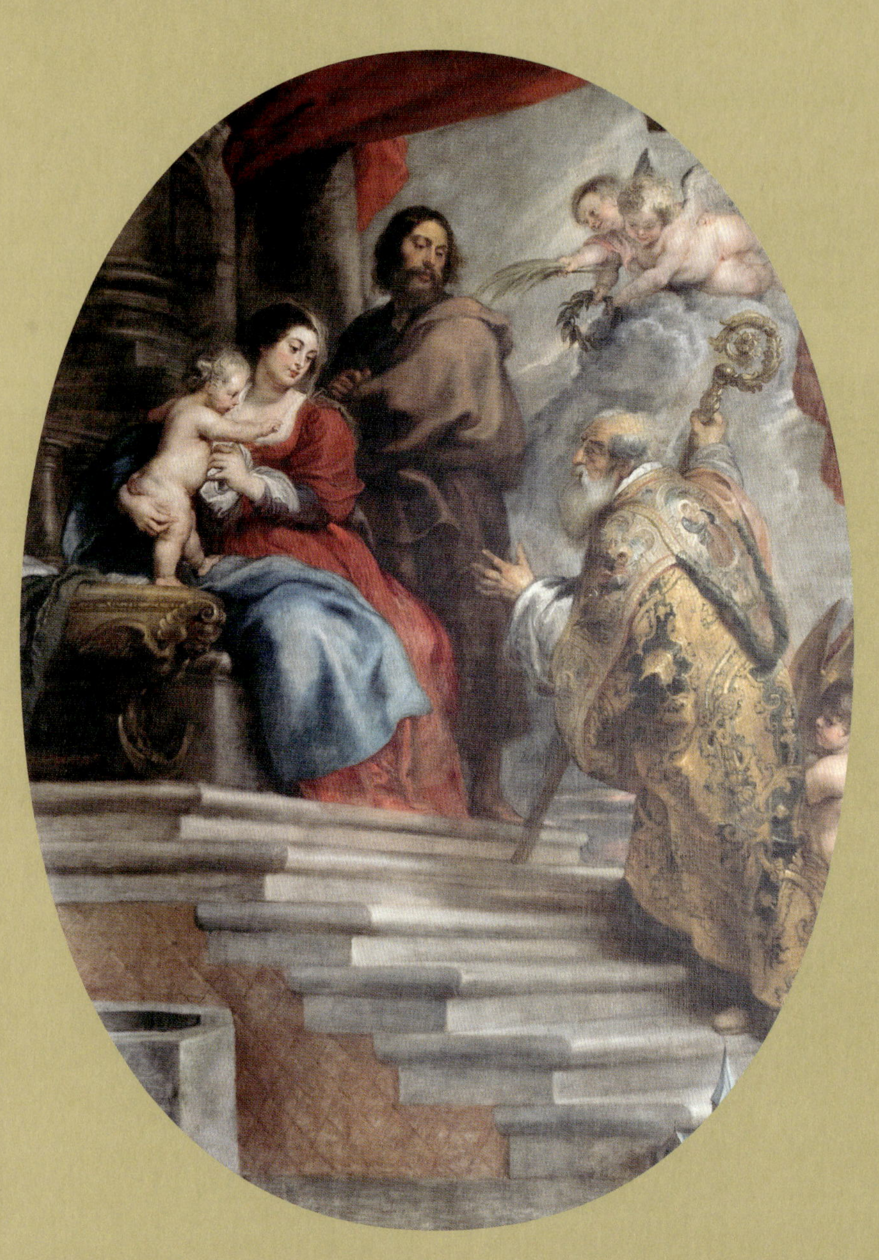

St. Willibrord's Church

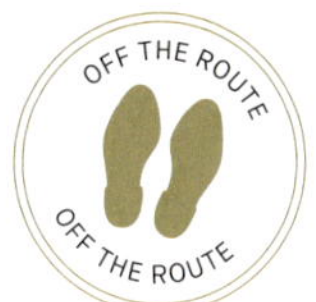

Kerkstraat 89, 2060 Antwerpen
+32 (0)3 236 62 10
www.topa.be
Mon-Fri 9:00-12:00, Sun 9:00-13:00

Today, St. Willibrord's Church in the Kerkstraat is situated well inside the ring road around Antwerp, but in medieval times the parish was outside the city walls. When hostilities recommenced in the Low Countries after the expiry of the Twelve Year Truce, and so the area around the city was no longer safe, it was decided to move the parish and its treasures to a more secure location within the protection of the walls, where it shared the Burlers' Chapel in the Keizerstraat. Whilst there, the Brotherhood of Our Lady, which also temporarily shared the chapel, was gifted a Rubens' altarpiece by a generous benefactor. Later, after the end of the war in 1648, both the brotherhood and the parishioners returned to their damaged church on the Kerkstraat, taking with them their precious relics and possessions. This included the Rubens painting, which since then has been on display in the new St. Willibrord's, a church that has been significantly renovated on several occasions throughout its long history.

St. Willibrord in Adoration of Mary, the Mother of God ca. 1630-1631

This canvas, in which the workshop certainly had a hand, was originally rectangular, but was altered in the first quarter of the 18th century, when oval-shaped altarpieces came into fashion. In this form it was incorporated into a richly decorated Baroque altar, with the church's famous statue of Our Lady as its focal point.

The painting depicts Bishop Willibrord as he humbly greets the Holy Family, who are standing on a platform at the top of a flight of stairs. A number of angels serve to emphasize the celestial nature of the scene. Rubens used this composition - a saint ascending a staircase, looking skywards towards the Virgin Mary and the Christ Child - in a number of his other works, since it was a device that easily allowed him to suggest movement. Some of these compositions are animated in the extreme, but this canvas is more restrained, with soft colours and a generally calm ambiance. This intimate simplicity was no coincidence: Rubens knew he was making the altarpiece for the Burlers' Chapel, where space was limited.

When the painting was converted to its oval shape, a section at the bottom was lost. This was probably when the stone font on the left and the small church on the bottom right were added. These are both references to St. Willibrord and his role as both a proselytizer and a founder of churches.

Canvas, 395 x 315 cm
Altarpiece for the Chapel of Our Lady
in the Burlers' Chapel in Antwerp.
With some elements completed by the workshop

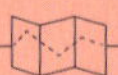

WALK

From the Keizerstraat return to the Minderbroedersrui, but then leave the city centre by taking a left turn into the Lange Koepoortstraat, immediately followed by a right turn leading to the Veemarkt via the Zwartzustersstraat. The Veemarkt is home to the imposing St. Paul's Church. You are now once again close to the River Scheldt, in the heart of the old shipper's quarter.

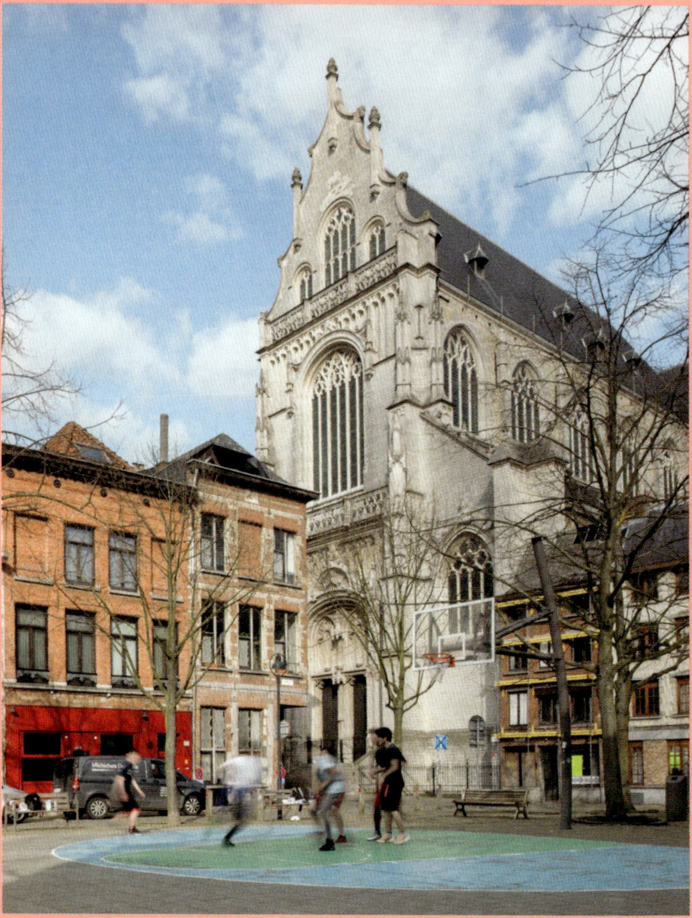

St. Paul's Church

Nosestraat / entrance: Veemarkt 13
www.topa.be
Apr-Oct Mon-Sun 14:00-17:00, Nov-Mar Sat-Sun 14:00-17:00

The original Late Gothic church was built in 1571 for friars of the Dominican Order. From the end of the 16th century onwards and throughout the 17th century it was significantly altered and enlarged. The Baroque decoration was added in the middle of the 17th century, which means that Rubens never saw the church in its finished state. This applies equally to the impressive Calvary alongside the church, which was only erected in the 18th century.
The church's rich Baroque interior includes exceptionally beautiful carved furnishings, various altars, a historic organ and paintings by several of the great masters, such as Rubens, Jordaens and Van Dyck.

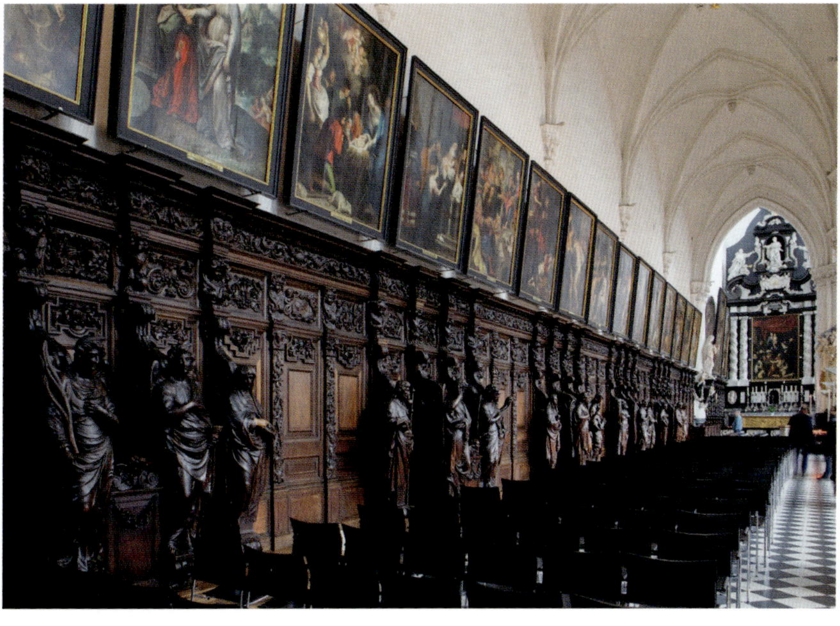

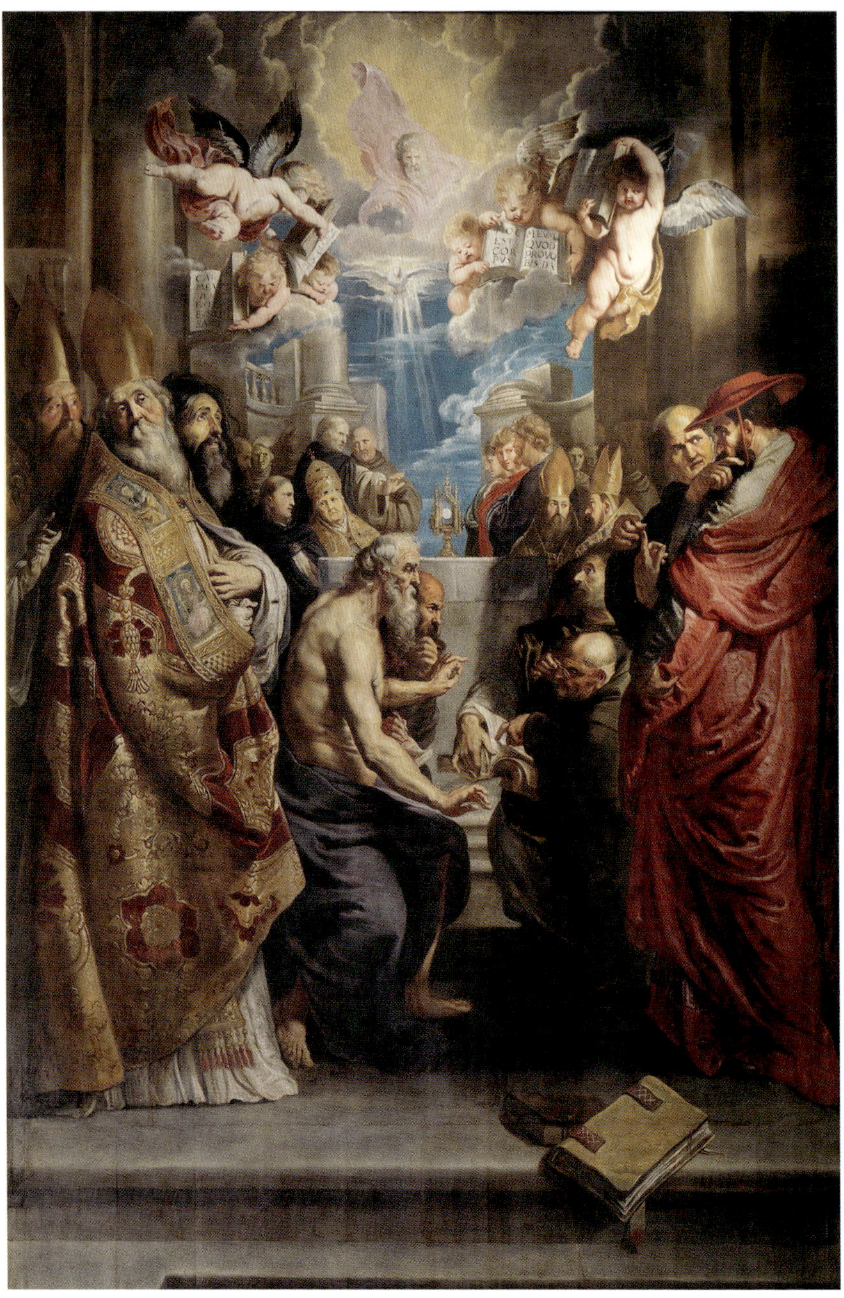

The Veneration of the Blessed Sacrament ca. 1609

The painting (referred to in older sources as *The Disputation of the Nature of the Holy Eucharist*) was one of the first commissions Rubens received following his return to Antwerp in 1608. The slightly elongated figures in the foreground, the glossy brown colouring of the skin, the Venetian blue-green in the background and the strong architectural accents are all typical of the artist's style during the final years of his stay in Rome and his first years back in the Southern Netherlands.

Panel, 377 x 248 cm
Altarpiece for the Chapel of the Blessed Sacrament in the Dominican Church in Antwerp (now St. Paul's Church)

The work was commissioned by the Brotherhood of the Holy Sacrament for the altar of their chapel in the Dominican Church, which is clearly reflected in the painting's theme. A company of bishops, monks, church fathers and other learned saints are gathered around an altar, upon which stands a monstrance containing the Sacred Host. Above them in the sky hover God the Father, the Holy Spirit (in the form of a dove) and angels displaying sacred texts. All the elements in the composition are intended to forcefully confirm the doctrine that the bread and wine are transformed into the body and blood of Christ during the celebration of the Eucharist. This mysterious act of transubstantiation was a key article of the Roman Catholic faith, which was fiercely disputed by Protestants and therefore just as fiercely defended during the Counter-Reformation.

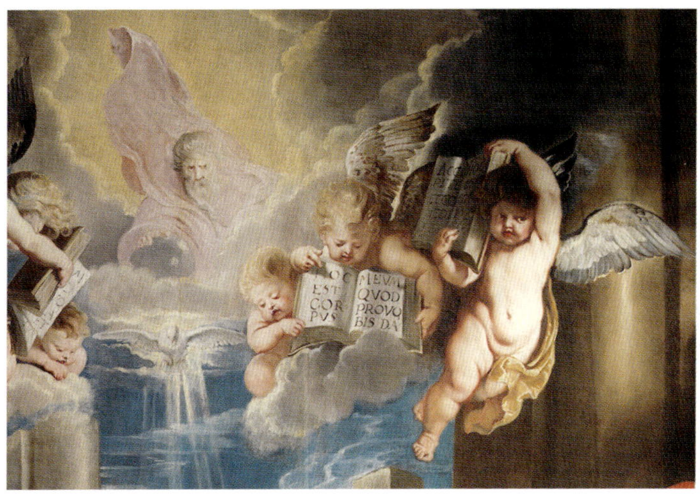

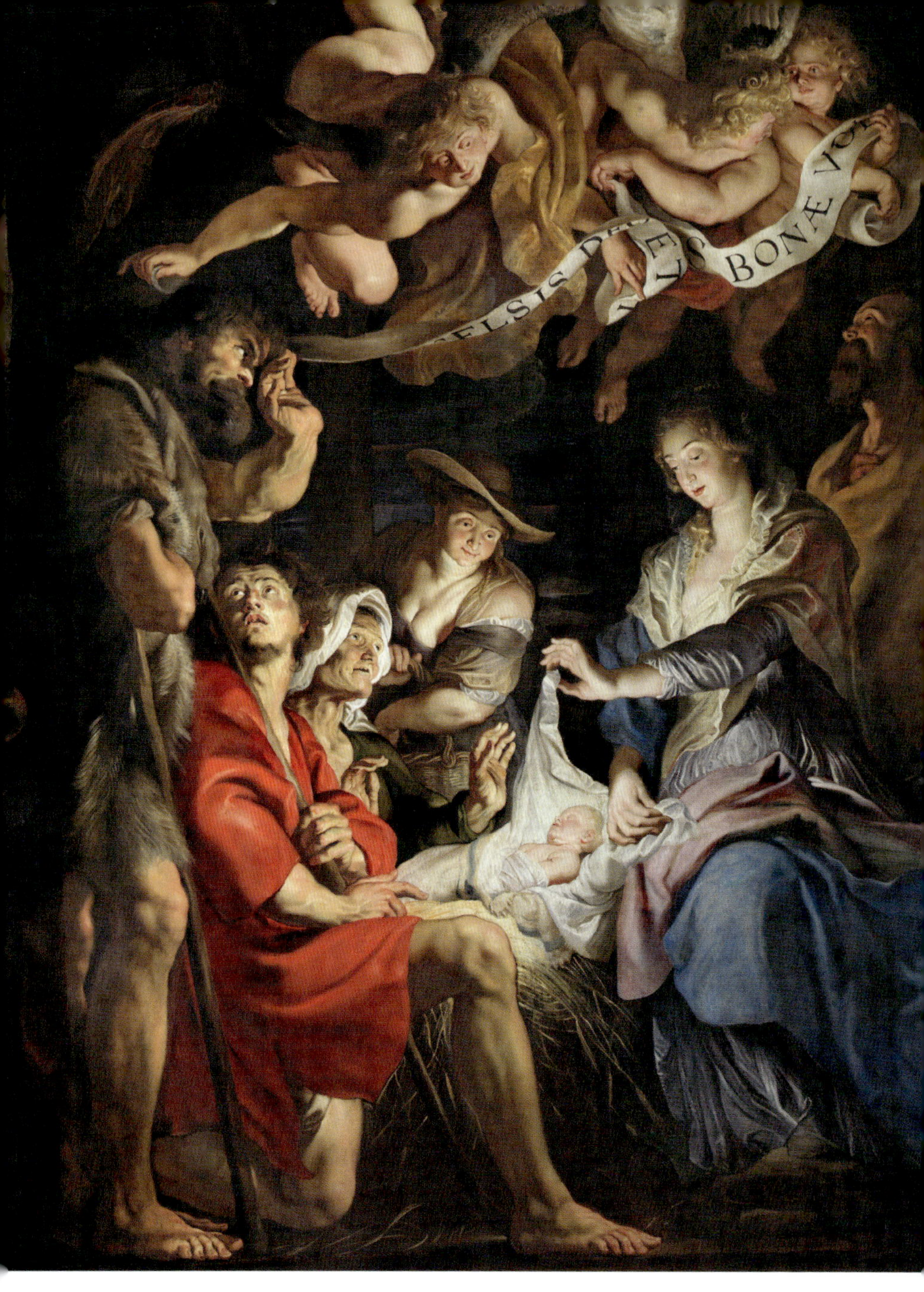
BONÆ

The Adoration of the Shepherds ca. 1610

It is not known who commissioned this painting, nor when it was first displayed in the church, but it is reasonable to assume that it was intended for this location and placed there soon after its completion, sometime around 1610. This makes it another one of Rubens' earliest works after his return to Antwerp.

The composition shows clear similarities with an 'adoration of the shepherds' he had already painted in Italy in 1608 for the Oratorian Church in Fermo. His depiction of a Christmas night in which the divine Child is the source of all light was probably inspired by Correggio's famous painting *Notte*, which Rubens may have seen in Italy. The light is reflected on the bystanders and on the angels above, creating a strong chiaroscuro effect. However, this contrasting use of light and dark, as well as the use of ordinary 'peasant' folk for his figures, also suggests the influence of Caravaggio. And there is little doubt that the colouring has all the hallmarks of the Venetian palette that so impressed Rubens on his travels and is evident in many of his other works from this early period.

In later years, the artist returned to this kind of 'Christmas night' scene on several occasions: in a design for a book illustration, in a *modello* for a ceiling panel, and in several other paintings, drawings and an oil sketch (the latter now part of the collection at the Rubens House), all of which had features in common with the Fermo version and this more dramatic and more monumental version in the Dominican Church.

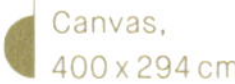
Canvas,
400 x 294 cm

The Flagellation of Christ ca. 1617

The generosity of wealthy Antwerp citizens made it possible for the Dominicans to decorate their church with a series of 15 panels portraying *The Mysteries of the Holy Rosary*. These mysteries form an important part of Roman Catholic devotional practice. Apart from Rubens, other known and less well-known Antwerp painters contributed panels to the series, including Anthony van Dyck (*Christ Falls Under the Weight of His Cross*) and Jacques (alias Jacob) Jordaens (*Christ on the Cross*).

In his composition, Rubens took account of the location in which the painting would be displayed, high against the side wall of the church. As a result, his figures are clearly delineated in the foreground, much like a group of sculptures, highlighted against a neutral architectural background. It almost seems as if Christ wishes to turn towards the faithful as they pray the rosary, but is prevented from doing so by his chains and by the foot of the black torturer.

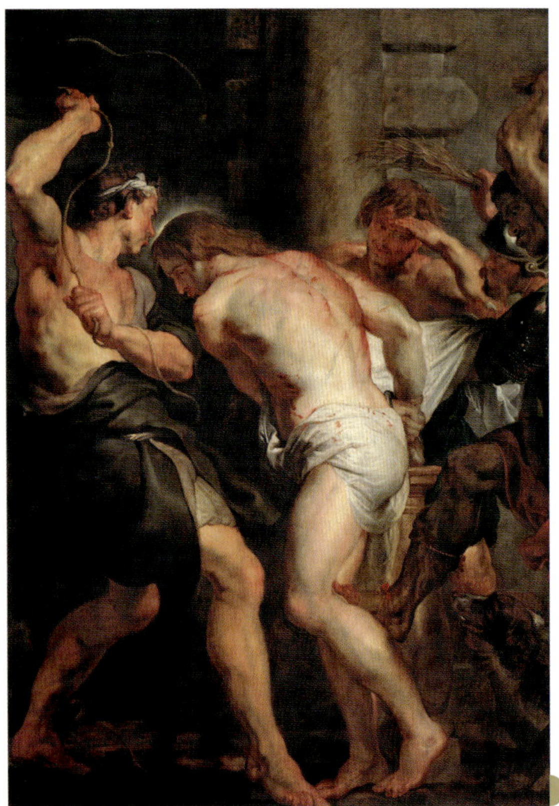

Panel, 219 x 161 cm
Panel from the series **The Mysteries of the Holy Rosary** in the Dominican Church in Antwerp (now St. Paul's Church)

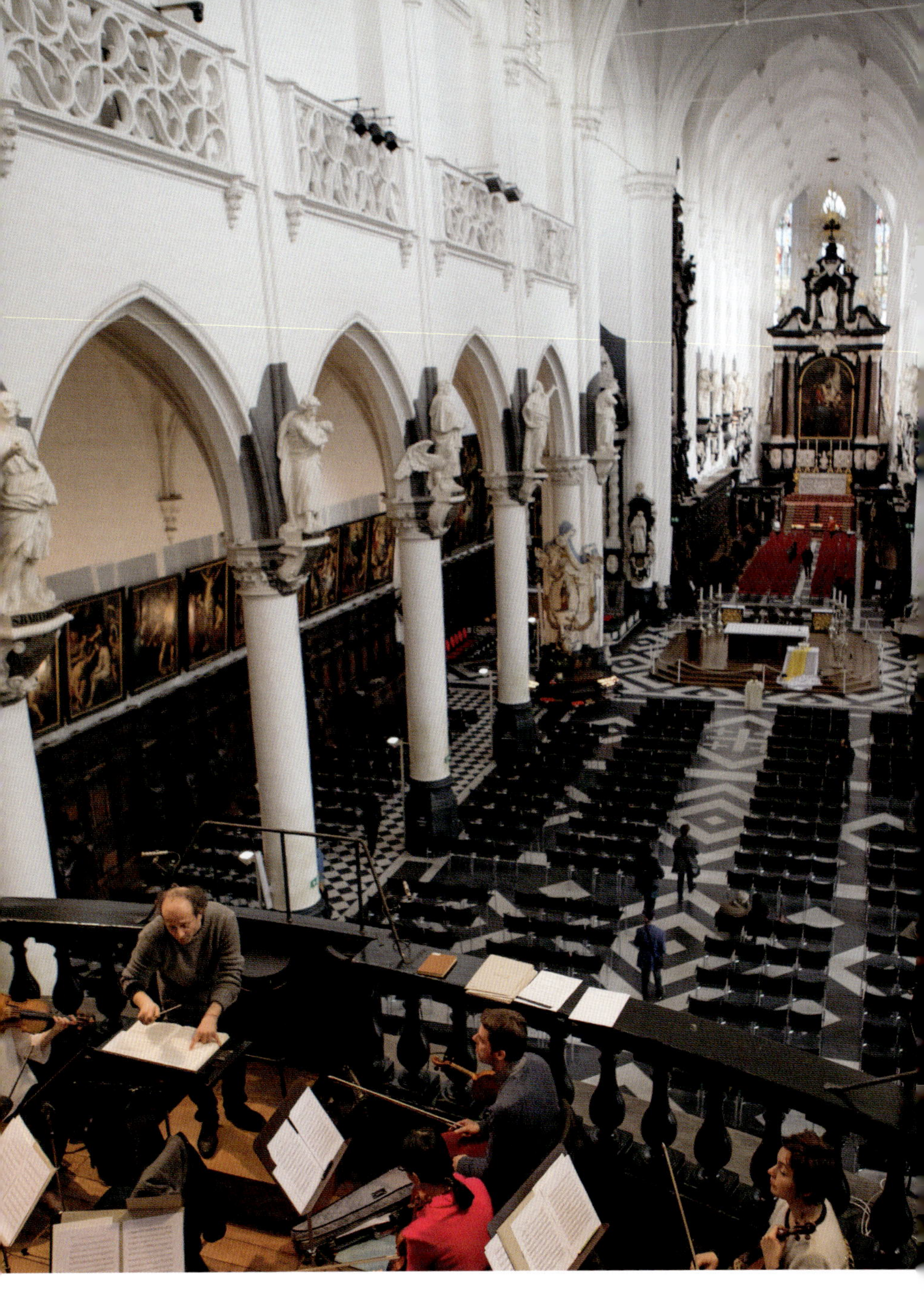

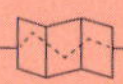

WALK

To reach our next destination, return from St. Paul's Church by the same route to the Minderbroedersrui. Cross over the Koepoortbrug and follow the long and rather boring Klapdorp until you reach the Paardenmarkt, where you will find St. Anthony's Church. Klapdorp may be dull, but in Antwerp even dull streets have treasures to discover. Level with no. 93 you will see another delightful 18th-century Madonna, sitting serenely under a large canopy.

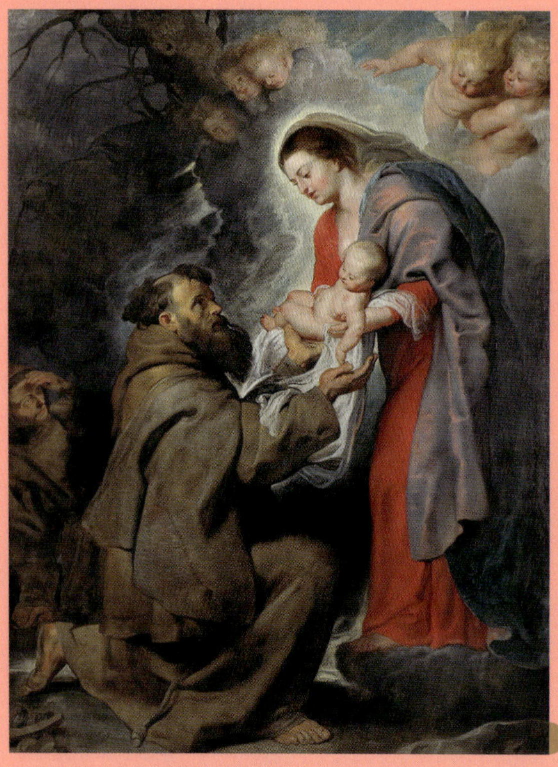

Canvas, 230 x 173 cm
Altarpiece for the Capuchin church in Antwerp

St. Anthony of Padua's Church

Paardenmarkt 109
+32 (0)3 231 74 23
www.topa.be
Jul-Aug, Thu-Sat 13:30-17:30

St. Anthony of Padua's Church is a large parish church of an imposing size and scale that is not uncommon in Antwerp. It was built at the start of the 20th century on the site of a 17th-century Capuchin church that was demolished in 1908. One noteworthy remain of the original monastery is the 18th-century calvary in the garden on the right, between the church's side wall and the rectory.
The monumental interior of the church is in white stone. The decoration is partly Neo-Gothic and partly 17th-century, since many of the furnishings and works of art were transferred from the old Capuchin church and another church that was demolished around the same time. This rich collection of artefacts includes a number of paintings by celebrated Baroque artists, including one work by Rubens' own hand and one by his workshop.

St. Francis of Assisi Receives the Christ Child from the Virgin Mary (undated)

This canvas was painted for the monastery church of the Capuchins, a branch of the Franciscan Order, which was situated on the Paardenmarkt in Antwerp. The present-day St. Anthony's Church, where the painting is currently displayed, was built on the site of the monastery at the start of the 20th century.
The church that the Capuchin monks had built in 1613 was an aisleless structure with just a nave, choir, side chapel and bell tower. Rubens crafted a painting that perfectly matched this church's modest size. The clearly delineated contours and the 'classic' Madonna figure suggest that this undated work probably belongs to his early period.
Leaving aside the angels circling in the air and the friar in the background, all of our attention is focused on the supernatural meeting between the saint and the Mother of God. The scene is formal, yet at the same time also realistic. The Blessed Virgin, surrounded by her heavenly aura, is all motherly tenderness as she places the Child in the hands of St. Francis, who is clearly deeply moved by the moment.

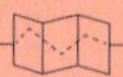

WALK

From the Paardenmarkt, a short walk through the Kleine and Grote Kauwenberg and the Prinsesstraat will lead you in double-quick time to St. James's Church in the Sint-Jacobsstraat. If, however, you are more curious and have a little more time, it is much more interesting to follow the Rodestraat, which starts a little further up the Paardenmarkt, just beyond the 16th-century Boys' Orphanage.

The Rodestraat, which runs into the Ossenmarkt, contains the former - and charmingly atmospheric - beguinage, which is now a residential complex. Nearby is the Lange Winkelstraat, with the Protestant Church known as the Brabant Mount of Olives. In Rubens' time, this was a convent for the Sisters of the Annunciation, with a Late Gothic church dedicated in 1620. It is interesting to note that, until 1785, Rubens' painting of *The Miracle of St. Just* (now in the Bordeaux Museum of Fine Arts) was displayed in this church. A member of the Moretus printing family commissioned it from Rubens in 1629 and donated it to the Annunciade church, where a relic (a piece of skull) of St. Just of Beauvais was venerated. The Pieter van Hobokenstraat and its continuation, the Prinsstraat, are both historic streets in the heart of the university quarter. In short, a fascinating place to be! Sooner or later - no doubt after a few unexpected detours - you will eventually reach our penultimate destination: the entrance to St. James's Church on the corner of the Lange Nieuwstraat.

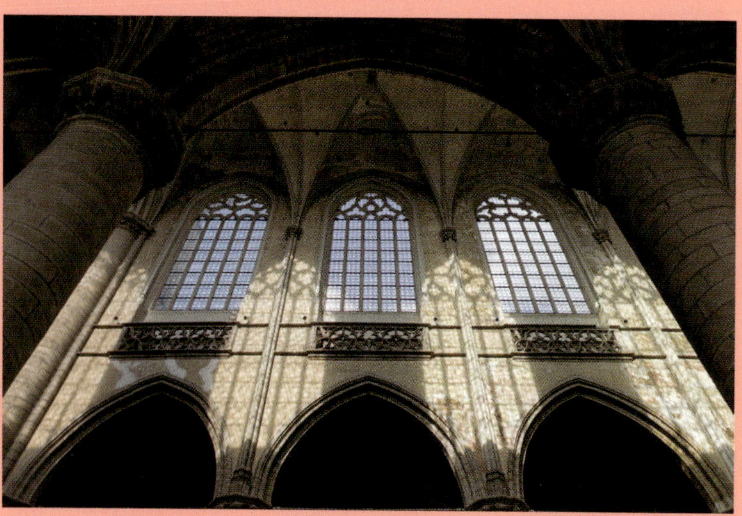

St. James's Church

Sint-Jacobsstraat / entrance: Lange Nieuwstraat 73-75
+32 (0)3 225 04 14 and +32 (0)498 33 04 05
www.topa.be, www.sintjacobantwerpen.be
🕒 1 Apr-31 Oct, Mon-Sun 14:00-17:00

In the Late Middle Ages, this part of Antwerp was home to merchants, bankers and noblemen. As the city's leading figures, they wanted a parish church that reflected their wealth and status. Its construction began in the final years of the 15th century and took over 150 years to finish. The result was an impressive Gothic church, which, construction time notwithstanding, displays a coherent and harmonious architectural unity.

St. James's was also Rubens' parish church. It was here that he married Helene Fourment, it was here that his children were baptized, and it was here that he was buried. The exterior of the church was not fully completed in his lifetime, but its interior was beautifully decorated in a Late Gothic and Renaissance style. In 1656, this interior was given a luxurious Baroque conversion, but by then Rubens had already been dead for almost 15 years. The altars and other furnishings, as well many of the paintings and statues, were donated to the church by trade guilds, religious brotherhoods and distinguished patrician families.

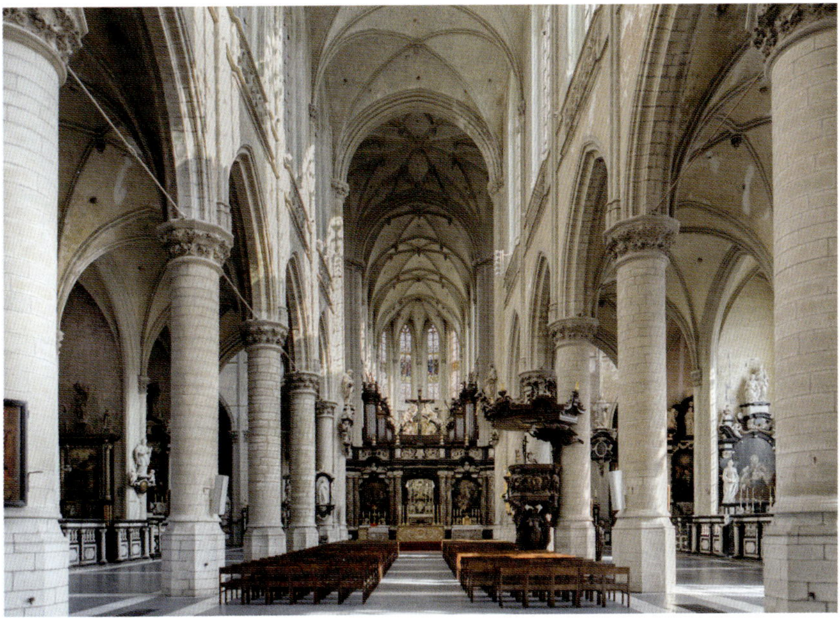

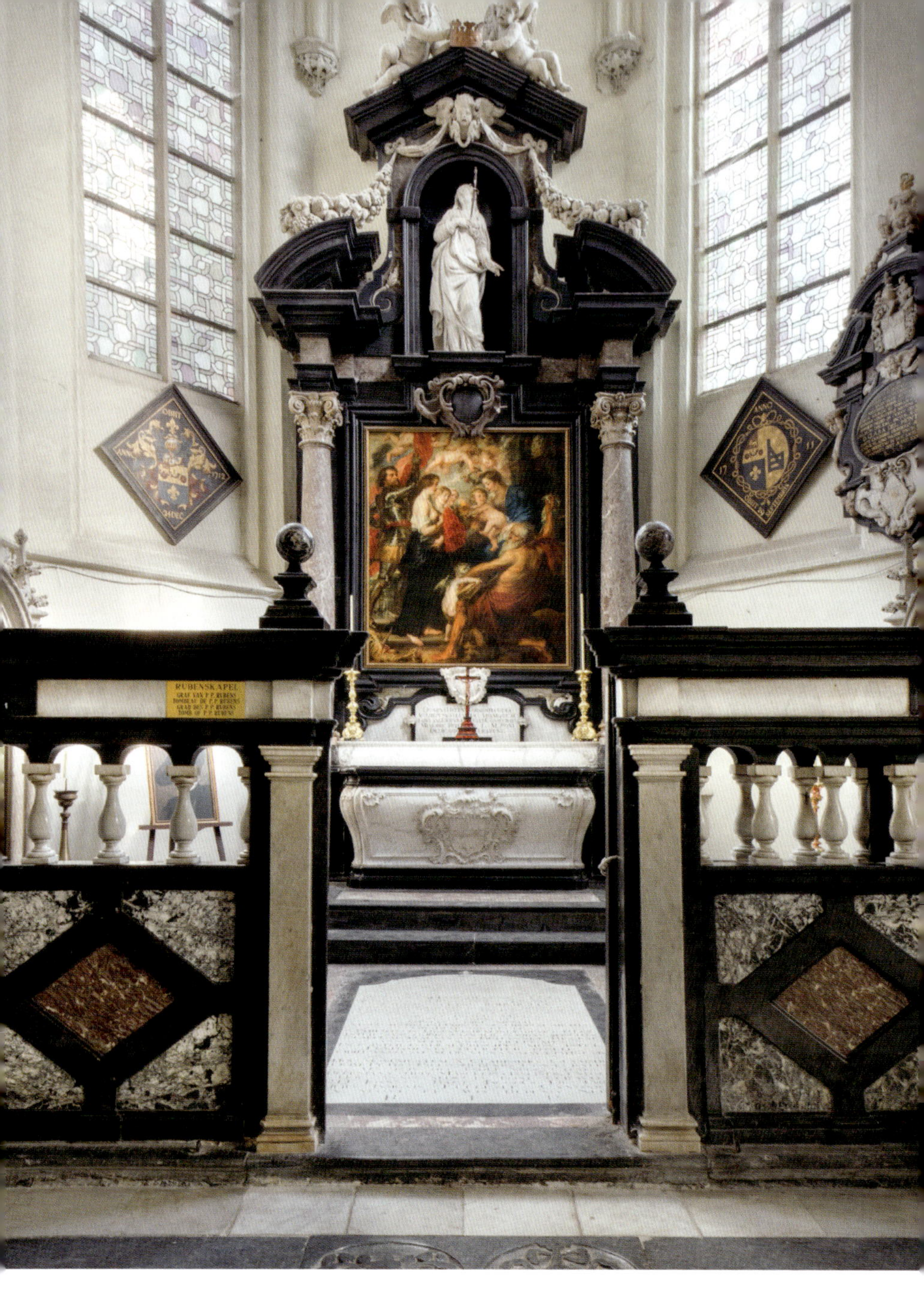
RUBENSKAPEL

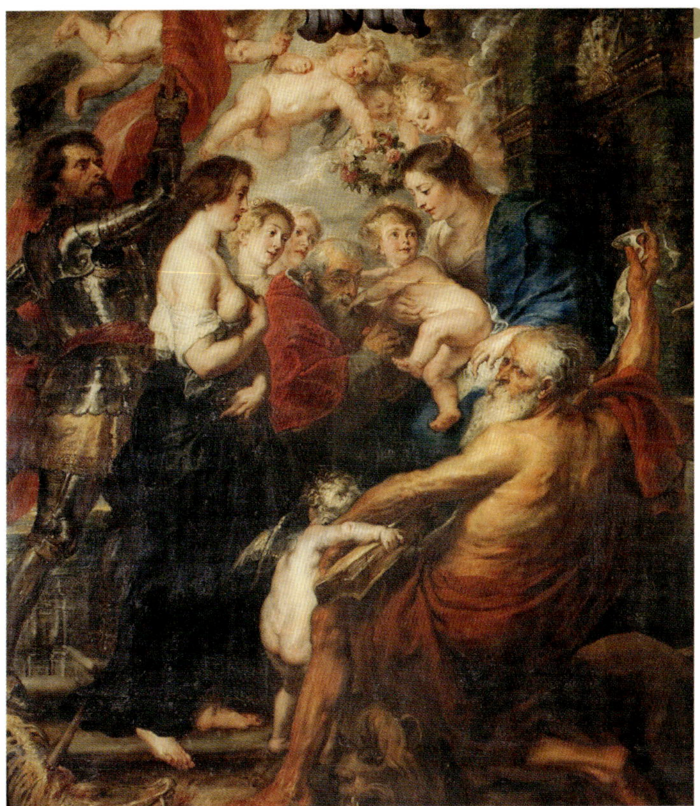

Panel,
211 x 195 cm

The Blessed Virgin and Child Surrounded by Saints 1638-1639

Just days before his death, Rubens said that he would like this painting to be displayed in the burial chapel that the Fourment family would prepare for him in St. James's Church. His wish was granted: the chapel was completed a few years later and the painting was hung in a place of honour above the altar. Because the work was not completed with a burial chapel in mind, its theme is not directly related to death, resurrection or eternal life.

The significance of the saints surrounding the Virgin Mary and the Christ Child is unclear. The saint dressed in armour is St. George. The woman is Mary Magdalene. And the half-naked old man in the bottom right corner is the learned church father, hermit and penitent Hieronymus, a figure who often appears in Rubens' works. Jesus has the facial characteristics of Frans Rubens, the artist's first child with Helene Fourment. This panel, one of the last works Rubens ever painted, illustrates his exquisite brushwork and the warm tonalities of colour that characterize his oeuvre in the 1630s, his so-called lyrical period.

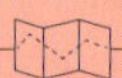

WALK

From St. James's Church, you can reach the Rubens House on the Wapper. This means that after passing through the Eikenstraat, you have to cross over the busiest shopping street in Belgium: the Meir.

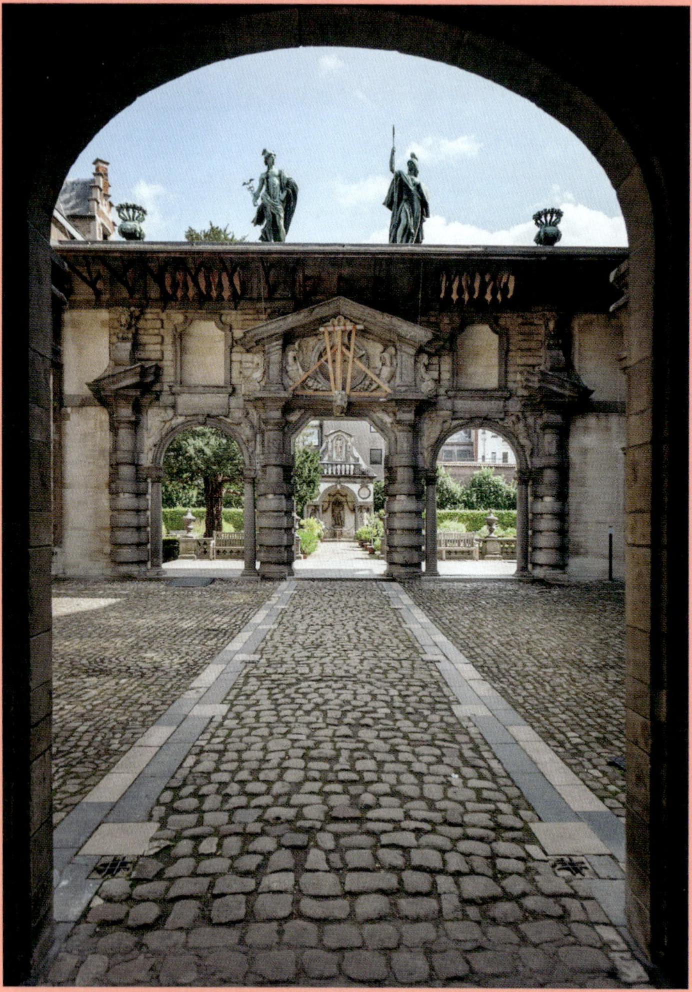

Rubens House

Wapper 9-11
+32 (0)3 201 15 55
www.rubenshuis.be
Tue-Sun 10:00-17:00, closed 1 Jan, 1 May, Ascension Day, 1 Nov, 25 Dec

It is impossible to ignore the fact that you are now in the commercial heart of Antwerp. The Wapper connects the Meir, where you can find branches of all the major chain stores, with the parallel streets of Hopland and Schuttershofstraat, home to the more exclusive shops and boutiques. The Rubens House is an oasis of calm amidst the hustle and bustle of the city. Behind its elegant facade, you will discover the artist's mansion and workshop, a courtyard, a portico and a garden with a pavilion. Rubens lived here from 1615 until his death in 1640. It was also the place where he painted most of his masterpieces.

The monumental building in Renaissance and Baroque style was carefully restored and in part rebuilt during the 20th century, using original sources, such as contemporary descriptions and prints, as a guideline. Since art historians know a great deal about Rubens, based on his own copious correspondence and the many testimonies of his peers, it was possible to decorate and furnish the house in a manner that closely matches the tastes and the spirit of his times. Within this authentically reconstituted whole, the original architectural elements, such as the Baroque portico and the garden pavilion, are enhanced to maximum effect.

The Rubens House is also a museum with an important art collection, including several works by the master. The Rubens Experience Centre, which opens at the end of 2019, will immerse visitors in a fascinating and complete virtual experience of Rubens' life.

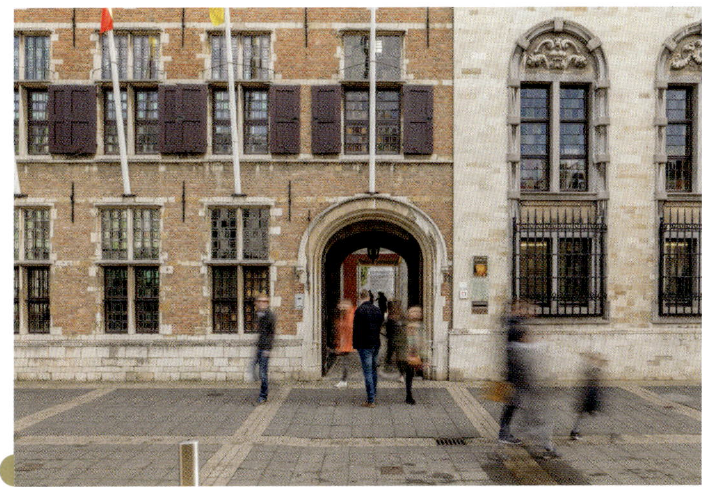

Facade of the Rubens House

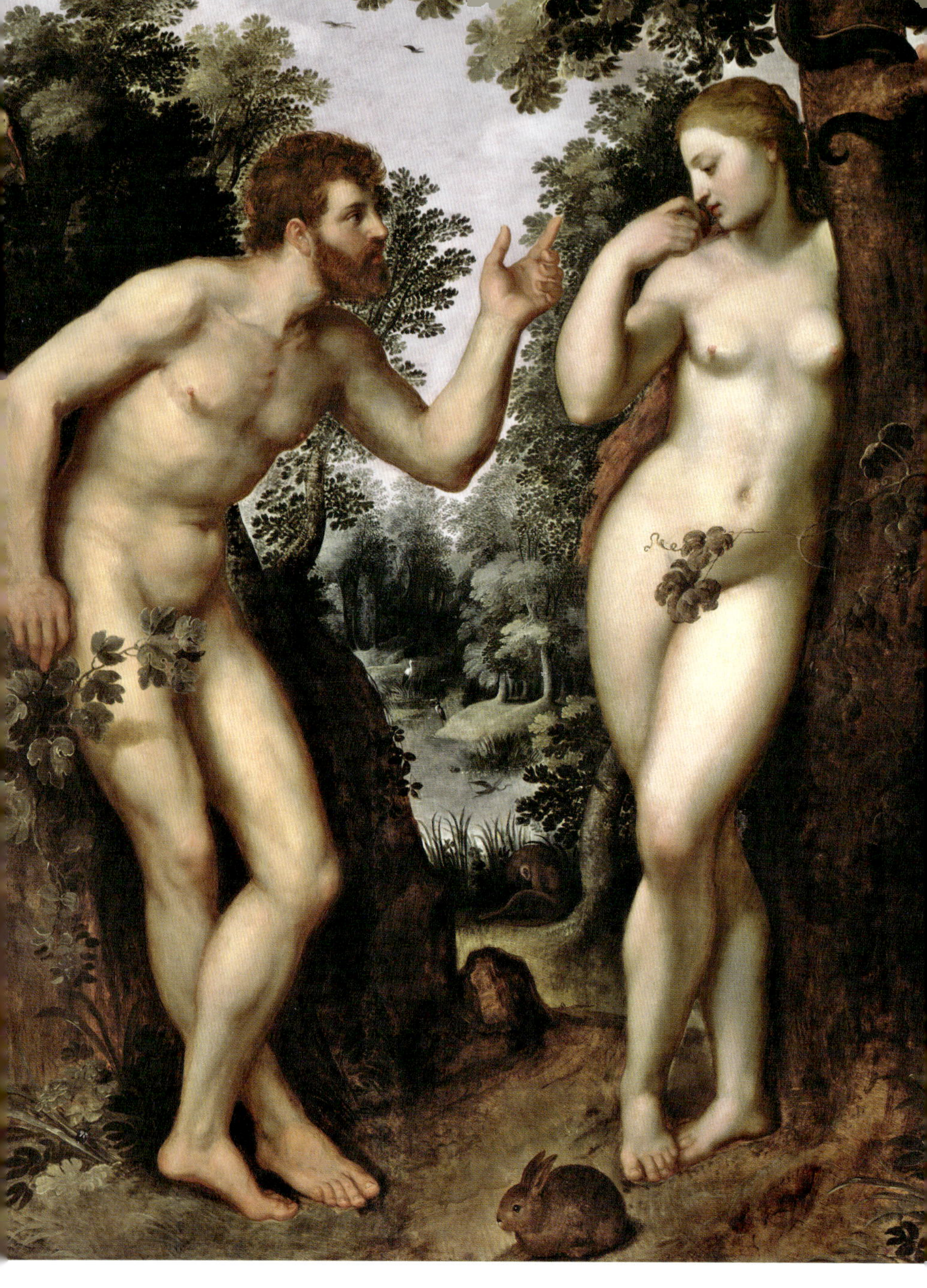

The Fall from Grace (or **Adam and Eve in Paradise**) before 1600

Adam and Eve in Paradise, also known as *The Fall from Grace*, is now generally accepted by scholars to be a rare Rubens work dating from before his departure to Italy. At that time, his style was strongly influenced by his mentor, Otto van Veen. The figures and the landscape are depicted in a classical manner and lack natural vitality, notwithstanding an attempt to make the hand gesture of Adam more expressive and more powerful. The classic profile of Eve, the bearded head of Adam and the crossed legs are all typical characteristics of late 16th-century painting. The use of colour is also highly traditional.

It was only as a result of his experiences in Italy that Rubens was eventually able to develop a looser and more innovative style with a more expressive palette, so that his later compositions are more animated, more intense and more personal.

Panel, 180 x 158 cm

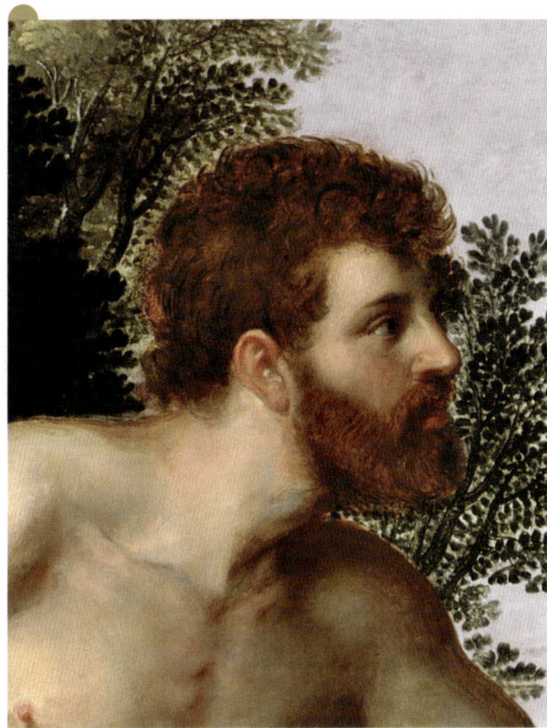

St. Sebastian beginning of the 17th century (?)

Sebastian lived in the third century A.D. He was a captain in the Praetorian Guard in Rome and much favoured by the Emperor Diocletian. In the left foreground we can see Sebastian's armour. When the emperor learnt that the commander of his personal bodyguard was a Christian, he had him sentenced to death by arrows. Miraculously, Sebastian survived the attempted execution and was nursed back to health by St. Irene, the widow of another martyr. However, in Rubens' version of the legend it is angels who come to Sebastian's aid.

This undated work only recently came to light. It was probably painted by Rubens towards the end of his stay in Italy or shortly after his return to Antwerp. He based his portrayal of the head of the saint on a Renaissance sculpture he had seen in Florence.

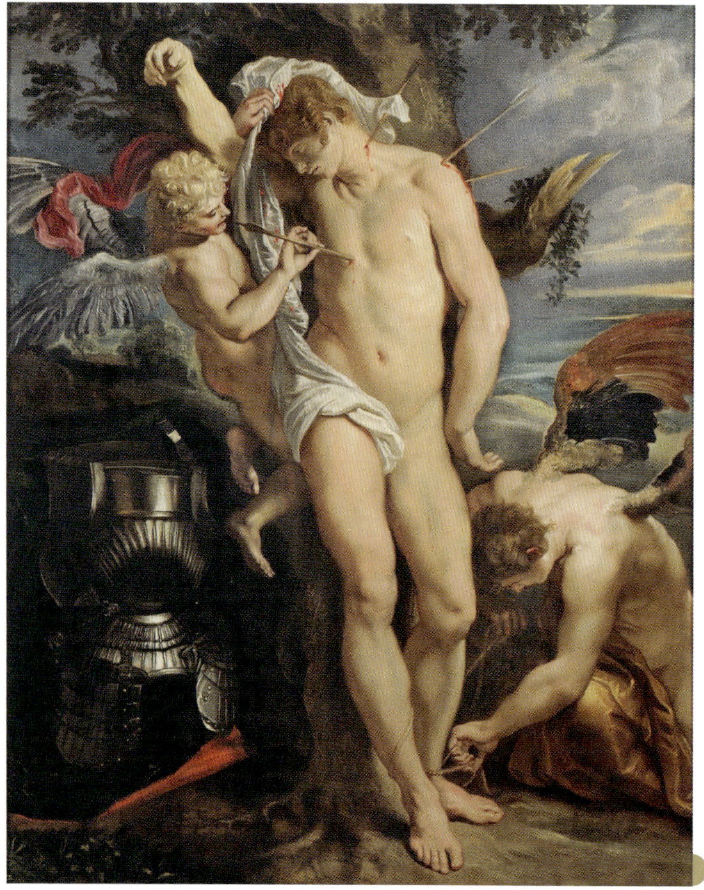

Canvas, 123.8 x 97.8 cm
On long-term loan from the Schoeppler collection, Germany

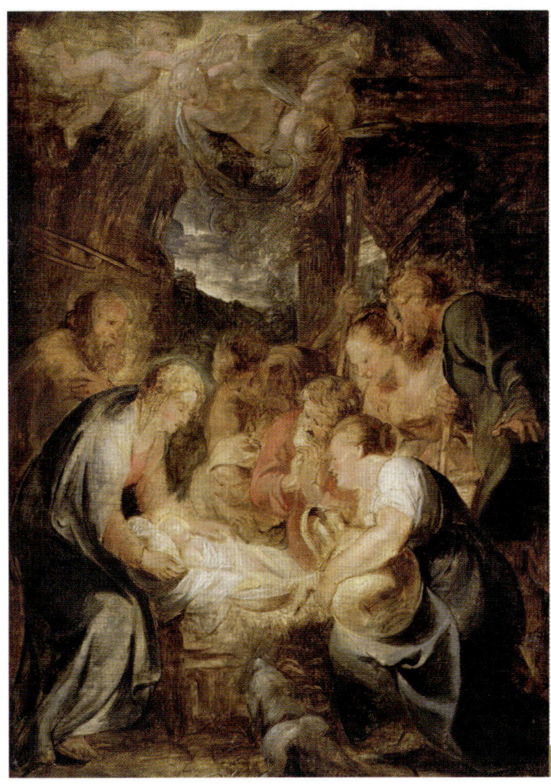

Panel, 46 x 34 cm
Oil sketch

The Adoration of the Shepherds (Design for a Christmas night scene) ca. 1615-1616

In this finely balanced composition, Rubens makes clever use of colour to create harmony and coherence. The contrast between light and dark is not intensified in the manner of Caravaggio, but is toned down and richly nuanced.

The Virgin Mary and the farmer's wife holding the copper jug counterbalance each other, as do St. Joseph and the standing shepherd. The darker colours of the clothing and the background surround the warm centre of the scene, painted in shades of white, gold, ochre and red. From each bottom corner, a diagonal works its way up towards the opposite top corner, giving structure to the scene. All the figures are positioned just under these diagonal lines, apart from the inconspicuous brown-coloured shepherd in the middle, who is positioned immediately above the point where the diagonals intersect.

Rubens painted several versions of *The Adoration of the Shepherds*, with a number of variations but also with recognizable elements that recur in a number of the different renditions. There is, however, no known painting based on this particular sketch.

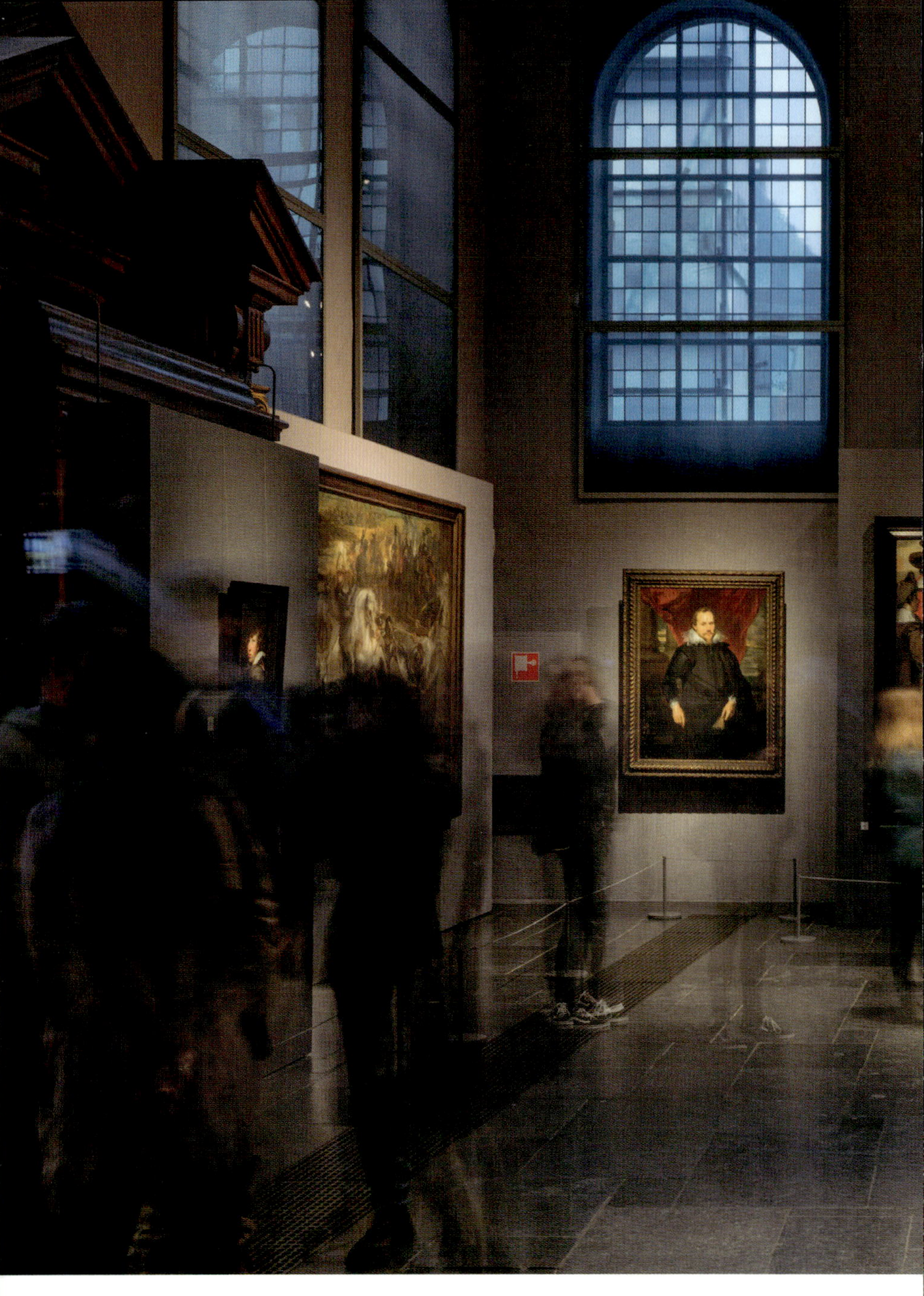

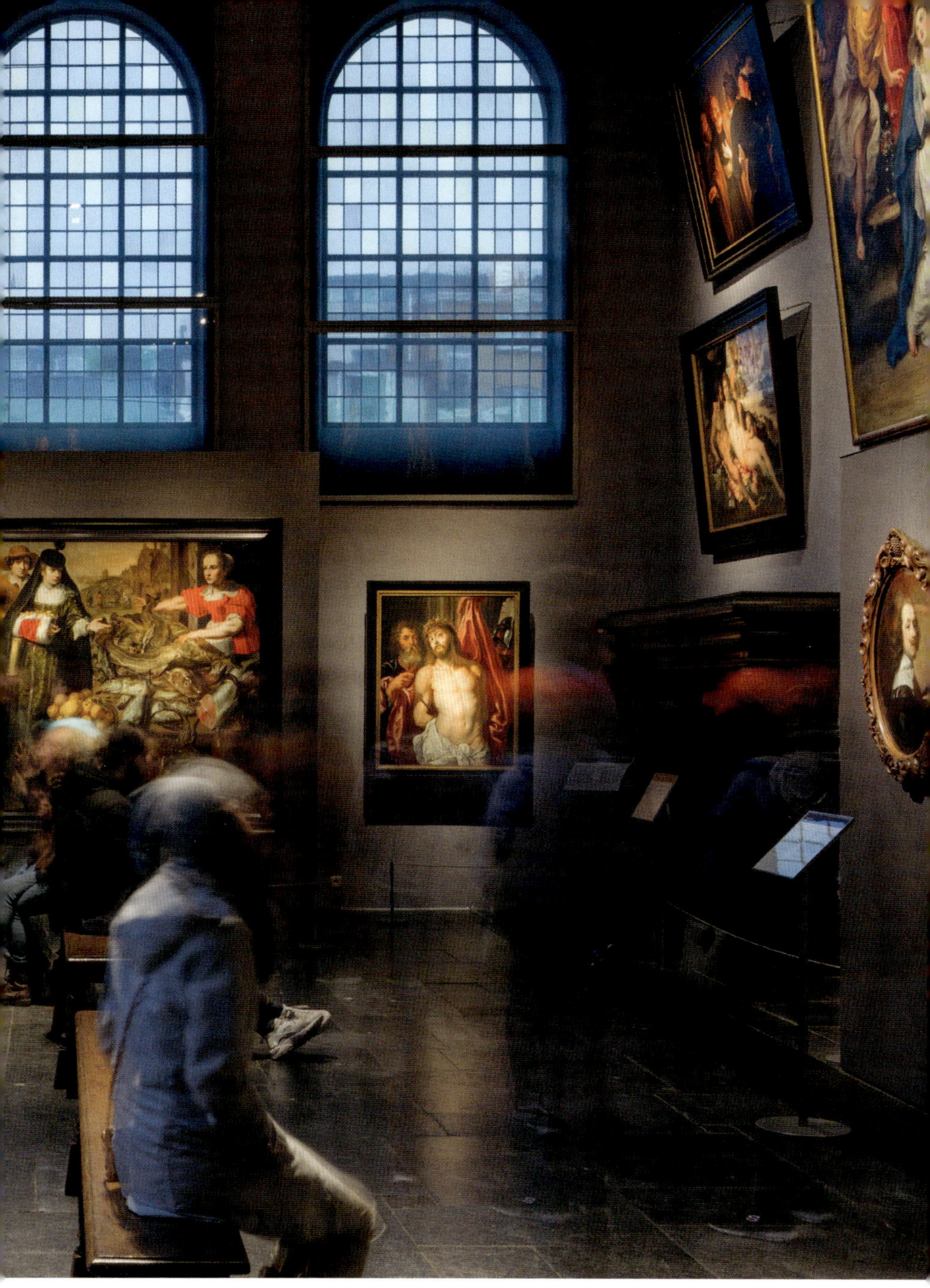

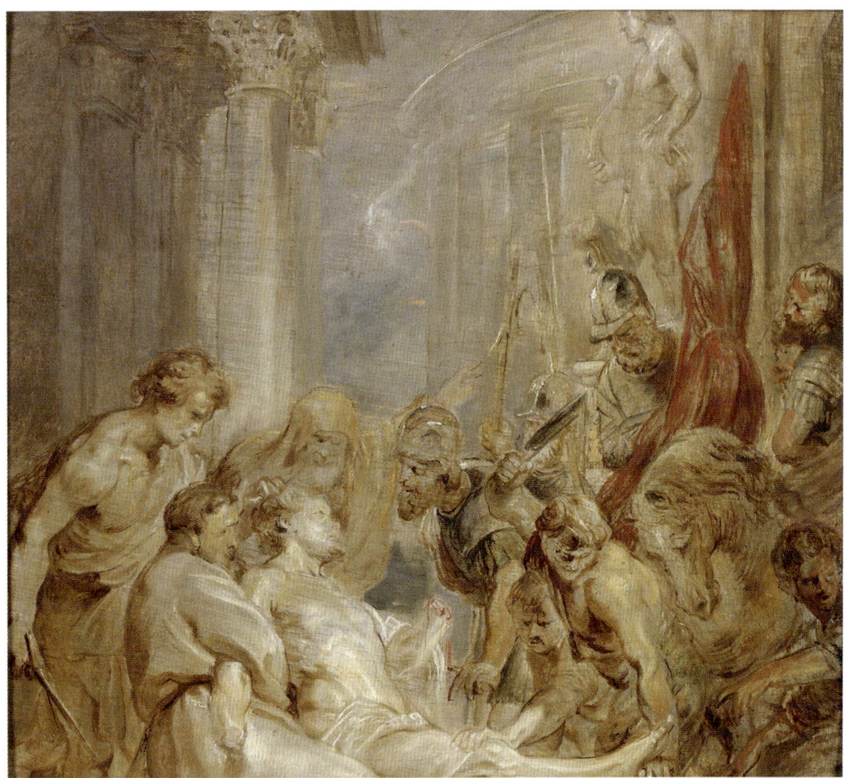

The Martyrdom of St. Adrian before 1620

Rubens' virtuoso oil sketches are a remarkable and valuable testimony to his talent. These small-scale sketches were made in preparation for much larger-scale paintings and were therefore the most important phase of the creative process. It was during this phase that the artist designed his composition and it was something he always did himself. For this reason, of all the works in the Rubens House it is in these oil sketches that we can most clearly see the hand of the master at work! And the sketches are all the more valuable because many of the paintings for which they were made have since been lost, including the painting that was based on this particular sketch of the death of St. Adrian.

Martyrs occupied a prominent position in the religious art of Catholicism in the 17th century. The powerful emotional content of their stories made them ideally suited to play either a leading or a supporting role in the visual propaganda of the Church. Like most artists of his day, Rubens also frequently depicted martyrs in the paintings he made for religious institutions.

Panel, 35.3 x 40 cm
Oil sketch

St. Clare Holding the Saracen Army at Bay with the Blessed Sacrament 1620

Rubens painted this *modello* in 1620 in preparation for the execution of one of a series of 39 ceiling panels for the Jesuit Church in Antwerp. A *modello* is a design piece in oils developed in more detail than the brief initial sketch or *bozzetto* in grisaille. According to the contract for the series, Rubens was obliged to make the *modelli* himself, though it was agreed that for the actual painting of the panels he could use the assistance of his best pupils, including Anthony van Dyck.

The title of the design tells us exactly what it depicts: according to legend, an advancing Islamic army turned and fled when the Holy Sacrament was pointed in their direction from a nearby hilltop by St. Clare.

Panel, 28 x 36.5 cm
Oil sketch, modello for a ceiling panel for the Jesuit Church in Antwerp

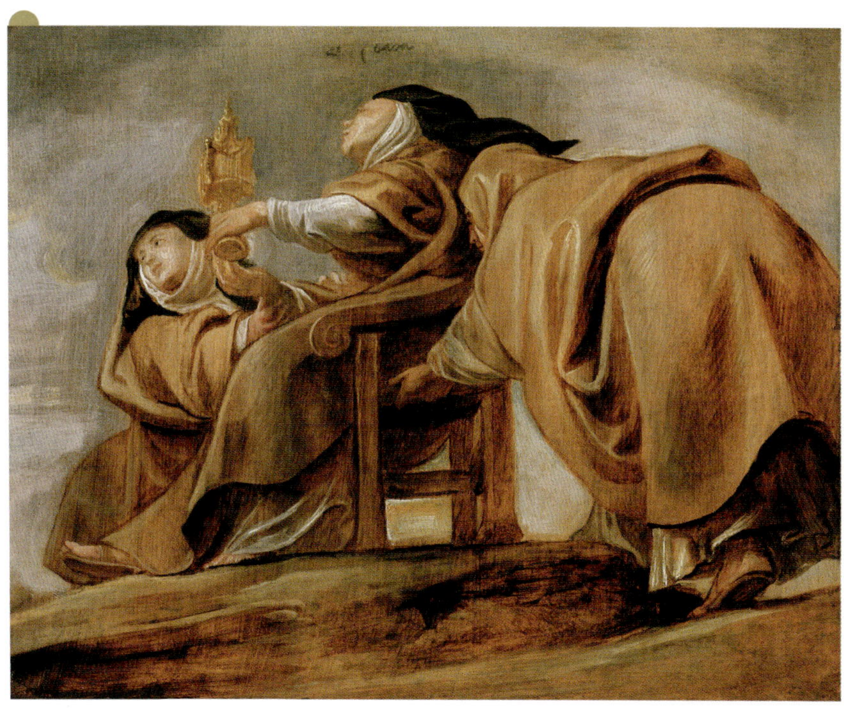

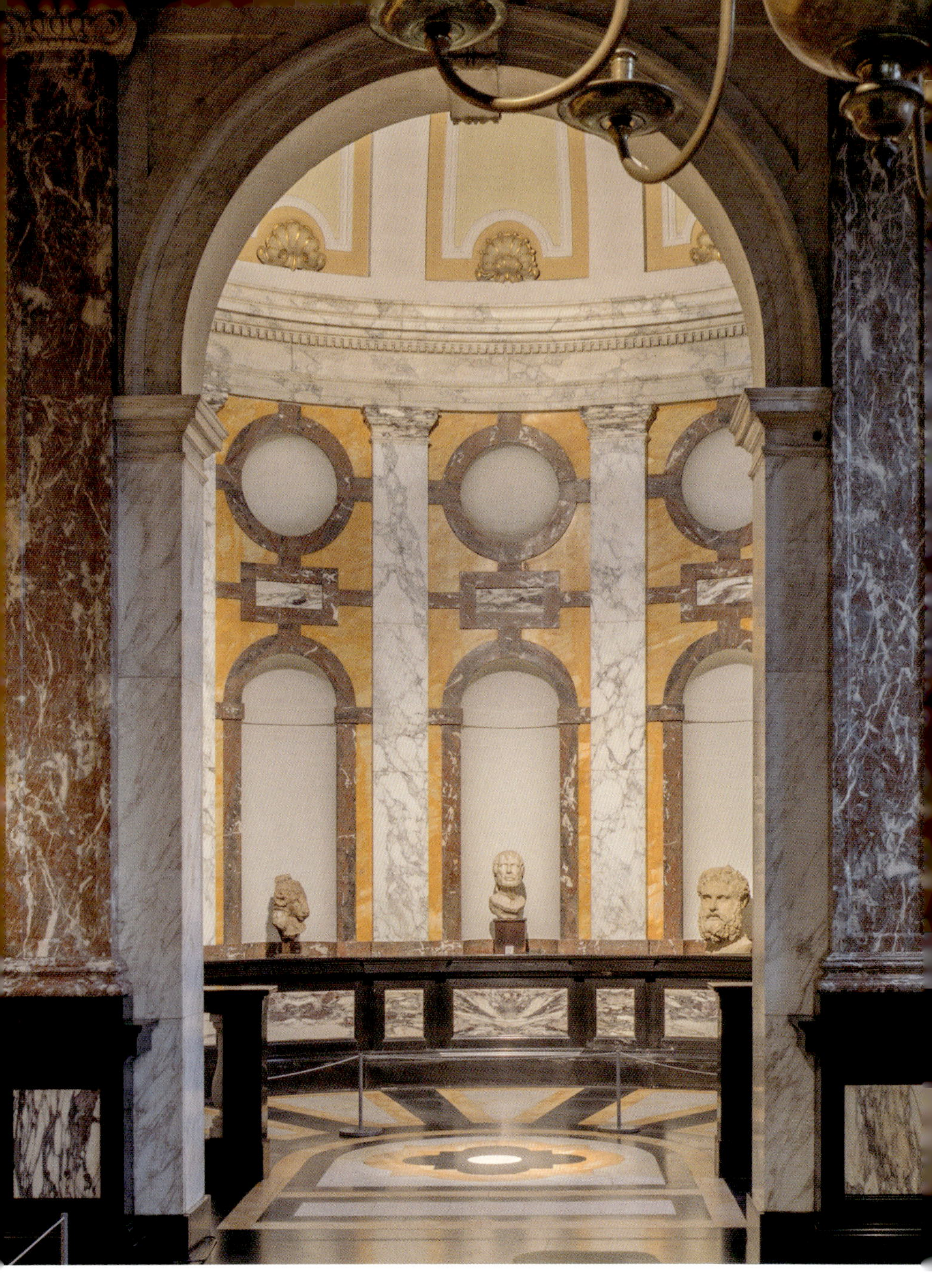

In terms of composition, this painting is a dynamic and quintessentially Baroque depiction of the angel delivering God's message to the Virgin Mary, making use of a number of traditional attributes, such as the sewing box, the sleeping cat, the vase of flowers and a prayer book.

When Rubens was sent on a diplomatic mission to the Spanish court in 1628, he took this painting with him (or had it sent after him) and sold it in Madrid to Don Diego Mexia Felipez de Guzmán, the first Marquis of Leganés. This military commander and diplomat in the service of the Spanish king owned an impressive art collection and had Rubens' masterpiece installed in his private chapel.

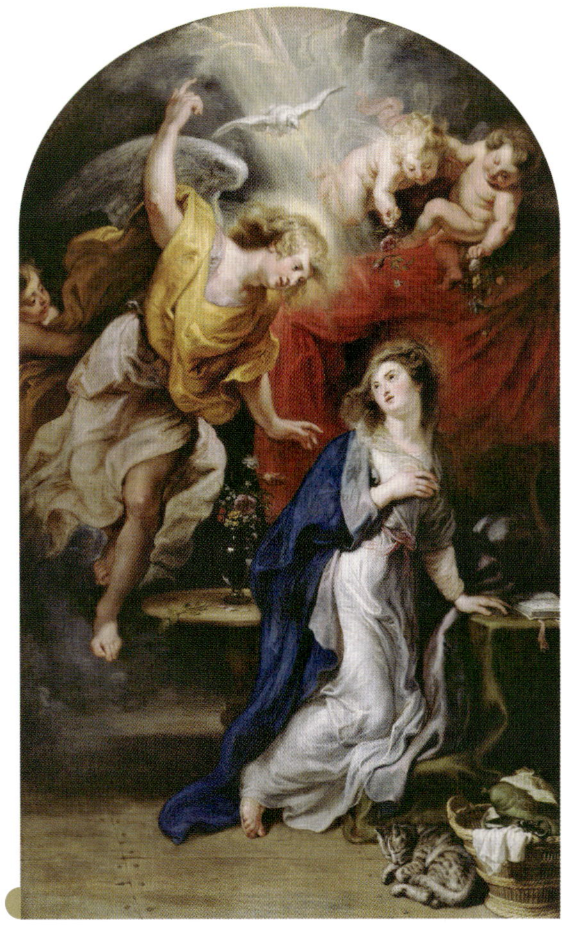

Canvas, 310 x 178,6 cm

Canvas, 174 x 260 cm
Unfinished painting
Landscape with battle
by a different artist
(Pieter Snayers, 1592–1667)

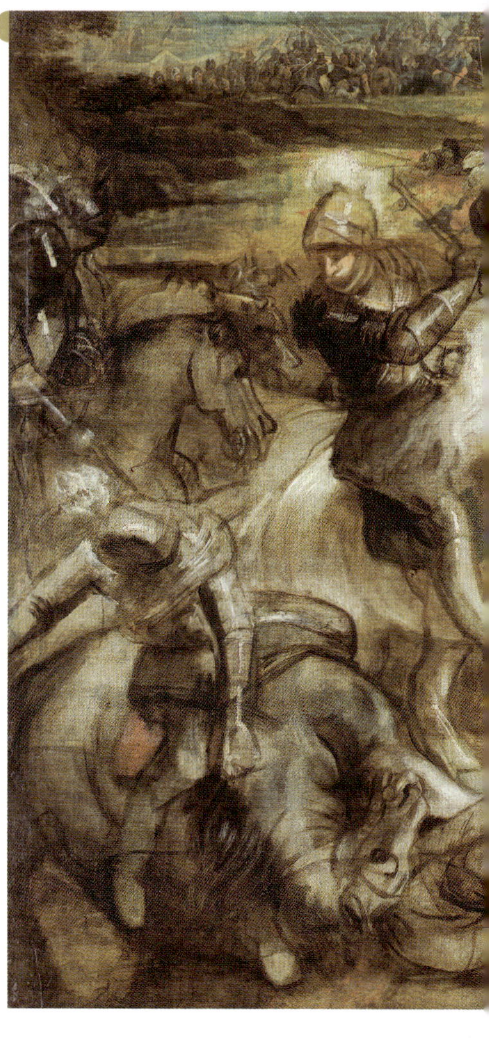

Henry IV at the Battle of Ivry ca. 1628-1630

In the inventory compiled after Rubens' death, this work is listed as 'one of six large and unfinished pieces, comprising sieges of towns, battles and victories of Henry IV, King of France, which was begun a number of years ago for the Gallery of the Hotel de Luxembourg, at the request of the dowager queen of France'. The artist was commissioned to paint this series about the life of King Henry IV by his wife, Maria de Medici, but the changing political situation in France - the dowager queen was forced to flee from her own son, the new King Louis XIII - meant that

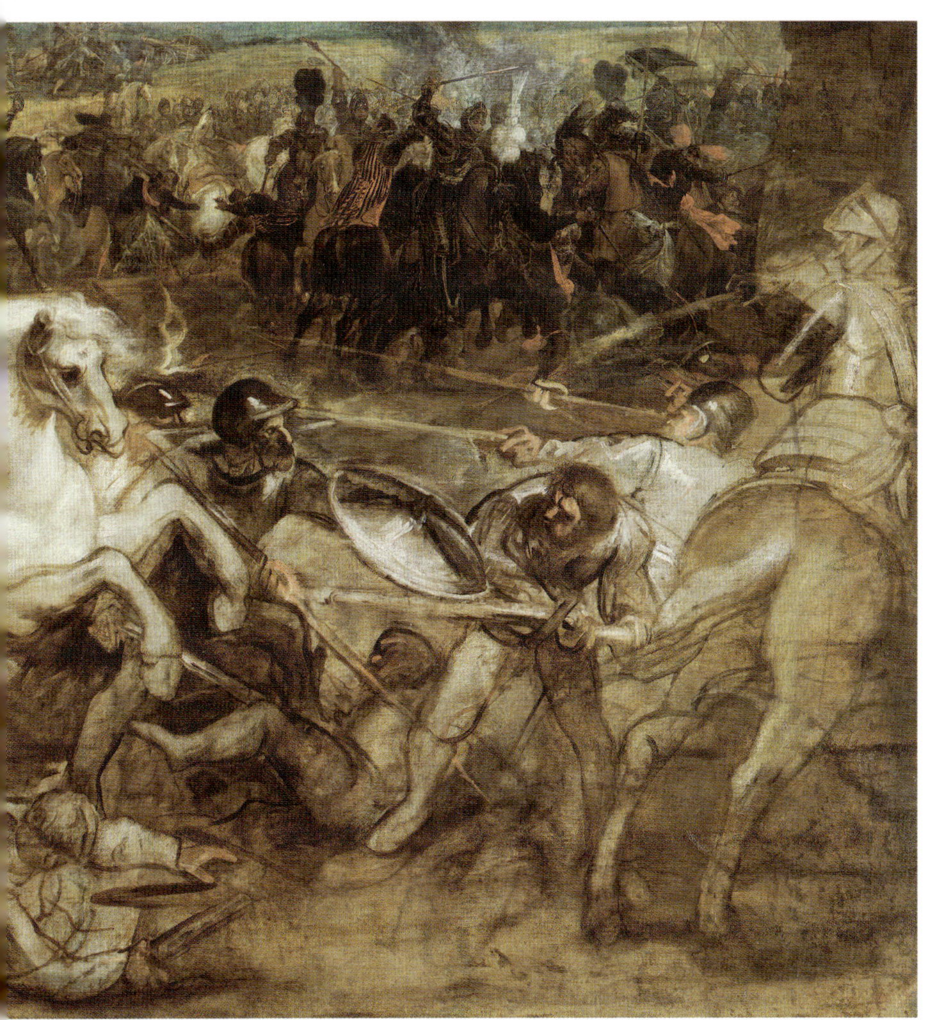

the paintings were not completed.

The canvas depicts the battle at Ivry on 14 March 1590, where Henry IV defeated his political enemies in less than an hour's fighting. This monumental composition was developed in collaboration with a second artist who specialized in battle scenes. The background with the battlefield was probably painted by the Brussels landscape painter Pieter Snayers. Sadly, the previous owner had the painting significantly reduced in size, so that much of Snayers' landscape has disappeared.

Portrait of Helena Fourment after 1630

The beautiful Helene Fourment was just 16 years old when she married the widower Rubens. She not only became a key source of his artistic inspiration, but also gave him a new and happy family life. Helene bore him no fewer than five children and Rubens often painted them together with their mother. In comparison, there are only very few portraits of Helena alone, including this partial copy of the elegant portrait now held at the Old Picture Gallery in Munich. She is dressed in the elaborate fashions popular in the 1630s. The manner in which she is leaning forward and slightly to one side adds something dynamic to the composition. In her hair she wears a conspicuous spray of orange blossom, a symbol of love and fertility.

Panel, 73 x 57 cm
Workshop of P.P. Rubens
On long-term loan from Amsterdam, Rijks Museum, loan from the Municipality of Amsterdam, A. van der Hoop Bequest

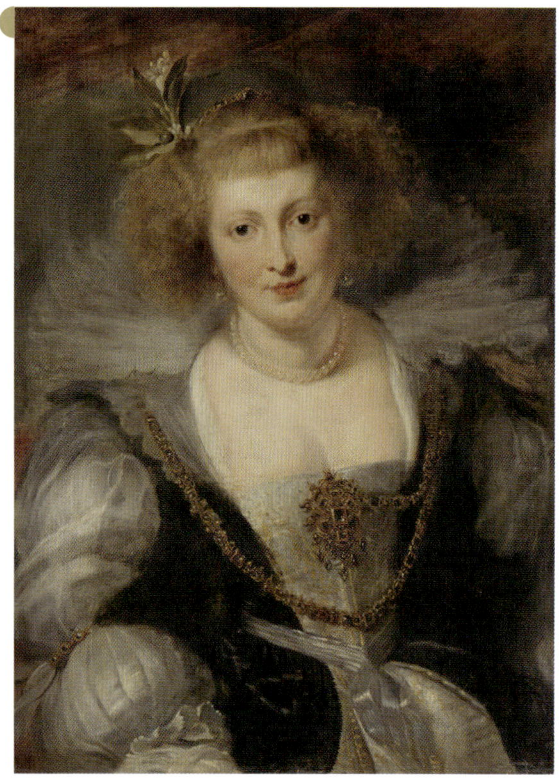

Self-portrait ca. 1630

Apart from the works in which the artist portrayed himself with his family or friends, there are only four known self-portraits of Rubens, one of which is on display in the Rubens House. It shows the artist, about fifty years old at the time, looking directly at the viewer with friendly interest. This amiable expression matches the many contemporary descriptions of his character and appearance. Here we can see 'the likeable Mr. Rubens,' who was 'so gentle in his manner' that everyone loved him and admired him for 'the great mildness of his conversation'. This portrait also expresses his stoic equanimity and refined humanist erudition.

Panel, 61.6 x 45.1 cm

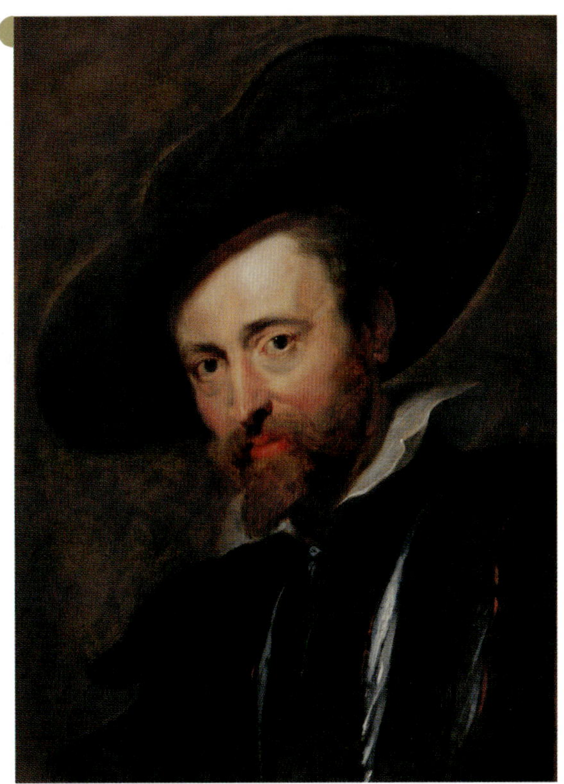

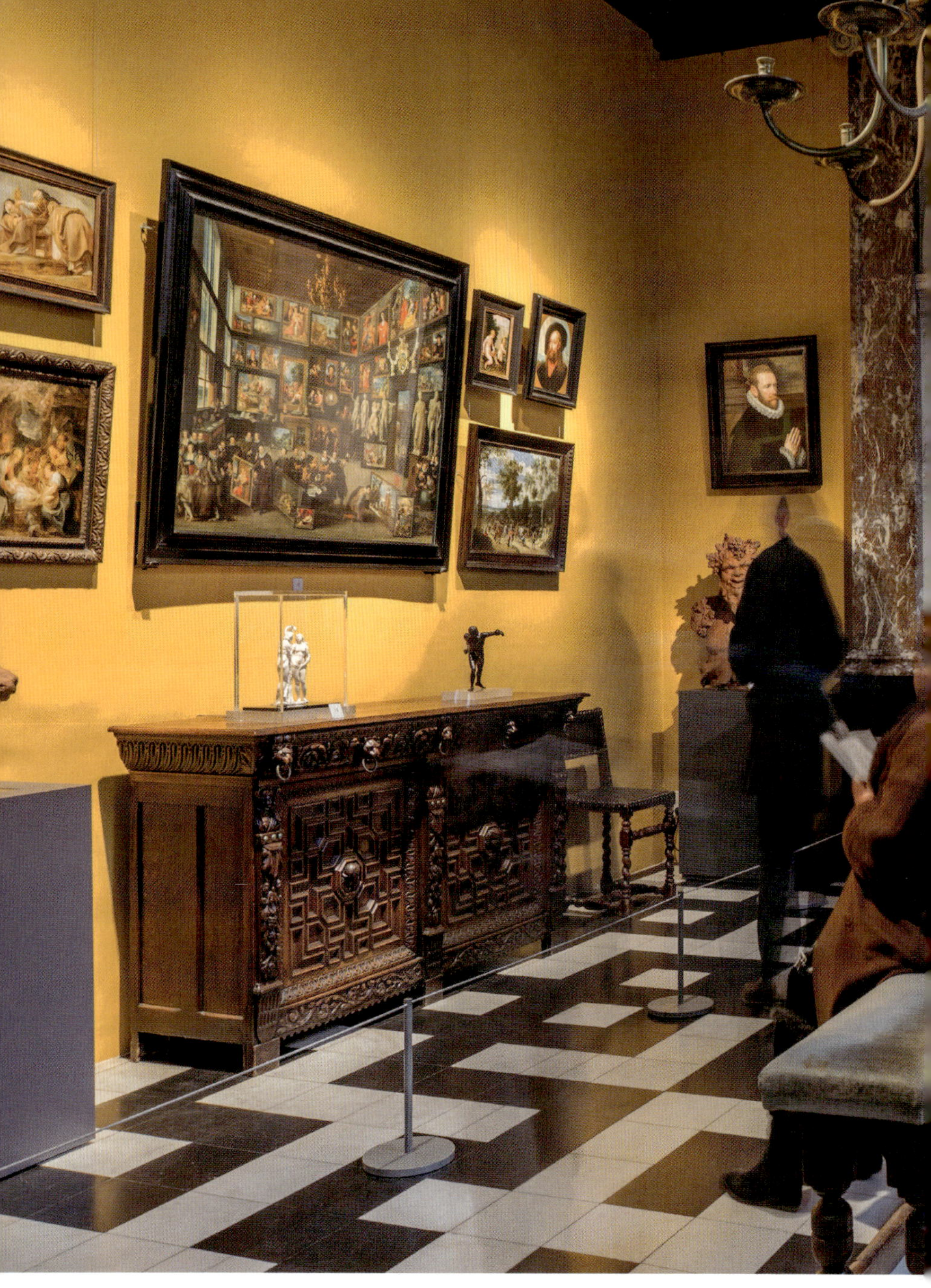

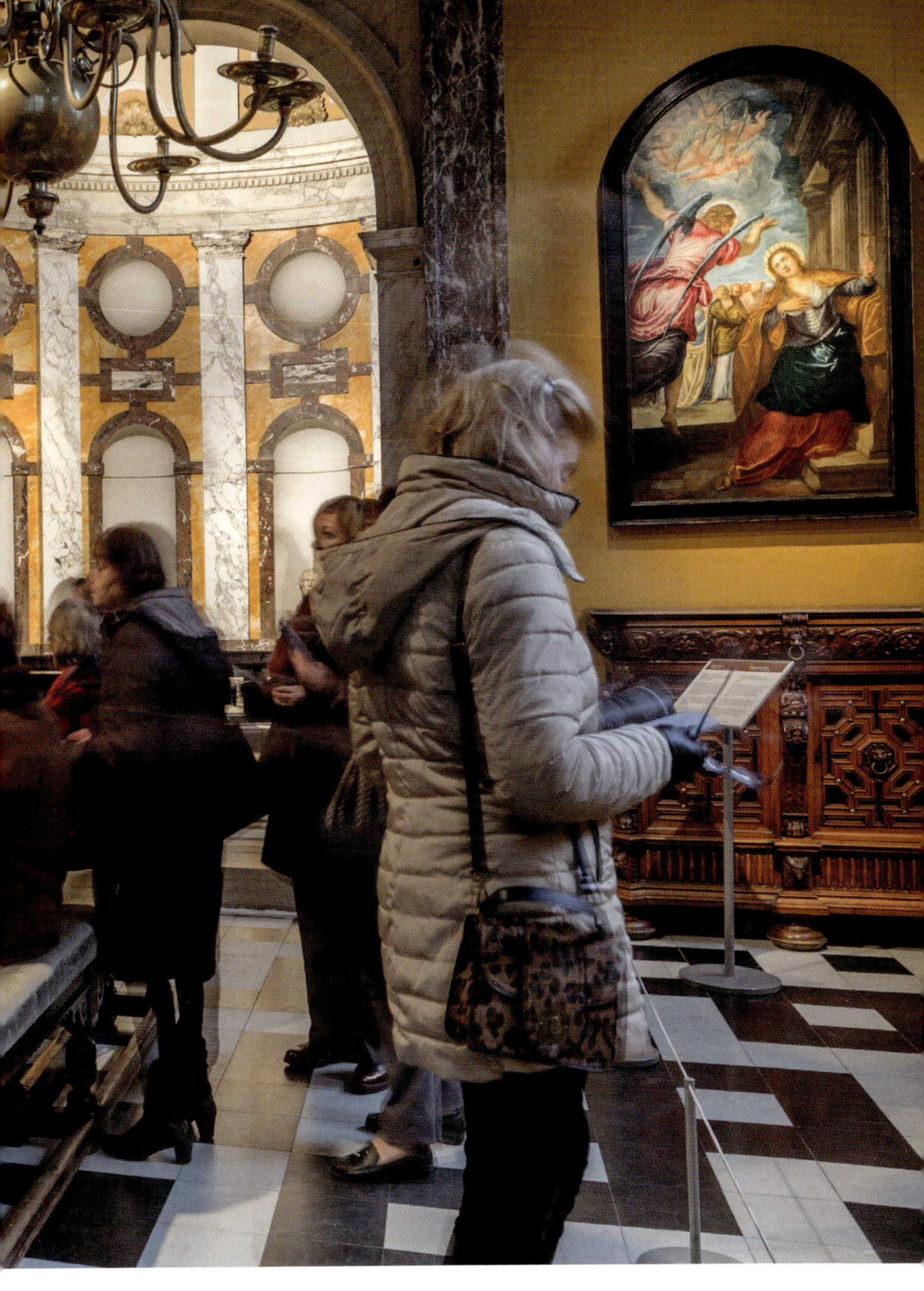

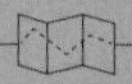

WALK

For the time being, your walk in the footsteps of Rubens ends here - or perhaps even better in one of the many nearby bars and restaurants that the vibrant modern-day city of Antwerp has to offer, where you can relax and reflect on your Rubens experience over a glass of something pleasant and a bite to eat. By now you should have worked up a good hunger and thirst. After all, you have walked more than five kilometres and taken over 10,000 steps (museum and church visits not included)!

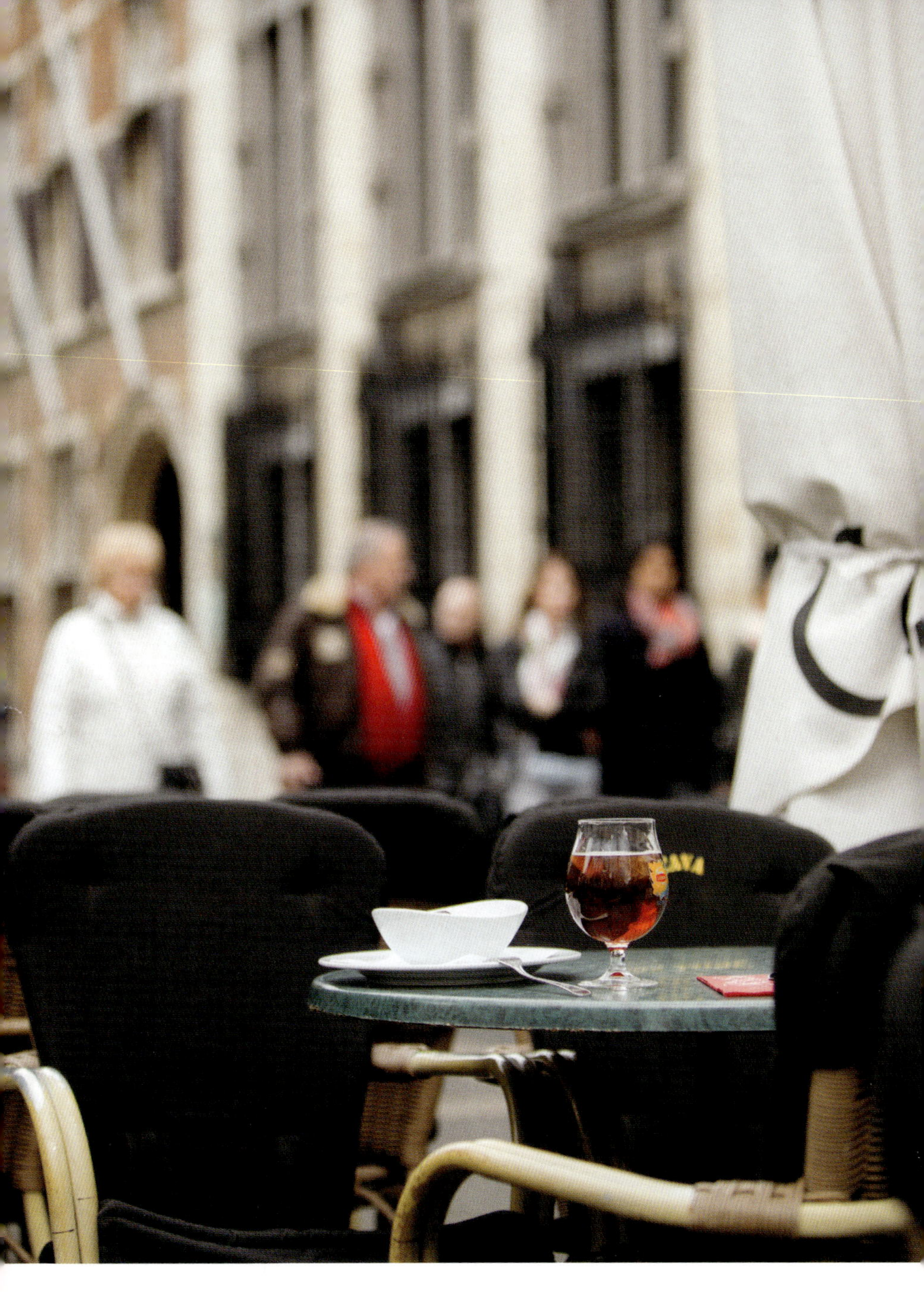

Photo credits

Belfius Art Collection: pp. 68 t., 68 b.
Imageselect: pp.18 t., 19, 24, 25 l., 25 r., 27, 30, 31, 34, 41, 46, 47, 48, 55, 59, 61, 63, 62, 64, 66, 69, 75
KIK-IRPA, Brussels: pp. 120, 121, 134, 139
Lukas - Art in Flanders VZW: pp. 15, 17, 20, 23, 26, 32, 36, 37 t., 42, 50 l., 53, 54, 65, 67, 76, 79, 80, 82, 83, 84, 85, 86, 87, 101, 103, 107, 109, 128, 130, 132
Plantin-Moretus Museum, Antwerp - UNESCO World Heritage, Collection City of Antwerp: pp. 28 r., 51, 57 l., 91, 95, 16, 58, 92, 93 l.; Michel Wuyts: pp. 29, 35, 56, 57 r., 93 b., 93 r.; Michel Wuyts and Louis De Peuter: pp. 94
Rubens House Antwerp; Collection City of Antwerp: pp. 18 b., 21, 52, 148; Ans Brys: pp. 12-13, 140; Joris Luyten: pp. 37 b; Louis De Peuter: pp. 43; Michel Wuyts: pp. 38; Michel Wuyts and Louis De Peuter: pp. 22, 28 l. ,33, 44, 45, 46, 142, 145, 149, 151, 153; Long-term loan from Rijksmuseum, Amsterdam: pp. 154; Long-term loan from London: pp. 50 r.; Long-term loan from the Schoeppler Collection, Germany, photo: Peter Maes: pp. 144; KIK-IRPA, Brussels: 155, cover
Shutterstock.com pp. 39, 96
Jesse Willems: pp. 2-3, 73-74
Juan Wyns: pp. 88, 90, 97, 98, 99, 104, 110, 112, 113, 115, 116, 117, 118, 119, 122, 123, 124, 126, 127, 133, 136, 137, 138, 141, 148-149, 150, 156-157, 159

Texts Irene Smets
Translation Ian Connerty
Design Mirror Mirror: Evi Peeters
Typesetting Keppie & Keppie
Coordination Uitgeverij Lannoo: Anne Haegeman
Photography Juan Wyns

www.lannoo.com

ISBN 978 94 014 5377 6
D/2018/45/451 – NUR 511/502